Samuel Jackson Pratt

Gleanings through Wales, Holland and Westphalia

Peace and War at Home and Abroad

Samuel Jackson Pratt

Gleanings through Wales, Holland and Westphalia
Peace and War at Home and Abroad

ISBN/EAN: 9783744727891

Printed in Europe, USA, Canada, Australia, Japan

Cover: Foto ©ninafisch / pixelio.de

More available books at **www.hansebooks.com**

GLEANINGS

THROUGH

WALES, HOLLAND AND WESTPHALIA;

WITH

VIEWS OF PEACE AND WAR

AT HOME AND ABROAD.

TO WHICH IS ADDED,

HUMANITY;

OR

THE RIGHTS OF NATURE.

A POEM,

REVISED AND CORRECTED:

———

By Mr. PRATT.

———

VOLUME III.

———

" He who is diligent to feek will always GLEAN fomething."
DR. JOHNSON.

———

LONDON:

PRINTED FOR T. N. LONGMAN, AND L. B. SEELEY,
PATERNOSTER-ROW,
1795.

Convents—Story of the Carmelite sisters, Isabel
and Fanchette.   p. 158.

LETTER LXVII.

The conduct of two sisters when taking the veil—
Their lovers—Illustration of some passages in
Pope's Eloisa and Abelard—Some affecting circumstances, the Convent is glean'd cautiously—
inside and out.   p. 182.

LETTER LXVIII.

An excursion into the beautiful country of Cuych,
and some neighbouring principalities——Their
resemblance to certain parts of England—Reflections thereupon—Miscellaneous subjects, and
Gleanings in different places omitted, brought together—Slipshod and barefoot servants—Barber
surgeons—English tradesmen resident abroad—
Curious Dutch custom respecting divorces—visiting ceremonies, and funeral condolence—Caution
against some petty impositions in making bargains
abroad——Price of timber in Westphalia——
Instances of simple curiosity—The popularity of
English manufactures in every part of the Continent—The delighted cobler and the triumph of
an English pair of shoes——Anecdotes of the
King of Prussia—Remarks on the German the-
atres—Confined ideas of foreigners on the extent
of British territory—Hardyhood of the German

education and nursing of children—Manner of
serving at table—Description of a Dutch drum
or rout—Fire and smoke!—A contre-visite—
Its etiquettes and singularities—A Dutch supper,
and bill of fare—Free towns, and places of
sanctuary in different parts of the continent—
The beautiful town of Neuwied distinguish'd—
An enquiry into the civil policy or impolicy of
the feasts and fasts so common in catholic
countries—The influence of these institutions on
the people, especially the servants—The Gleaners adventure at a Prussian wake, and at the
house of a happy family, in whose good company
he hopes the reader will be happy also—A canal
scene, and the parting of friends, to whose
society the reader is invited—The Gleaner is
courteous—and his courtesy is rewarded by a
pretty Dutch woman—The Dutch love ornament, yet affect simplicity——Instances—A
Dutch humourist—Over-cleanliness of the Dutch
in certain particulars—their attention to symme-
try—The German peasantry resemble the Welch
in their dress—The historical cause of this—
Pleasure of finding out likenesses—Comparative
view of the ancient Germans with the ancient
Britons——their Wars—Religion——Priests,
Bards, &c.—more than all, their spirit of independence—A Gleaning from Gibbon to illumi-
nate this subject—Anecdote and character of

the

TABLE OF CONTENTS

OF VOLUME III.

LETTER LVI.

A Difquifition on the fubject of Liberty, Equality, &c. &c.—The author ventures his opinions. p. 1.

LETTER LVII.

The author gleans the two laft infurrections of Hol-land—An inftance of Dutch revenge in private life—Reflections on the public mania in different countries—The progrefs of political difcontent. p. 9.

LETTER LVIII.

The calamity of the times generally fpoken of—The author's promife to glean *them more particularly in the courfe of this* laft Sheaf—*The author gleans the German theatre—Some of its beauties and defects—Analyfis of fome of their dramatic pieces—The Ger-man Romeo and Juliet turned into an opera; but managed with uncommon addrefs—Its fable and fcenery—Defcription of a gala play, at which three princely perfonages, in honour of whom it is re-prefented, fall faft afleep.—The author gleans them in that fituation, and literally takes them* napping —*The Stadtholder's birth-day, or* anniverfary martyrdom—*More advantages of little folks over*

great:

great: with more reflections thereupon—The ridicule of the popular term Equality, when the lowest station even under a Monarchy is thus happier than the highest.—Marching of troops out of the Hague to the frontiers—A second wet jacket for his Highness of Orange—Disaffected state of the Dutch soldiery, and of the Dutch people—This important subject investigated—The author reasons a little with the Dutch patriots.—The Gleaner's farewell to Holland and Guelderland.　　　　p. 24.

LETTER LIX.

The Gleaner enters Westphalia—Contrasts it with Holland—Describes the charming Duchy of Cleves—Its similitude to the most agreeable parts of England—It exhibits the beautiful though not the sublime of nature—The Cleves wood—Its abundant graces public and private—Summer—Autumnal, Winter, and Spring views of it—Gleans them all, and moralizes en passant—An account of the environs and town of Cleves—A contrast in favour of Holland as to neatness—Illustrations— "An ounce of Civet to sweeten the reader's "imagination"—The story of the ox, the sheep, and the lamb—Reflections addressed to those who happen to have hearts.—Passages from Pope and Otway exemplified. Cambrian and Westphalian sheep contrasted. The author gleans a Westphalian shepherd and dog, the latter the merriest, and most useful

useful fellow of the two—His daily labour described—First recommended to the sad dogs of England, then recanted—An excellent Westphalian custom respecting mad dogs, worthy of adoption. p. 44.

LETTER LX.

A Westphalian tea-party, and the curious method of baking, boiling, and smoke-drying themselves in the open air—General character of the Prussian and German concerts, clubs, societies, and other social meetings—Dissertation on stoves and tobacco-pipes—The author gleans the mouths of the West-phalian and Dutch gentry, and is obliged to give them a blow in the teeth—German, particularly Westphalian, customs—Hat-pulling—Kissing ceremony—Resistance to the habits of a country, and the author's advice on that subject—Prussian imposition—A very grand action of a very little person—The Gleaner converseth with him. p. 57.

LETTER LXI.

The great, little, person writeth an epistle to the Gleaner—The mischief done by English travellers to their countrymen and to foreigners—This subject gravely discussed—A scale of imposition, expence, and œconomy—The English teach foreigners to charge—Proofs—Average of expenditure in different countries, an humble, but useful Gleaning—Imposition and the art of bill-making in England,

Holland,

Holland, and *Weſtphalia*, and parts adjacent—
Reaſonable and unreaſonable—The black landlords
ſeparated from the white—A week in *Weſtphalia*
and a day in *Holland* are about par as to tavern
charges—Proofs poſitive—The author promiſes to
glean the Pruſſian coins—Advice to travellers,
who mean to reſide abroad—The Gleaner aſſiſts
their menage—Correct ſtatements—Advice to the
poor and proud—The miſery of the Pruſſians,
Weſtphalians, &c. in their habits of kitchen ex-
pences—The author gleans a Pruſſian pantry—and
a gentleman's table—The frugality of foreigners—
Curious inſtances—Modes of living—Twelve
o'clock dinners—An accommodating appetite
amongſt the bleſſings of a traveller—The author
gleans himſelf—Apoſtrophe to good-humour!—
and the letter concluded with wiſhing the reader
the poſſeſſion of that treaſure, and a good appetite.
P. 70.

LETTER LXII.

Weſtphalian churches—with obſervations on literary
brick-work, and travelling ſtone-maſonry—The influence of the Catholic faith on the ſubordinate
claſſes of mankind—This ſubject gleaned at large,
and oppoſed to the preſent ſyſtematical infidelity of
a once moſt Catholic country—Half an hour's walk
by moonlight and the blaze of bonfires—The occaſion of them. P. 97.

the present Emperor of Germany—A Gleaning for the Reader's affections—The Gleaner apprises his friend and readers that he is going to enter on trembling subjects—Dutch patriots—Prussian patriots — French influence — The Gleaner refreshes his friend and reader with an instance of Dutch loyalty—and another instance of Dutch perverseness, with which he closes this letter of a mile.

LETTER LXIX.

View of the country from Cleves to Cologne, as to its present political situation—Comparative survey of the beauties of art and nature in times of trouble and of tranquillity—The Gleaner's sensations in course of this afflicting survey—The effects of republican confraternity abroad—A family in ruins—Gratitude to the poems of Thomson and Goldsmith, the travelling companions of the Gleaner. Application of several passages in each: with a view of actual circumstances too powerful for the pencil of either—A Gleaning of the victor and the vanquish'd in a tour through conquering and conquer'd countries—!

LETTER LXX.

The author's reflections on the subject of his last letter, and on public wars.

LETTER

LETTER LXXI.

A comparative view of the monarchy and of the republic of France—The difficulties of the future historian who shall detail these horrid deeds for the information of posterity——The general outline,   p. 290.

LETTER LXXII.

The history of the murder of the Princess de Lamballe—and her character—The Gleaner's private opinion on the subject of revolutions in general—France and Poland in particular—Reflections drawn from a survey of the whole. Particulars of a prophecy in the year 543. CONCLUSION.

Considerations on the origin, progress and conduct of the French Revolution: and of a reform in governments—Anecdotes of a great foreign personage—All is not gold that glisters—A gleaning of state-jugglers—The author takes his leave.

HUMANITY A POEM. p. 331.   p. 302.

TWO DIALOGUE LETTERS.

Containing necessary first questions and enquiries for the use of all travellers.

LETTER I.

Necessary questions in English, Dutch, and German, for travellers who mean to pass only a few hours or days at a place.   p. 421.

LETTER II.

For the service of those who wish to reside abroad.

p. 435.

LETTER LXIII.

The injuſtice of national prejudice—A freſh attempt of the author to remove it—He gleans a Pruſſian cottage, where he finds hoſpitality that would have done honour to a palace—The general pains attendant upon parties of pleaſure—A definition of a party of pleaſure recommended to dictionary makers—Man and woman of the world's day, and a lover of nature's day, compared—In this letter will be found a great deal of love and friendſhip—and an old invalid Pruſſian ſoldier—and another moonlight Gleaning. p. 107.

LETTER LXIV.

Begging friars—Sunday aſſemblies—and contraſt of neighbour nations—The author, after much heſitation, gleans a certain place, and a certain family, who are all anxious to make the author admire it as much as themſelves. He goes over very trembling ground, and in his way meets with difficulties—Is in danger of the Engliſh reader's diſpleaſure, but averts it by a handſome and well timed compliment to the certain places of Great Britain. p. 122.

LETTER LXV.

Weſtphalian ſuperſtitions—The Gleaner regales his readers and friends with ſeveral witches, men, wolves, and cats, very different in their character

A 4 *and*

and disposition from the same sort of personages of the British empire—Adventure of the bird catcher and his Canary—Cleves fair, and strolling musicians—The family ducat—and a circumstance which the reader will peruse, for his own sake, more than once.

P. 139.

LETTER LXVI.

A week or two of gleaning in the nooks and corners of different countries—Their scenery—manners—hospitality—cheapness—accommodations, &c.—The windings of the imagination—The author gleans the Maise and Rhine—A noble castle, and a nobler chaplain, one of its inhabitants—Imitations even for Englishmen—The Pont Volant—The peasant pilgrims—An hill—A valley—After gleaning which, the author goes farther into the country by every possible direction, and journeys with his reader and friend " many a mile," but he hopes without weariness—A set of Westphalian day-labourers at dinner—May the reader be as content and as grateful for more costly fare—The liberty enjoyed in the Prussian dominions—and the abundance of the peasants, notwithstanding their disaffection and the poverty of which they complain—The difficulties of the Prussian Noblesse—Their hardships—The Author gleans the beautiful little Signiory of Boxmeer, by favour of a friend's communication — Its singular situation—Its peculiar verdure—Its Convents—

GLEANINGS, &c.

LETTER LVI.

I HAVE purpofely put off, hitherto, one important but difaftrous fubject, to the laft moment; although I have now for the fpace of fome years, in my different traverfings of the continent, been placed, as it were, in the very eye and ear of it. You feel that I mean the dreadful public, and yet more fatal private, wars of this and many other countries on this *unhappy* fide of the Englifh Channel.

What, my loved friend, is the matter with them all!

> " Sure 'tis the very error of the moon,
> " She comes more near the earth than fhe was wont
> " And makes men mad."

Does it proceed from the facred flame of liberty? which exalts the human, almoft to the divine nature; or are the nations filled with

clamours " for that which no man felt the want
" of, and with care for freedom, which has never
" been in danger?" Springs it from a due
fenfe of that proud principle within us, which
points at the right which every honeft individual has to rank with the loftieft of the fpecies,
when meafured by the ftandard of nature? or
from that factious and difcontented fpirit,
which prompts the worft of mankind to trouble
the repofe, and plunder the poffeffions of the
beft?   Comes it from true patriotifm, or from
that party rage, which " robs it of its good
name?" It proceeds from all thefe.   But with
refpect to *Equality*, on the literal idea, as the
mob are encouraged for reafons they cannot
penetrate, to conceive it, was there ever fuch a
day-dream? To make the abfurdity more egre-
gious, yet more palateable, it is called *natural*
equality! Prepofterous as falfe! What, dear friend,
in nature is equal?   Survey her productions:
from the firft to the laft, from the moft gigantic
to the moft minute, as well in animals as man,
what is there which fhe has not *created*
UNEQUAL, even by exprefs order of the Creator?
And by that very *inequality* intending to promote
the wifdom, force and felicity of the whole?
Amongft the fifhes of the fea, and the fowls of
the air, and the beafts of the field, the grand

line

line of fubordination drawn by nature goes on.
Would you give to the linnet the wing of the
eagle, or to the turnfpit the fpeed of the grey-
hound? To what end? Would not nature, by that
exchange, be violated in her general laws, and
would the beings themfelves be the better for
it? Am I told, that all thefe creatures were
put under the fubjection of man, and that he,
as the lord of all below, can have naturally no
fuperior but the God that gave him life. The
argument refts then, it feems, on the natural
equality of *human* creatures. Fallacious again.
For of all the beings in the fcale of the univerfe, man, (if we except his origin, concerning the *equality* of which he has no more right
to be proud, than the worm that devours his
carcafe), is the moft fubject to the laws of
natural *in*-equality. The point which places
him at the top of the creation is certainly his
foul; for his body, whether a mafterpiece of
beauty, or a mafs of deformity, is alike cor-
ruptible, and rather an object of humiliation
than triumph. But, were you difpofed to
felect, from the diverfified works of nature, any
fpecimen of her wonderful variety and irregularity, could you fix on any thing fo proper to
difplay that irregularity, that variety, as the
human mind? So far from there being herein
an univerfal equality, there is nothing fo *une-*

qual amongst all the performances of Creation. The strength of the lion is not more remote from the feeblenefs of the gnat, nor the fwiftnefs of the rein-deer from the tardinefs of the fnail, than the diftance between the power and weaknefs, velocity and flownefs of men's fouls and underftandings. Nature, by uncontroulable laws, has eftablifhed, that to one man fhould be given an head to plan, govern, and command; to another, hands to toil and obey. Innumerable are the gradations, from thofe who guide the helm of the ftate, to thofe who regulate the fteerage of a fimple fkiff, from the nobleft architect to the moft ordinary artificer. The harmonies of civil fociety are carried on by the joint affiftance of all thefe in their *proper places*; take them out of which, and tranfpofe them, put the one into the ftation of another; and, in fhort, jumble them together, on the plea of natural equality, according to the new fyftem, and what refults from all this? What becomes of civil fociety, and of the world? Doth not fuch a farce upon the decent fubordinations and arrangements of nature, fill it with difcords, diforders, and death? Look into the page of ancient annals, and into the more fanguinary hiftory of modern times—what do they exhibit but a tiffue of abfurdity, horror, and blood?

Can

Can it be fuppofed, that were thefe at length to fubfide, by the eftablifhment of Republicanifm on the ruins of Monarchy, that the happinefs of mankind, which ought to be the aim and end of all governments, would be the effect? Let the toiling hand govern, and the projecting head obey. Would not confufion be indeed confounded? Or fhall all men have an equal fhare in the direction of human affairs? Shall there be no governors, no governed? Shall families, focieties, ftates, and empires be without an head? Shall all be common right, and common fellowfhip? The comet, my friend, were it " to rufh lawlefs through the void," would not trail fo much mifchief in its courfe, as fuch a number of licentious orbits out of their proper fpheres. The wolves and tygers of the forefts acknowledge, it is true, no fuperior, and they fometimes troop, in grim affociation and fell banditti, to lay wafte the countries through which they pafs; they are, it muft be owned, notable republicans, and are unanimous to deftroy whatever they meet with; but they deftroy each other alfo; and are bad examples of the fuccefs of an univerfal republic, inftituted on the levelling principle. The wolves and tygers of human kind, if fuffered to roam through the wildernefs of life, without any check on paf-

fions

sions more fierce and fatal than any beftial appetite—or, if controuled only by thofe laws which are inftituted by what are called patriots, only becaufe they avowedly differ from and oppofe any order in a creation that is fuftained by order only—would foon make the univerfe more intolerable to its inhabitants, than any abufe which power has yet introduced into the government of the world; and the moft dif-loyal being would again call out, like the frogs in the fable, for a king, and rather than any longer be left to the anarchy of being delivered over to themfelves, would pray for one tyrant (fuppofing no honeft prince would then accept of them) in exchange for an univerfe of def-pots.

But farther, how egregioufly abfurd, my friend, is this new doctrine! Are not all large bodies of men compelled to have governors and chiefs? And do not thefe imply command and obedience? and do not thefe argue in their very name and nature, authority and fubjection? What are the Admirals, Generals, Colonels, Captains, and Subalterns of the prefent French armies, but heads? What are the foldiers and failors they govern or direct, but fubordinate members? In what confifts the difference betwixt thefe and former commanders, whether

minifterial

minifterial or military? Alas, nothing but "the whiftlings of a name." Call jt Ariftocracy, and the gentleft government becomes tyranny: give it the name of Democracy; and there is no flavery too hard to be endured. Nay, the very men who are fuch fticklers for equality, who have even fought and bled for it, continue to this very hour to make the proudeft diftinctions amongft men, even in a ftate of mutual captivity. The firft thing that ftruck me in my vifit to Weyzel, a celebrated town, as you know, of Weftphalia, was the feeing a number of Republican French officers, (prifoners) walking on the parade attended by their *fervants*. Two of thefe latter, were receiving the orders of their mafters, with their heads uncovered, and their bodies bent in a very unrepublican manner. What! in a ftate of common calamity, are thefe nice diftinctions to be made, thought I? are brother prifoners to keep up this lofty difference? Are thofe who have levelled the earth, fo foon unmindful of their leading maxim? "All men are equal!" One of the fuperiors (I thought there were to be no fuperiors) grew angry, chid his domeftic, and fent him from his prefence. Could the old conftitution—could defpotifm do more! I faw the obedient flave with the moft fervile fhrug of his country, and of his condition, go flinking away. So much for confraternity.

My friend, a fkilful ufe of words, fubftituting one for another, as time and circumftance may require, will apparently change the nature of things: but real liberty and flavery are the fame beautiful and bitter potions, denominate them what you will, and the tyrant is not lefs an oppreffor, for altering his name to that of a friend to freedom: indeed, fome of the worft enemies that freedom ever had in all ages and countries, have affumed this facred character.

Point out to me the Defpot, that has not called himfelf a lover of his people, and of his country. Under this fpecious mafk I have, within a few years, been an eye-witnefs to no lefs than two formidable infurrections in this little Republic, on the verge of which, I am now writing. I am far from being fure, that I fhall not be fpectator of a * third: though one would have thought either of the two former might have written on the hearts of the people, the WISDOM OF CONTENT, in characters of blood. That which raged in 1787, is fo well and faithfully written, by an Englifh author, who calls

his

* The third has come to pafs.

his work an history of the late Dutch Revolution, that I shall not only refer, but recommend
you to a perusal of it. A few of the miserable
particulars, I shall give you on the authority of
personal knowledge. But not till I again resume the pen to assure you, amidst the storm
of contending nations—"the wrecks of matter,"
and the almost "crush of worlds," I am,
affectionately, yours.

<hr>

LETTER LVII.

TO THE SAME.

WE talk much, and with much
reason, of the wild excesses of our English
mobs, my dear friend. Their sanguinary
disposition has been compared to that of our
English bull-dogs, which are said to be in-
satiate of blood, when they have once drawn it
from the objects of their attack. Our British
insurrections are, no doubt, marked like others,
by some of the prominent features of rebellion
in all countries, devastation, flames, and untimely death. But I did not know, how great
an enemy man could be to man; nor had I a
clear idea to what an extent human beings
could go in the destruction of one another,
although

although I am not unread in the bloody ſtory of my own country, till I began to glean the more dreadful annals of others. The ſix years that have elapſed ſince I beheld in Holland the demon of civil fury aſſociated with party madneſs, far from having abated the memory of their dire effects, are felt, methinks, with a ſtronger horror, from having obſerved ſimilar outrages in other quarters of the agitated globe. Unhappy Holland! while one party were attempting to deſtroy thee and themſelves by fire and ſword, rapine and ſlaughter, the other were wreaking vengeance againſt thy beſt, faireſt, and moſt innocent poſſeſſions—upon thy wives and children.

While one ſide, I ſay, my friend, were thus outraging all order, decency, and compaſſion, the other manifeſted no leſs fury. The party of the Stadtholder, and that of the patriots were alike infected with the poiſon of the times. It reached the boſoms even of the gentler ſex: as an inſtance of which, pardon me, if I make your nature recoil, even as mine did on the day my flowing eyes bore teſtimony to it. A party of patriots had taken, and killed, in the town of Bois-le-duc, one of the Princes adherents, who had been active in the cauſe of the Stadtholder. His defeat was,

therefore,

therefore, a kind of triumph; a groupe of people foon gathered round the body, yet ftruggling betwixt life and death. Amongft the reft, were two women who had been fetching water from the public fountains. One of thefe no fooner underftood the caufe of the mob's collecting, than fhe poured out about two thirds of the water from her pail, which fhe placed under the wounds of the murdered citizen, whofe blood was thus mingled with the water, when pledging the furrounding populace, fhe exclaimed, as fhe drank with more than favage fury, " May rivers of this flow through the ftreets till our enemies are vanquifhed!" And to fuch a pitch of enthufiafm was this carried, that, as one more example, I muft inform you, another patriot quarrelled with the beautiful rainbow, and fhot at it, becaufe the orange mingled in its hues: this was nearly as mad and irreverent as the dreffing up the figure of the Virgin Mary with a red bonnet, and writing under the crofs of our Saviour, the man Jefus, the *ci-devant* Redeemer of the world.

All comments of the moralift, my friend, are loft, and all effufions of the peaceful lover of mankind abforbed on occafions like thefe: for breaches of this fort in nations, like old and incurable wounds, though they are often

fkinned

fkinned over, conceal an unfubdued venom,
which gathers ftrength and virulence, and then
again break out. Private families, we know,
may, after " fome imminent and deadly
breach," reunite from policy, or principle, or
from fome reliques of affection : but even this
is a patched up accommodation; and after a
violent open rupture, whether in empires, or
the little domeftic common-wealths that form
them, the whole hiftory of mankind furnifh few
examples where the parties have fincerely for-
given one another. Many months after the
Prince's party had been reinftated in its privileges, and the patriot faction, not only yielded
to authority, but appeared to have forgot its
animofity, I had but too many illuftrations of
the foregone remark. On the breaking out of
the rebellion in other countries, I again heard
the voice of fedition, and the more than *murmurs*
of difaffection in various parts of thefe dif-
united ftates. Sacred be the love of rational
liberty. But the fever of freedom is a wild-
fire that is more defolating than any other con-
tagion: that of Conftantinople is not fo fuddenly imbibed, nor does it travel with unim-
paired venom fo far or fo faft. It is a peft
that feizes diftant nations, and ftrikes with the
rapidity and the force of lightning. Even
when Holland feemed to have got the better of

this

this political plague, its poifons were under-
mining her conftitution, and like thofe fires
which are burning in the bowels of the earth,
unfeen, are inwardly confuming its entrails, and
making their way to the furface. I was in
Holland when fhe was precifely in this fituation, prepared for her fecond fhock, and waiting only for the fignal of her *expatriated fire-
brands* (the banifhed Dutch patriots then
forming a part of the French army) to give the
explofion. Breda was taken, Gorcum was
inundated, and the cannonade of Williamftadt,
thundered to the very fea, and prepared the
patriots of the provinces for the reception of
their exiled friends.

In my way to Helveotfluice, in order to em-
bark for England, every countenance I looked
into carried the marks of fear, loyalty, ambition, or revolt. Notwithftanding the cautious
jealoufy natural to power, and all the vigilance
of the magiftrates, little knots of people were
to be obferved gathered together, in corners of
the ftreet, and in bye-places, where it was
thought the eye of authority would not penetrate. My wandering fteps, which fo often
led me into unfrequented places, and thereby,
as you have feen, make me tread upon many
a fecret, led me to the haunts of thefe Dutch

male-

male-contents. They were always to be feen in that earneft and ear-approaching whifper, which fo often betrays its treafons; the fore-finger extended, the button caught at, and held faft, or fhook moft rebellioufly; the mouth of the fpeaker contracted, fo as to fend forth only the unbetraying voice of confpiracy, and that of the hearer, on the contrary, opened to its width, to fwallow the treafon, while the eyes of the party communicating, like a pair of fentinels, ordered to defend the door of the lips, feemed to keep double watch, left, as Shakfpeare fays,

> " The babbling goffips of the air
> " Should prate of their *where-about!*"

Artizans, burgomafters, priefts, and peafants, were thus infidioufly, or fearfully, gathered to-gether, either to exprefs their apprehenfion, their hope, or their defpair, were to be de-tected in thefe communities; and had not the whole country been threatened with a very ferious calamity, it would not have been un-amufing to a Gleaner, who delights

> " To catch the living manners as they rife."

It is not unentertaining to fee the little fhifts which perfons, engaged in fecret converfations of any kind, make to prevent being difcover-ed: the immediate change they make on the

firft

first view of an intruder—the sudden alteration from an aweful to a carelefs air as the
faid intruder approaches; the tones varied
from almoft in diftinct whifpers, and porten-
tous meetings, to louder accents; now walking
on, now ftopping a little, as if engaged in
ordinary converfation, the fubject of which,
while you have an eye on them, is changed as
often as their pofitions. I took notice, while
I paufed at Helveotfluice, that as their friends
on the other fide of the water, that is to fay,
the enemies of their country, were more rapid
in their advances, while their very fires were
in fight, and the patriots, on the Helveot
fide, were almoft opening their arms to receive
them, thefe fecret meetings were lefs vifible.
It is a crifis at which the *mind* of a confpiracy
is made up, the component parts of which,
perfectly underftanding their plans, lie in wait
to put them in execution, affuming, in the
mean time, the mafk of well-diffembled loyalty: for, ftrange as it may feem, vice, when
fwelled to its *height*, and juft about to fhew itfelf, borrows the femblance of its oppofite virtue, in the robes of which it is then moft affidu-
ous to cover itfelf. Thus, drunkennefs affects
temperance, incontinence chaftity, avarice generofity, detraction candour, impiety religion,
and faction, which would hurl a fovereign
from

from his throne, in that moment is the loudeft
to fing forth the praifes of royalty.

But treachery, my dear friend, is never fo
perilous, never fo fatal, as when it thus hides
itfelf, and would feem the thing it is not.
From a foe, whom I obferve taking aim at
me, I may efcape by accident, by courage, or
by addrefs, but from the ftroke of an affaffin,
whom, though I once knew him to be my enemy, my believing heart at length confiders as
a penitent friend, I am fo far from being
guarded, that to ufe the words of one of our
old poets,

" I lay my fleeping life within his arms."

Thus it was with the feveral inhabitants of
Holland. They had done fpeaking and were
now prepared to act, and the moment of that
action was waited for with the fullen malignity and gloomy paftime which characters a
cold and determined nature, fuch as many of
the natives of Holland poffefs. They waited
for their long-wifhed revenge in filence, but it
was a filence that refembled the fearful ftillnefs
of the fky, when the thunder is gathering
force : but the filence of a Hollander, when
once his part is taken, is more to be apprehended than the thunder itfelf, of which I
                                            gleaned

gleaned an inftance that is in referve for you. Perhaps I have raifed your curiofity, and therefore you fhall have this dire example of Dutch revenge here.

Two brothers, on fome very flight occafion, quarrelled, and, from being inmates, feparated houfes, neighbourhood, and at length broke connexion : their alienation was neither foftened, nor embittered by correfpondence. After about eleven years paft in this manner, one. of the brothers married a beautiful woman. The fingle brother, who had been watching his opportunity of vengeance, made his appearance very unexpectedly on the wedding-day, and defiring an interview with the married man in a feparate apartment, was no fooner perceived than welcomed; the latter taking it for granted he came to be reconciled, and had chofen this diftinguifhed day to render it more acceptable. The bachelor thus addreffed the bridegroom. " Brother, we have not met fince our difagree-" ment divided us, this day eleven years : I " come now to remind you of the circum-" ftance.—Thus,"—ftriking a poniard into the heart of the bridegroom, who had juft power to gain the apartment of his bride, who was then dancing with one of her hufband's friends. Scarcely could he exclaim that he was murdered, ere he sunk down and expired at her feet; and while the company and servants were employed about their friend and master, the assassin coolly mounted his horse, and made his escape.

Alas! my friend, it is with the patriotism that embraces all my fellow-creatures, and their happiness, that I apprize you, that our present sheaf must be deeply spotted with their blood! the mingled blood of beauty and deformity, innocence and guilt. The scenery, which is yet in store, was partly painted amidst the tranquillity of returning peace, and partly amidst the horrors of returning war.

Often have I been within sight, not seldom within hearing, of two of the fiercest oppositions that ever desolated the works of man and God. You will not be surprised to learn, that the impression which such scenes has made upon an eye and ear-witness, should have filled his mind with materials that lie fresh in his memory, and bleed in his heart. How many towns, villages, and all that they inherit, have I seen blooming on the one day with beauty, wealth, content, and happy countenances, despoiled, deformed, impoverished, and deluged in tears and in blood, upon another. The pictures of these, taken both in the one position, and in the other, must be given. They
shall

ſhall be delineated with ſimple hiſtorical truth, for neither romance nor fable, in their wildeſt, warmeſt colourings, could, can, or has ever reached them.

Poſſibly the Gleaner is the firſt travelier who hath yet deſcribed the happineſs of nations at peace, and the miſery of ſuch nations at war, in a reſidence immediately *before*, and *after*, the violations of public tranquillity. He has viewed as well the havock of battle in its moſt intenſe rage, as the cold horrors that ſucceeded conqueſt. He has luxuriated in countries, when the horn of plenty filled them with fertility and fragrance, and deplored, even as if his property were mingled in the common wreck, the withering effects of victory, after the enemy had torn up all the works of nature, and of man, the moſt fair, and the moſt cheriſhed. He has been amongſt the laſt to quit, and the firſt to reviſit, a threatened country and evacuated town, and has obſerved the labours of a life ! a century ! annihilated in a ſingle day ! the deſolations of every work of art, and the more affecting ruins of human beings ! Before he ſet out on this laſt tour, of which he has here drawn the faint outline, he had ſeen public miſery, and felt its effects : his reading had furniſhed him

with

with recorded horrors in the bloody hiftory of his own country : but all this was but the *fhadow* of the difafter, which the excurfion alluded to, has brought clofer under his eye, and yet clofer to his heart.

Defcending by degrees, in a ftep that receded in proportion as the enemy advanced, I found myfelf almoft imperceptibly once more in Holland, whofe armies, ftill freezing upon the banks of the Maife and Lower Rhine, muft, perhaps, again have recourfe to the affiftance of her great *water-dog*, to whom fhe has more than once owed the falvation of her Republic; and indeed this fturdy guardian ought to do infinite good, fince he cannot be let loofe upon the enemies of the ftate without abundant mifchief—an inundation of the country being, next to captivity and its confequences, the greateft evil. Would you believe, after all which has happened fince my former gleaning of the United States, after all the faithful traditions of horror, bloodfhed, pillage, and blafphemy, which have been placed before them, that I find again here the felf fame fpirit of difaffection grown more gigantic, and with increafe of ferocity proportioned to augmentation of force ? For the difaffection of more *arbitrary* States, of France herfelf, for inftance,

I can

I can more eafily allow and account, but one would have thought that a Republic,—attached as is that of Holland to all thofe things which the French people now moft hold in fcorn, perfon, property, life, and religion; and with the bleeding teftimonies of rapine, devafta-tion and death before their eyes,—one would have thought, I fay, that in fuch a country, amongft fuch a people, who have much to lofe and nothing to gain, the fury of party, by which they have fo often unmercifully fuffered, and are fuffering at this moment in every limb and artery of the Republic, might have been moderated, if not deftroyed. Surely the defpe-ration of liberty, like that of love, baffles all reafoning, and mocks at all fober laws. Even the richeft merchants of the United Provinces, men who muft, on the very principles of equality, at leaft, divide the labours and gains of life, with thofe who fubfift only by an oppofite fet of principles, which levels idlenefs and induftry—even fuch men pant for the complete triumph of the common enemy, and are ready to facrifice, not only their fortunes, but their families—to what? to falfe ideas of freedom, and to revenge. What could they acquire? the gratification of an ancient grudge. What muft they lofe? Every thing elfe. But fo cold and fo dark is their feeling on this fub-

 ject,

ject, they would confider it as a cheap * purchafe,

But the fpreading flame is not confined to
Holland ! The Gleaner has traced its progrefs
through the provincial, petty towns of Auftria,
where a flender paffage of the Rhine feparates
the inhabitants from their utterly ruined neighbours, friends, and countrymen on the other
fide; he has feen and heard the look and tone
of determined Revolution: and, if he has at
one moment obferved one man retreating with
fear, he has, in the next, noticed more than
one remaining fixed to his houfehold, in hope
of the deftroyer. In numberlefs places, believe me, a *protecting* army is an object of filent,
yet obvious, hate, and one which menaces captivity is welcome. Along the banks of the
Maife, as of the Rhine, even though their
waves may be almoft faid, from the alchemy of
commerce, to flow with *gold*, the very worfhip-
pers of that precious mifchief would gladly
tinge its billows with blood ! In Weftphalia,
in Pruffia, he has followed, in every direction,
the like power. You cannot get into a public-
houfe, boat, or carriage, but the water and the

* The purhafe has been made; we fhall fee how long they
continue pleafed with their bargain.

land

land re-echoes with the ill-diffembled voice or loyalty, or the avowed and bolder tones of faction.

In fhort, the fever is more univerfal than any other that has yet raged in the world. It feizes on all ages, fexes, and countries; and though millions have already died of it, the fury rather increafes than abates. I have feen old fellows in their grand climacteric (to whom an eafy chair and a warm peaceful hearth, one would think, might comprife all the liberty fighed for), I have feen fuch receive with ex-ultation every account of a fortrefs deftroyed, a village burned, or a city defolated, even though adjoining their own. Like the malig-nant Zanga, but unfupported by Zanga's motives of revenge; they

    " Love the rocking of the battlements;
    " It fuits the gloomy habit of their fouls."

In a word, in a circuit of many hundred leagues, I have feen a fpirit of revolt to the ruling power, (whether emperor, ftadtholder, or king) that rifes amongft the ruins, and ftirs up infurrection amidft the very afhes of thrones and dominions! Adieu!

LETTER LVIII.

TO THE SAME.

YOU told me, I remember, in one of your late favours, that I had mingled in my sheaves many a bloody wreath. Alas, it is but the blushing signal of those events which are doomed to outrage the feelings of every gentle heart. In the character of an historical Gleaner I shall, ere long, be called upon to afflict the reader, and my friend, yet more: the moft terrifying truths are to be told; truths, over which I have wept and shuddered; but, over which, I neverthelefs hope (should the perufer of thefe pages shed a tear, and shudder alfo) he will find a balm sufficient to the wound. Amidft the pangs of *general* philanthropy, every *Briton-born reader, at leaft,* will feel at his heart the beatitude of his *particular* happinefs, in being a member of *that* ifland, which, although (by comparative extent) it meafures but as a fpeck in the map of the world, is the natal refidence of the fortunate, and the almoft fole fanctuary of the unhappy proportions of the globe.

3   But,

But, however, my countrymen, and my friends, are to be felicitated on this circumstance, I forrow to diftrefs them by delineating the fad reverfe, and, therefore, will

" Spare the telling, fince it be a pain."

as long as poffible.

The hurry and agitation of public affairs have led me to fome anticipations; the crouding incidents of the moment; the now gathering, now difperfing ftorms of war, have made me break in upon my referves prematurely; and *that* to the neglect of many a more pacific and fmiiing fcene. To thefe I fhall return with a fatisfaction that, I flatter myfelf, you will fhare, as it will, for a while, fufpend every more turbulent fubject, and empower me to conduct you gradually along, till you almoft forget we are approaching fcenes of devaftation. By fuch means, too, I fhall rather break the blow upon your feelings than take them by furprize: nay, more, as our paths to the feats of war lie through fome of the moft charming parts of Weftphalian Pruffia, I fhall even ftrew thofe paths with flowers.

I am now again addreffing you from Nimeguen, the laft confiderable town of the Dutch
territory,

territory, where, after having employed the reft of this letter, in a few Gleanings properly belonging to Holland, and the Provinces, we will journey onward,

" Sedate to think, and watching each event."
and, with our accuftomed privileges, -

" Try what the open, what the covert yields."

You have in recollection, I truft, my Gleanings of the Dutch theatre, when the ghoft of Hamlet ftalked upon the ftage of Holland, during the Hague fair. On a re-vifitation of that celebrated town fome days ago, I found that a troop of German actors had been permitted to take poffeffion of the playhoufe, fituated in the Cafuary-ftreet, which the French comedians (convicted of Jacobinifm, as I informed you), had evacuated. The firft piece, at the reprefentation of which I attended, was called, I think, The Robber; in which, amongft feveral very fine-wrought, and as fine acted, fcenes, was *one* turning upon an event fo prepofterous, that I muft relate it to you. The hero of the performance is a young man, who, in the firft inftance, robs his own father, and, eloping from his paternal houfe, carries his plunder to a defperate banditti, who have their haunts in a deep foreft, and with fuch affociates he fhares the plunder and the crimes. Notwithftanding

ftanding his companions have had ftrength
enough over the virtues of his youth to extin-
guifh his fenfe of duty to an aged and almoft
helplefs parent (and one of the tendereft that
ever bore the name), and even to make him
forego the endearing fociety of a lady to whom
he was powerfully attached, they had not force
of feduction fufficient to eradicate, entirely, the
vital principle of nature and confcience, which,
at various periods, broke forth in fighs of remorfe, and blufhes of fhame. The " cunning
of the fcene" affords many difplays of thefe,
and in the lucid returns of his heavily-fmitten
heart, he refcues that very parent, and that very
much-loved, though deferted, miftrefs, from
the barbarity and machinations of an elder
brother: This brother is, alfo, by his means,
(and by the moft equitable laws of human
life, as well as of the drama) brought to
juft punifhment; and, by arrangements no lefs
proper, the father is reftored to the freedom
and honours which his eldeft fon had ravifhed
from him, and the young lady is preferved
from violation. By fuch means, the parties,
long divided by the vices, are brought together
by the virtues of this heroic robber. Forgive-
nefs of the father, and of the miftrefs, are
matters of courfe, and the reconciliatory fcenes,
which exhibit thefe, are as naturally fuftained

as the incidents by which they are brought about, are artfully contrived. Every thing is in the faireft way of being fettled to the fatisfaction of the characters and of the audience. I never witneffed the *denouement* of a tragedy more comfortably arranged for the feelings. But the author was of a different opinion, for in the moment that you are about to congratulate this good ending of as bad a beginning, the poet ftarts a difficulty, which I conceive neither nature or reafon fuggefted to him. The almoft converted robber, even while fupported on the one hand by the love of a father, and on the other, by that of an adored miftrefs, finds out, that having *fworn* to live and die with his foreft companions, he cannot violate his oath ; and that, even if he could, his delicacy would not fuffer him to carry pollution into the arms of an innocent woman.

Now, if you approve of this *ftroke of delicacy*, I could wifh to ftop at it; but, as a faithful Gleaner, I muft proceed to inform you, that our delicate hero by no means contents himfelf with this declaration ; but while his hand is joined by a parent to that of a miftrefs, who covers it with tears of joy, and kiffes of love, he literally

" Throws it like a noifome weed away."

observing

obferving that, although he feels it impoffible to marry the lady himfelf, he cannot endure the thought of her living for another. This new misfortune finks the father to the ground, upon which he is left to die on one fide of the ftage, while the lady ftands ftatue-ftruck with grief on the other. Neither of thefe objects go to the heart of our hero. On the contrary, he intimates that there is no way left to pacify his fears on this curious point of delicacy, but the death of this beloved miftrefs. Hereupon the poet makes her obligingly take the hint by throwing herfelf into an attitude to receive the blow from the hand of her lover; who, however, rather hefitates about it, upon which the lady prefents her beautiful bofom (all heroines you know *muft* be beautiful) to any of the robbers; none of whom can be found to

" Scar that whiter fkin of her's
" Than monumental alabafter."

when men, who live by pillage and murder, are thus tender-hearted, I am juftified in applying the quotation; though, I fhould confider myfelf as having a fufficient fanction on the *determined* laws of the drama, to enrol amongft their unities, thofe of heroifm and perfonal beauty.

The

The Ruffians, however, all unfheath their fwords, and might, perhaps, have been wrought upon to cut in twain the filken bonds of humanity, that held them a moment uplifted, had not the hero come forth in all the *might* of his delicacy, in the fhape of *a rant*, (loud and vehement as ever pierc'd " the ears of the groundlings)," to affert *his* fole and exclufive claim to the affaffination. Saying which, and a great deal more, he takes the woman of his heart, *gently* in his arms, then buries his dagger *gently* in her breaft, then fupports her *gently* as fhe finks on the earth, where, *gently* placing her on the fide oppofite that of his dead father, on whofe body by the bye, dying or dead, he never beftows a glance, and then *gently* embracing his robber-friends, he ftalks off to kill himfelf at a more convenient feafon: and thus concludes this *gentle* piece of bufinefs: of which if any thing *could* add to the abfurdity, it would be the circumftance of having juft before found himfelf wholly incapable of ftabbing his worthlefs brother, becaufe, though ftained with the fouleft offences againft his dear father and dearer miftrefs, he was, forfooth, a good for nothing—brother! If this is not *refining upon refinement*, and *out-fentimentizing fentimentality*, the deuce is in it! Few of my readers but muft allow this was carrying the

point

point of delicacy a little too far: and, for my part, if this is the German method of settling the point, I remain a steady admirer of the coarse English fashion of stabbing *any body*, and, indeed, almost *every* body, rather than the woman of one's heart.

But the truth is, this is *not* the German mode any more than it is ours, as I have shewn, and shall still shew, in various instances. It is the act and deed solely of the *author of this drama*, who has therein not only put his heroine to death for his own amusement, but has committed an assassination upon a much greater character, even *nature herself*, and this is one example (out of an hundred) that has made me wish, gentlemen, who have the life and death of their characters, as dramatick writers, in their hands, would be a little less lavish of human, at least of poetical blood, without shewing cause in the courts of *reason*, *nature*, and *conscience*. Not that I mean to attach this strain upon dramatic or natural laws, to the productions of the German poets in general. They very frequently write, and act, with the most accurate knowledge of the human heart, and seldom fail to find their way to it, when their purpose is to interest its affections.

I was,

I was, indeed, foon recompenfed for the
above related outrage of probability, by the
performance which I faw at the fame theatre,
a few nights after, when all was

" Nature to advantage drefs'd."

It was, properly fpeaking, a gala play, being
reprefented in honour of the Prince Stadtholder's
birth-day, one of the few very occafional events
which bring a fufficient number of people to
fill the Hague theatre; for, although it is not
larger than Colman's in the Haymarket, there
is rarely audience enough to pay for the few
pounds of candle beftowed to illumine the
gloom, and, doubtlefs, this is one reafon why
there is not more light thrown upon the
audience of the Hague. On this great occafion,
however, there were about *half* as many lamps
ftuck over the Stadtholder's box as would have
been placed on the board of his Britannick
Majefty's corn-cutter on the 4th of June; and
even the under tier of fconces, that ufually ftand
unoccupied, were filled with wax!   In a word,
I beheld the aftonifhing circumftance of a
Dutch theatre *crowded*; and, inftead of " *the
beggarly account of empty boxes,* I found myfelf
amongft the flower and fafhion of the Hague.

After being waited for by the actors and the
audience the decent time, that is, juft long
enough

enough to wind up expectation to the proper
pitch, without ftraining its fprings, his Serene
Highnefs and his Royal-blooded partner made
their appearance, the firft in a modeft fuit of
flightly-ornamented blue broad cloth, the laft
according to the etiquette made and provided,
in thefe cafes, glittering in white filver tiffue.
Brunfwick's eldeft hope was fhining at their
fide, and his Duchefs attended the graceful and
lovely Princefs Hereditary in the ftage-box, de-
corated, for that night only, to receive them.

But, alas! all this was but the gay difguife
of a concealed anxiety; or rather, it was but
the trapping and incumbrance of a comfortlefs
fituation, too mighty for difguifes. Three
days and nights previous to this theatrical exhibition of themfelves, had the Prince, Princefs,
and train been made the illuftrious victims of
this anniverfary martyrdom: and every moment that was not devoted to the bendings,
bowings, and other pliabilities of the court,
was feized upon by the camp, for it was the
time when above a thoufand foldiers were preparing to replace the devaftations of the laft
campaign in Flanders. The Stadtholder is
indefatigable in his military duties; and thefe,
happening to fall at the period when he was to
receive the compliments of the nobility and

gentry, on gaining the forty-fixth year of his age, you will not wonder to hear that he brought to the play-houfe a weary head, and, perhaps, an aching heart; the more efpecially as it was faid an heavy piece of public news had been received from the frontiers, which it was neceffary to hufh up in his own mind, and in that of his auguft partner in diftrefs, left it fhould check the ardour of the troops about to take their departure. There is, you know, a crifis in fplendid, as well as other mifery, at which the oppreffed fpirits and faculties take refuge in fleep. It appeared to be exactly this crifis, when the party above-mentioned gained the theatre; for fcarce had the natal falutations been received and acknowledged, than a deep fleep fell upon both their Highneffes, and upon the Prince of Brunfwick. Never did I fee three illuftrious perfonages fo oddly difpofed of. They funk fubdued into a comfortable nap, as if it had been a preconcerted thing to refrefh them-felves at the theatre with a doze of this fort; and which, to fay the truth, they ftood fadly in need of. It feems they had been exhaufting themfelves in public affairs and ceremonies, from five in the morning to midnight of the preceding day. But that the anodyne was very powerful, may be gathered from their enjoying it, almoft unbroken, through the three long acts

of

of a German opera, spun to the length of as
many German miles. Once, indeed, his *Serene*
Highness opened half an eye, and cast it, in a
dizzy way, first at the sleeping princess, then
at the snoring duke, as if to explore the cause
that roused him; but, perceiving it was only
the crash of instruments, in a general chorus
by way of *finale* to the second act, he again
bid adieu to unwelcome recollections, in the
oblivious arms of that power which is very
justly called the kind " restorer of nature." I
could not help a reflection on the different allot-
ments of human kind, as I saw the most illustrious of the audience the only parts of it which
were unable to enjoy either the harmony, or
the pleasantry of the entertainment, and altogether insensible to the surrounding splendours.
We rave about, and we are bleeding at every
pore, and fermenting in every vein, for *Equality*,
my dear friend; we are hearing perpetually of
the necessity of bringing the poor on a level
with the rich, nobles with peasants, and kings
with beggars—ah, God of them all, with how
little reason! with how little recollection of the
history of *human conditions!* The worst and the
most unhappy is probably that which winds up
the climax! and so on of the series: since it is
most likely the houseless beggar, who eats his
morsel of alms under a hedge of thorns, when

the

the rude hand of winter had torn off every shel‑ tering leaf, in remembrance of the day that brought into the world the brat which he buckles to his back, has a more exquisite relish of that morsel, and is more soothed by the gra‑ tulations of his weather-beaten companions, than the Prince and Princess of the Republic of Holland, sleeping amidst the felicitations of a theatre, or, in truth, any prince, or princess in these times. Equality! alas, were all men reduced to a level *like this*, how soon would those who, till then perhaps, without being con‑ scious of it, had experienced the blessings of an humble state, wish again for the refuge and distinction of poverty. Whosoever has looked on the fatigues, weight, and peril of the ele‑ vations amongst mankind, must know this, and it is strange there should be found any one so unreasonable as to envy the exalted this gild‑ ing of their care and misery. As to the emi‑ nent examples in question, happy to see them enjoy this temporary respite, I was sorry when the fall of the curtain awakened and dismissed them to new fatigues.

Whatever might be their fate for the rest of that night, to new fatigues the Stadtholder, at least, was destined the succeeding morning. The troops which had cost him so much trouble

to

to make ready, were to march at eight o'clock. Without ufing literary privileges, which allow authors to blot out the fun, or command him to fend forth his moft effulgent beam (having, you know, a charter from Parnaffus to do as we pleafe with the elements) I affure you, in the profe fimplicity of truth, that, *really*

" The dawn *was* overcaft, the morning low'r'd,
" And heavily in clouds brought on the day."

Nay more, thofe clouds, very foon after the Stadtholder reached the parade, broke on his unfheltered head, for the indifpenfible ceremonies of a field-day were to be exchanged, and his Royal Highnefs (princes not counting amongft their prerogatives the liberty of controlling the fkies to their purpofe) got a ducking more fevere than that I have recorded in a former letter. One would again be led to think that " there was more in thefe matters than philofophy can find out:" for really had the clouds been in combination againft him, they could not have fpouted down a more inaufpicious torrent. It was not, however, of fufficient vehemence to damp his martial attention: neither had it the force to chill public curiofity: confequently it was fet at defiance by powers ftronger than either curiofity, or martial ardour. Never, on any public occafion, did

 I fee

I fee fuch a collection of human beings. Every paſſion of the heart, and every feeling of nature, were here met together. In the form either of patriots, princes, men, wives, miſtreſſes, children, officers, or foldiers, you might have obſerved hate, allegiance, love, hope, and defpair. You might have remarked alſo a few fmiles of heroifm, amidſt many bitter tears of apprehenſion. The difaſters of the laſt campaign were had in *bleeding* remembrance, and there were thofe amongſt the difaffected inhabitants, who exclaimed, " See what a brave " ſhew of fellows are waiting *orders to march* " *to the ſhambles!* " *

Infidious whifperings of this kind had been in circulation for fome time, and feveral defertions had taken place in confequence; upwards of twenty on the night immediately preceding their march. Nor was this the worſt: a difpiriting kind of alarm pervaded the foldiery,

---

* Alas! this exclamation has fince proved, in fome late inſtance, fo late as the 15th and 16th of April laſt, but too prophetic ; and, although the military entré of the young Imperial Monarch has been marked with glory, one cannot but regret it has been marked with fo much of the blood of his allies. Many of the very men whom the Gleaner beheld that day leaving their country have bade it an eternal adieu. It is the fate of war: but one ſhrinks from the thought ; and I wiſh I had not cen them all alive. It is weaknefs, perhaps, but forgive me.

who performed their military preparations with reluctant delay. I had noticed many of them ftanding, the day before their departure, by the fide of their baggage waggons, as if they were taking a furvey of their hearfes, filling them with their beds, &c. as if they prefaged they would prove their beds of death. Others were following thefe vehicles with all their marching apparatus, not with eyes that anticipated victory, but with downcaft looks, and folemn fteps, to dirge-like meafure, as if they were moving after the coffin of a comrade ; and the beat of the drum that acts fo wonderfully upon the fpirits in certain moments, now feemed to found in their ears the dead march.

Examples of every kind are known to be contagious ; in no inftance, perhaps, more than in their influence upon our hopes and fears : courage and cowardice are communicated in a moment : they are even *transferred* with electric rapidity from one man to another ; the bofom of the brave, catching an unwonted apprehenfion, and the breaft of the daftard, glowing with even an unnatural ardour, as the poifonous breath of difaffection, or the exhilarating powers of loyalty, are diffufed amongft them. It is a lamentable thing when private houfes or public empires are fet againft them-

felves. States are only large families, united
by the fame laws, and bound by the fame intereft. The connexions of the neareft ties in
private life are fcarce more clofe, nor ought
they to be more facred. As the welfare of
man and wife, fo the profperity of nations, my
friend,

> " When thofe whom heav'n ordains to will the fame
> " Look different ways, unmindful of each other,
> " Think what a train of wretchednefs enfues!"

Unfortunately for the well being of thefe *United
States* (which, by the bye, is, and has long been,
a mifnomer) the two parties that are difmem-
bering it are in perpetual counter-action.
While the one is diligently labouring to knit
the provinces together, the other, perhaps
more induftrious, for mifchief is a very active
power, works day and night, though working
often under-ground, to render that honeft dili-
gence ineffectual : and vigilant malignity will
always be more or lefs fuccefsful.

On this important morning, however, the
Stadtholder rallied the half-feduced energies
of his foldiers; he faluted them firft generally,
then particularly ; he complimented, and with
great juftice, their martial appearance, cheered

them

them with a prince's fmile, diftributed amongft them a prince's bounty, beftowed, with well-timed addrefs, a prince's eulogy on their known valour, &c. &c.

" A little flattery fometimes does well."

He manifefted, by fifty little attentions, that he confidered them as the faithful defenders of the Republic, and, in fhort, put in motion every wheel of a good general, a good-natured prince, and a good man. His deportment had a vifible effect on the troops, into whofe countenances there came, as if by reflection, a fudden and promifing brightnefs: the morning itfelf began to look more cheerfully, and the officers with their men duly equipped, from the orange branches in their hats, to the neat knapfack at their backs, took their march through the ftreets leading to Schedam—their firft day's march—accompanied to the outer gate of the town by tens of thoufands of fpectators.

If fome few of thofe thoufands heaved a fin-cere figh of loyalty for the return of the troops, victorious and uninjured, how many, fecretly, or, to fay the truth, openly, defired and hoped, they might be vanquifhed and cut to pieces! How ftrange does this feem, how unnatural does it found?

" Is it not as if this mouth

" Would tear this hand for lifting food to it?"

With refpect to the Hollanders, the liberty to fay and do what they like, in defiance of all inhibited things, and, as ufual, with the more eager audacity, becaufe forbidden, is * *their's*; and as to their being taxed, do they confider that they live in a country made by induftry in defpight of nature, who intended it to be only one of her enormous bogs, while the anceftors of this grumbling but hard-working hive, fet " doggedly to it," as Dr. Johnfon fays, to make it into productive land, and a more pro- ductive water? a pile of ftupendous art, from one end to the other, and not to be kept in repair without extraordinary taxation? Do they grudge this? Would they let the edifice run to ruins, and be buried amongft them? Would they heap up their money bags to fink them with themfelves more profoundly in the *returning* bog? Will the French, or their native patriots, mend either their country or

* Not one of the motives that urged the French people had the Dutch

" to fpur the fides of *their* intent,

" Save vaulting ambition,"

which, the Gleaner thinks, will, in *their* cafe, at leaft, be found to have

" O'erleap'd itfelf."

their

their commerce? Let them try! Ingenious, laborious, abſurd, wiſe, fooliſh, prepoſterous people!

Here then let us bid a long, and probably a laſt, adieu, to the United Provinces, on which we have beſtowed more liberal obſervation than they have been wont to receive, but not more than they have deſerved, as the moſt curious and aſtoniſhing efforts of a patient, powerful, and vigilant people: A like fare-well to Guelderland, for whoſe proſperity I ſhall have a warm wiſh were it only for the ſake of the opportunity it gives of *loſing one's way*, and *finding the Man of the Foreſt*. Bleſſed be every leaf of every tree which comes under the axe of that man! And bleſſed be you, my friend! aye, and ye, my readers! Weſtphalia invites; but I cannot quit one country, and take you into another, without ſeparating them and their inhabitants by a little pauſe in our corre-ſpondence.

LETTER

LETTER LIX.

I HAVE in a former gleaning noted the wonderful progreſſive relief from low to high land, and from wet to dry, from ſtagnant canals to running ſtreams, as you proceed in your journey from the United Provinces to the Upper Countries. This is leſs ſenſibly felt after a few days or weeks ramble in Guelderland; but could the traveller be ſuddenly tranſported from the Province of what is properly called Holland, to thoſe blooming edges of Weſtphalia, to which I am now conducting you, he would imagine, that *one* was the purgatory of ſinful, and the *other* the paradiſe of happy ſouls: The fabled waters of the Styx and of Elyſium, are not more ſtrongly contraſted. The very air, as well as the water, takes a purer breath. Not that in point of vegetable or rural grandeur, Weſtphalian Pruſſia is to be compared to ſeveral parts of Dutch Guelderland; but in point of unambitious and ever-ſmiling ſcenery, I have never ſeen any thing ſuperior. The houſes and the land, and, indeed, the inhabitants of Holland, reſemble nothing but themſelves,

felves. The charming Duchy of Cleves, and "all that it inherits," refembles the moft beautiful unaffuming parts of England. You have fcarce reached the firft Pruffian town, which is mid-way betwixt Nimeguen and Cleves, the name of which is Cuylenberg, ere your native country preffes on your heart: you feem to be carried, by fome magician into the midft of its alluring fcenery; its whited cottages, comfortable farms, and cultured grounds, are all within your view. You are ftruck at almoft every ftep with the fimilitude. It is the agreeable and beautiful, but not the fublime of nature. There is nothing of hill or vale, water or wood, to afto-nifh the traveller; but there are numbers of objects always frefh and always charming, and a profpect of great abundance. I am fpeak-ing here of the Duchy of Cleves in a circum-ference of its beft poffeffions, a *coup d'œil* of more than fifty miles; for, on a clear day, your eye can travel to this extent, if it takes fight from any of the delightful little emi-nences near the town of Cleves: particularly from a mount in the wood which gives you the command of half a dozen noble avenues, each a mile in length, at the end of which your view is bounded by the prettieft towns in the Circle of Weftphalia, and Province of Guel-derland. The eye refts fatisfied and refrefhed;

it

it wishes not to penetrate beyond thefe beautiful limits. The Cleves wood is, in itfelf,
full of charms, artificial and natural; but by
the former I only mean the ftately, and fomewhat formal, rows of trees, which fhade and
canopy the almoft numberlefs paths that are
cut through it. Yet, admitting this to be an
objection to the lover of nature in all her
graceful wildnefs, there are to be found in this
wood an infinity of bye-walks, where nature is
permitted to enjoy her utmoft romance, and to
fport her " virgin fancies," and which, perhaps,
derive additional charms from the contraft with
the more *difciplined* vegetation. This fine wood
is fenced round with the old Englifh-looking
park-paling, thatched, as it were, with grey mofs,
as with us, and, as with us, the chaffinch, green-
finch, goldfinch, and " all the other finches of
the grove," as the Critic fays, are feen peck-
ing at it on a fine fpring morning to build the
outworks of their nefts. I have haunted this
wood at all times and feafons, and truft, therefore, you will be pleafed with both a fummer,
and winter account of it. There appears to
be fomething remarkable in the foliage of
Weftphalia, to be obferved in the moft dreary
months. With us, even in our moft extended
forefts, the trees and bufhes are almoft ftripped
of their withered foliage. In Great-Britain
                                    and

and in Holland, autumn fcarce leaves a trace behind her when the " furly winter," as our poet of nature beautifully calls him " with his ruffian train," has ufurped her empire. It is far otherwife in Weftphalia: The underwood, not only of the enduring oaks, but of all other forts of more tender fhrub wood, fcarcely fuftain the lofs of a leaf; a general ruffet, fuch as we fee in the Englifh groves, when they put on their November robes, covers whole acres till the end of March, when it is moft likely nature is arrayed in her fpring drefs in Great Britain. Refpecting the trees of foreft growth, they are here, as in the general roads of France, and in the avenues that lead to our antique manfions of England, planted in the ftraight line, but their regularity as to height and extent gives them one appearance, at the prefent moment, fingular and agreeable. Three or four days of rain, with the intervals of a dry fouthern air, have given them fuch an univerfal blufh, that (though nothing like a leaf is to be feen in alleys of feveral thoufand trees, cut into different roads at right angles, and is fimply the effect of a fwell amongft the buds) you have the promife, that the very next funny day will *invert* Shakfpeare's much-criticifed expreffion, *making the green* ONE *red*, by making the *red* ONE *green*; for on cropping one of thefe bloom-

ing

ing twigs, and preffing the buds with your finger, you perceive them burfting into infant vegetation.

Eight and forty hours of genial weather fo changes thefe glowing branches, that the eye regales in a profpect of that tender verdure, which, in vegetable, as in human, life, gives the frefhnefs and complexional delicacy which belongs only to the moft *early youth of nature*; fo fweet to behold, and, alas! fo foon deftroyed: Neither the broad foliage of a more advanced Spring, nor the rich expanfion and colouring of confirmed Summer, offer any thing fo pure. There are, you know, the fame changes, productive of the fame effects, in the progrefs of life, in the feveral ftages of *its* Spring, Summer, and Autumn.

Suffer me now to carry you about Cleves Land. Imagine that you are feated on one of the ruftic benches, in a retired part of its delicious wood, while I recount to you the gleanings of feveral tours in its neighbourhood.

The town of Cleves in itfelf has nothing to recommend it, but the exceffive beauty of its fituation. It is a large, ftraggling, ill-paved place, with many good houfes and more bad.

It

It is, however, the capital of the Duchy, and
under the domination of his Pruffian majefty.
Though fo near to Holland, and with fuch an
example of neatnefs before their eyes, the inhabitants of Cleves by no means deign to follow
it. On the contrary, they are in their houfes,
ftreets, and not unfrequently in their perfons,
the moft difgufting contrafts:—but of thefe
difagreeable matters hereafter.

As I reached the environs of the town, the
firft day my affections were very fingularly
interefted: Indeed, I know not when they have
been more powerfully called forth, where the
objects of their fympathy were taken not from
the human fpecies, but from the animal world.
About a mile from the Weftern-gate, I perceived a man and boy bufied in doing fomething
to the moft beautiful ox I ever beheld: as I
came nearer I found they were adorning it
with a great variety of fanciful ornaments; a
large collar of yew branches, tied with ribbon,
and wreathed with other evergreens, were
thrown over its neck: painted papers, on which
were drawn herds, flocks, and fhepherds, and
folded into large beau knots, were fixed, I am
afraid, *pinned* with large corkers to its fkin, in
various parts of the body: bunches of the fame
were tied to the tail, braided into the mane,

and the brows were hung with a garland of holly, of which there was a twist fastened by red filleting even to the horns, on the tips of which were stuck little May-bushes in bloom.

My attention was presently called off from this, by the bleat of a sheep and its lamb: those creatures were bound to an hedge in a corner of the same enclosure. They were dressed nearly in the taste of the ox, with this variation in the lamb, a collar of several early spring flowers of the field, and some twigs of hawthorn, in bud, and which, betwixt sport and earnest, it was trying to get into its mouth. On asking the cause of all this finery, I was told it was upon account of its being a *jour-de-fête,* and also the day before that of the greatest beef, mutton, and lamb market, in the whole year!

And pray, friend, said I, where is the necessity of dressing the animals in that manner?

'Tis our custom, Sir, replies the man driving the ox towards the town, and the boy with the sheep and lamb, now unbound, following his example,

I had not time for more interrogatories, being wholly taken up with the anticks of the
lamb,

lamb, which frolicking sometimes with its mother, and sometimes with the boy, and sometimes even with its own shadow, brought so close, under my eye, and so near indeed to my very heart, the fine lines of Mr. Pope, that I repeated them over and over. Every image of his description had its immediate illustration in the objects before me:

> " The lamb, thy riot dooms to bleed to day,
> " Had he thy reason, would he skip and play?
> " Pleas'd to the last, he crops the flow'ry food,
> " And licks the hand just rais'd to shed his blood!

We gained Cleves as I pronounced, for the tenth time, that impressive verse which gives the moral of the former stanza—

> " O blindness to the future! *kindly* given."

The animals were led, or rather driven, through the principal streets, literally for a *shew*, it being the practice of Westphalia for the butchers to exhibit their meat *alive* the day preceding the slaughter. I pretend to question neither the use nor the necessity of all this; nor by any means to stretch pity or feeling beyond their bound. I only observe to you, that my affections followed these creatures in their *funeral* procession through the town of Cleves, and could not leave them till on turning a narrow lane, I saw, with a kind of emotion you

will

will eafily guefs, the door of the place deftined for their deftruction; it being a practice in this country to flaughter their meat, and a very filthy one it is,* in the open ftreet; the pavements and kennels of which are ftained and running with blood.

I will carry you no farther into this little adventure than juft to note, that being the next day obliged to pafs the end of the ftreet, where I took leave of my poor dumb companions, I obferved not only feveral parts of them hang upon hooks at the butcher's fhop, but feveral of the ornaments. Even the flowers that were wreathed about the face of the lamb were now crouded into its mouth, and fpotted with its harmlefs blood. Poor little fellow, faid I, thou wert yefterday the merrieft of the frifking tribe! Would I never had met thee!

If, in the courfe of the week, it was my lot to *eat* any part of thefe animals, at the tables where I then vifited, as it is moft probable was the cafe, confider *poor human nature*, and forgive me! I am not prepofterous enough to advife a being, who is made up of appetites to abftain from the gratification of fuch as are neceffary to exiftence, but while we yield to the ftern laws of our mortality, let us not, you, I am fure,

* The fame vile cuftom prevails in feveral parts of Holland.

will

will not, spurn all sort of feeling, like the man, who, on seeing some lambs at sport in a meadow, exclaimed,—" Ah, ye dear, innocent, beautiful creatures, would to heaven I had a joint of ye to-day for dinner, with nice spinnage and butter!"

A very different sentiment sprung up in my mind as I surveyed the amputated limbs of these my late associates. You remember what the heart-melting Otway says on the subject:

" Lead, lead me like a tame lamb to sacrifice,
" Thus in his fatal garlands, fine and pleas'd
" The wanton skips and plays————
" Trots by th' inticing, flattering, priestess side,
" And much tranfported with his little pride,
" Forgets his dear companions of the plain,
" Till, by her bound, he's on the altar lain
" And then too hardly bleats.

Never can this affecting passage be more touchingly illustrated than in the case of my lamb of Westphalia.

The sheep of this very beautiful country, however, are not so well-looking, nor so good, in point of food, as might be expected from the rich abundance of their pasturage, and the purity of their air. They are longer in the visage, body, and legs than ours : Their fleeces are more ragged and dirty. How different in colour and countenance, from the fair flocks

 gleaned

gleaned in our firſt ſheaf, that climb the mountains, and friſk along the valleys of our Cambria! A ſheep in Wales is really an intereſting
being; you ſee its mild face peep unexpectedly
from the fiſſure of a rock, in the midſt of an
enormous pile of ruinous ſtones; or you have a
full length view as it repoſes at the mouth of a
fine natural cave; or you obſerve it looking
down upon you from a ſtupendous ridge of
rocks, on the extreme verge of which it ſeems
to hang, till you feel ſomething like an apprehenſion it ſhould tumble into the vale below
and be deſtroyed: but, even while your ſympathy
is thus engaged in its welfare, the wanton creature, wild as the wind that bleaches it, and
romantic as the ſpots on which it feeds, will
bound from the dizzy precipice where it ſtood,
to an height yet more fearful, and projecting its
neck beyond where you imagine it poſſible for
it to keep the due equilibrium, will crop the
herbage that vegetates amongſt the ſtony ruins,
or the flower that makes its flinty bed in the
rocks, and will continue to climb and deſcend
places, the perpendicular of which makes your
eyes ake, and your head giddy; but the Cambrian ſheep takes its *paſtime* amongſt theſe
apparent dangers, with ſo much eaſe and gaiety,
you are ſoon convinced it is rather an object of
your envy than compaſſion.

Now

Now in Weftphalia, and in moft other parts of Pruffia and Germany, thefe animals, after they have outlived the frolicks of lambhood, have lefs of this playfulnefs, and, indeed, become very foon a fet of ferious, ruminating, ragged, and folemn creatures.

The dog that guards them, however, is generally a very pleafant fellow. He is taught to dance, and has many other laughable humours and accomplifhments, but in his bufinefs is indefatigable. Wholly unlike the curs of England, where the apathy of the mafter feems contagious, and where, even when following their flock, both appear to be *walking in their fleep;* the fhepherd dogs of this country are like fo many perpetual motions; if the fhepherd wifhes to have them driven from one part of pafturage to another, to divide, to congregate, or to conduct them to their fold, his dog begins his office, which is performed in the following manner. He runs round them in a circle, or rather three parts of a circle, leaving the fourth part open for their paffage, and he barks all the time. If any ftraggler loiters by the way, he enlarges his round, till it includes the wanderer, who is brought up with the reft. He does his work in two equal fpaces of ground, running from right to left, and from left to right. It is truly, a curious operation, and not a little fatiguing, fince it fometimes continues an hour together, without a moment's refpite from barking and running. But, like many others, it is, for the moft part, labour in vain. The fheep are fo much in the habit of hearing this eternal yelper, that fo far from attending to his cries, I queftion whether they hear his voice, like thofe perfons who live within the found of bells. At any rate, they pay no re- gard to it; for, while he is in full cry, the fheep ftep as leifurely as if he was fix feet under ground; even the ox I have mentioned in a former part of this letter, and my poor lamb, round whom he galloped in the fame way, heeded him not. The firft turned him as it were, into contempt, and the laft into ridicule, looking at him without fear, while his mouth was wide open, and, full of antic, joining him in his race. So that I begin to think our Englifh fhepherd's cur does the bufinefs more effectually.

While I am upon the fubject of the canine race, of which you know I am a profeffed friend and admirer, let me not forget to inform you of an excellent cuftom prevalent in Hol- land, and in Weftphalia, refpecting thofe animals in the dog-days, namely, the law

which

which enacts their being shut up during the sultry feason. The appearance of a dog of any kind in the streets at such times is punished with just severity. Now, as canine madnefs, perhaps the most lamentable distemper incident to human kind, is very rarely heard of in the various parts of the Continent that are the objects of these Gleanings, we must impute it principally to the caution here described. "Go, and do likewife," is an admonition worthy the adoption of the people of England, who suffer deplorable instances of distraction and death, arising from the want of some regulation on this subject.

Far, far from the friend of my heart be every malady of the body, and of the mind!

LETTER LX.

TO THE SAME.

CLEVES may be enrolled amongst the watering places, but as those waters contain nothing to distinguish them from a thousand others, whose basis is steel, with a certain mix-ture of falts and sulphur, I know you will easily

difpenfe

difpenfe with a defcription of them. Neither
will I take up your time by a detail of the
dinner or tea parties in the very wood I have
now placed you. Thefe fort of accounts re-
femble the pictures which were cenfured for
being, though vaftly pretty, all alike. Water
drinking, or dipping, places have, in themfelves, but one character, and a defcription of
any, will, like Mr. Garrick's prologues, ferve
as well for one place as another. If you turn
to any book of travels, through any part of
modern Europe, for mineral or falt water, (to
fave trouble look in the index) and take that
which comes firft to hand—no matter for the
country—you will have a defcription in point,
for what has been faid and done on thefe occafions, fince water-diving and drinking came
into fafhion; the fame talkings, walkings, in-
trigues, divorces, matches made, and matches
broken, covert whifpers, and open fcandals,
and all the old ftory of little and great con-
fpiracies, fince the paffions firft came into
public. There is not left a remark, *generally*
fpeaking, on thefe fubjects, worth a fingle
wheat-ear. So we will pafs them by without
gleaning, juft noting one or two *particular*
habits of pleafure that obtain in the neighbourhood of the Cleves Wood.

It

It is the practice for the Clevelanders to crowd on a fine Sunday to some very good tea-drinking houses, situate in the park, to see tumbling boys and girls, and dancing dogs, and learned pigs, and poultry. The spectators place themselves in extensive alcoves, open at both ends: they almost all are to be seen in the *hottest weather*, drinking the *hottest* tea, with a dozen, and often two dozen, *red-hot* tea-urns under their very noses. By way of auxiliary to this heat, the men all smoke, and take alternately a sup of tea, a slice of bread, or cake, and a whiff of tobacco. The married women snuff in proportion; the spinsters, born and educated amidst fire and smoke, disperse the clouds with which their lovers and parents thus envelope them: sighs of tenderness, and whiffs of the best Virginia are puffed forth and mingle in the same breath, and the young lady melts in the midst of them. I do assure you a kitchen fire in the dog-days is " dew-dropping coolnefs" to the being enclosed in this *long green oven*; and, what with the scalding water, on the one hand, and of the burning fires on the other, a stranger finds himself almost suffocated. The first time that I myself was stuck betwixt this Scylla and Charibdis, I feelingly saw the force of custom, which reconciled the most delicate young women (for, in point of form

and

and feature, Weftphalia has many fuch to boaft)
to this hideous practice. They feem as collected
during this double attack as Generaliffimos of
an army in the heat of action. After ftaying
till I was almoft boiled on one fide, and fmoke-
dried on the other, I fought my efcape in the
wood, the moft beautiful paths of which, as well
public as private, where nature breathed the
fweeteft air, difplayed the moft enchanting
pictures, and fung the fongs of gratitude and
joy among her branches, were comparatively
deferted. I am forry to fay that all the concerts, focieties, clubs, and other focial meetings,
are deformed by thofe infufferable fumigations,
with which every houfe, fhop, and even every
garden, is infefted.

It is thought to be falutary. Had it been
confined to Holland, I might have poffibly
come into this notion, as a corrector of bad
air; but when I found it laid all Germany in
fmoke and afhes, and thereby fpread over countries " where every breeze is health," I fet it
down as a vile cuftom that feeks to hide its
filthinefs in a weak apology.

I cannot but reckon it·lefs excufeable than
the ftoves amongft women—a practice not lefs
univerfal, but which the dampnefs of the
                                        air,

air, in the Provinces of Holland, may render neceffary. It is attended alfo, by worfe con-fequences; for there is nothing fo rare amongft the Dutch, Pruffians, or Germans, as a good fet of teeth: and as boys accuftom themfelves to the ufe of a pipe almoft as foon as they can fill, hold, and light it, their teeth are difcoloured at a time of life when the youth of other coun-tries are alike pure in mind and perfon. This defect is the more obvious in the German young men, becaufe the females of the fame age are remarkable for exhibiting rows of that pearly whitenefs, which, in Europe, at leaft, has been ufually thought fuch a conftituent in perfonal beauty. The ladies, however, of Pruffia and Germany, being in the habit of feeing a couple of black ranges in the mouths of their lovers and hufbands, and to receive a whiff of fmoke in their faces almoft every time they affociate, or are fpoken to by the oppofite fex (for imme-diately before and after, and fometimes *at* meals they fmoke) do not feem to feel the contraft.

I particularly remember to have been prefent at this very town of Cleves, when, amongft other company, were two young people, who had been given out as paffionately fond of one another. The lady was playing at her forte piano, her lover, holding a pipe in one of the

fil.hieft

filthieft mouths I ever faw, and accompanying
her in a very pretty German air. This air
fhewed the lady's fine rows of ivory to advantage, while it expofed her Coridon's ebony no
lefs to view, and, at the end of the fong, a fly
and quiet Gleaner, like myfelf, could perceive
that the company were fo well pleafed with the
performers, and the performers with *themfelves*,
that, not contented with the general acclama-
tion of the friends, they fealed the private applaufe they beftowed upon *one another* with fo
clofe an approach of faces, that, though their
confcious fatisfaction was not expreffed and
fealed in a kifs *heard* (or hardly feen) it certainly was in a kifs *felt*. No one who had been
a fpectator of this fcene, would have agreed
with the father of the fair-faced Defdemona,
in calling the love fhe manifefted for the moor
unnatural. She had, like the pretty Cleve-
lander, looked away the fable hue of Othello,
and, fince fhe could not find his mind in his
vifage, difcovered his vifage in his mind.
Poetry, and, efpecially, the poetry of Shakfpeare, which can do every thing, can,
of courfe, do this; but nothing, except that
cuftom, which the fame immortal bard in-
forms us

 " Can make the flinty and fteel couch of war
 " A thrice-driven bed of down."

or

or what is yet even stronger than custom, all-commanding love, could make a junction of the whitest and blackest, fairest and foulest teeth, a matter of delight!

Before I take you from this fair wood into the town of Cleves, I must prepare you for a few other customs which you will meet with there, and in other parts of the Duchy; and, indeed, in most places of Germany.

Expect, in the first place, to find the inhabitants here, as in Holland, too civil by half: The courtesy of hat-pulling prevails in Westphalia to a degree really painful. It is a settled point for all natives to make bows to strangers of almost every description, so that a traveller has little more to do in the considerable towns than to cover and uncover his head. Indeed, the hats themselves sufficiently shew the prevalence of the custom, being all of them squeezed into a long roll, as compact as a polonie, on the take-off side, with the continual gripe of civility. In one of my first excursions into this country, I took part of a carriage with a young man just come from the Independent States of America, and glowing with all the unrestrained spirit of his country. His objections went to almost every thing he heard or

saw

faw in monarchies: they began with the head
and defcended to the feet; for he neither
endured the uncovering of the one, nor the
flexibility of the other. I honour'd this ardour
of his principles, but wifhed to make them relax
a little to the cuftoms of a country. I began
with the affair of the hat, which he fwore fhould
be inveterately fixed on his head in his paffage
through Holland; adding, that he looked
upon obeifance to every body, without diftinction, as a fervility below the dignity of man's
nature. Let me advife you my friend, and
my readers, to be courteous; and to give
into this fomewhat fatiguing practife. It will
repay itfelf by many little urbanities you will
wifh for and find: the Germans and Weftphalians are an obliging race; and their excefs of
hat civility is better than the contrary extreme.
But civility abroad is by no means confined to
making you a paffing-bow: and if it were,
it is a flight tax upon a traveller to endure and
return it.

I recollect being much pleafed in Holland
with a union of two things that rarely meet in
any country. During my Hague gleaning, I
was at the Playhoufe, when the beauty of two
ladies, both on travel, excited the attention of
the audience more than the performance. But
the

the obfcurity and gloom of the Hague theatre
not clearly afcertaining that beauty, a great
number of the fpectators were anxious to fee
more of the truth, and accordingly had arranged
themfelves after the play, in two mighty rows,
as if by common confent, to fee the fair
ftrangers pafs from their box to their carriage.
In itfelf, this fet and determined ftare was
certainly one of the rudeneffes of curiofity; but
in order to fmoothe away its rough edges, the
paffing meteors no fooner appeared within the
lines, than, as if by common confent alfo, every
hat was taken off, and every head bowed refpectfully to greet them. Even if the curiofity,
which beauty very naturally excites, did not
carry, in fome degree, its excufe along with it,
it would have been impoffible for that beauty
to have been offended. In the prefent inftance
it produced, juft as it fhould do, a blufh of
courtefy and confcioufnefs as it paffed along,
not refenting, though not inviting, the homage
which it drew.

Who is there, my friend, that ever has paft
but a fingle winter in London, but muft have
often feen the heroes of the box-lobby forming
themfelves into a phalanx, hats on heads, and
opera glaffes at eyes, to ftare out of countenance, and out of the houfe, perhaps amidft in-

decent obfervations, both beauty and innocence. Let us not quarrel then with civilities that foften away our difguft; nor even with public curiofity when it is tempered with public refpect.

Be prepared, alfo, for the *kiffing* ceremony which you will find begin in Pruffian Weft-phalia, and extend over every part of the German territories. Neither treat it with ridicule or difrefpect; for although it is the cuftom for both fexes to embrace, and to prefent both fides of the face for falutation, after paffing only an hour together, and though but next door neighbours, it means no more than our exchanging the cuftomary civilities of the moment, *en paffant*, in our own country: it fignifies, in fhort, about as much as the mode of profeffing ourfelves the obedient very humble fervant of thofe indifferent people we meet with in the ftreet, or addrefs by letter of bufinefs or ceremony.

I muft repeat that thefe national habits ought always to be complied with. An obftinate refufal in a young countryman of mine to accept of a falute was intended by him to exprefs a fcorn of the cuftom itfelf, particularly in fuffering his cheek to come into momentary
contact

contact with that of a *man*; but, by the gentleman who offered the salute, it was conftrued
into his having a bad breath, and a fear to
difcover it.

Now as an imputation of this kind would be
more wounding to the felf-love of our petit-
maitres and maitreffes, than, perhaps, an expul-
fion from kiffing all the days of their lives; I
advife them to give and lend their cheeks for
the kifs of cuftom without any farther hefitation.

I feel it my duty likewife to prepare you for
a little impofition in the hotels and private
lodgings before you enter them, as well as for
the counterbalancing *agrémens*.

I muft lay it down as a firft general principle,
that a Pruffian and German landlord, if he
poffibly can, will over-reach you; not fo much,
I believe, from difhonefty, as from an almoft
innate idea of confidering the word *Englifhman*
finonimous with the word *riches*. An Italian,
French, and every other traveller, even a
Dutchman, whom, generally fpeaking, they
know is well able to pay up to any price demanded, may always get accommodated at half
price, in comparifon of the Britifh wanderer—
that felf-devoted victim of vanity and folly.
Of this I will give you an inftance, not pro-

duced in refentment, for it was rather a fubject of pleafantry, but in order to put you,
your friends, and every one into whofe hands
thefe Gleanings may fall, on guard.

On my firft tour to Cleves I wifhed to make
a ftop of a few months, and not readily fuiting
myfelf in an Hotel, I fought private apartments.
A tradefman, of whom I had bought fome
trifling articles, and who fpoke very good French,
offered to attend me to the houfe of a man
who, he faid, had rooms to lett; and added,
that he would have the honour to be my
interpreter.

We went accordingly, and I defired my Interpreter to afk the price of the Rooms, when,
by way of anfwer, came forth another queftion.

Mafter of the Houfe. The gentleman, I fuppofe, is French.
Interpreter. No.
Mafter of the Houfe. Dutch?
Interpreter. No; Englifh.
This information, confifting only of two
monofyllables, had the effect of a volume on
the man's mind. He intended, however, to be
cautious and manage the intelligence; but his
features betrayed him.

2   He

He *doubled* upon me every article, as I shall presently shew. I caused him to be informed, that, on the receipt of my next letters from England, I should be able to decide whether I remained in the town, or proceeded farther up the country; observing, that if I became his inmate, it would be impossible to do without a slip of carpeting, or some covering by the bed side.

That may be had, quoth the landlord; and so we parted.

The expected letters arrived, and finding it convenient to pursue my route as far as Emeric, on the other side of the Rhine, I gave him notice two days earlier than my promise, that, as I should be absent a month or six weeks, I would not hazard the letting his apartments to a more stationary tenant should any such offer. Now, that this notice might be formal, it was translated and delivered by my interpreter. Here, I supposed, we had done with one another; but the next morning, when every thing was ready for my departure, the master of the inn, where I had slept, presented me with a reply to my billet; written with a majesty of style that would have better suited the *Grand Frederic* (who, by the way, would have given a much

 more

more courteous anfwer) than the little great
man who was the author, or rather dictator,
for he underftood even lefs of the French than
I of the German, and was at the expence
of a notary—*Voilà le decret defpotique de mon
Maitre d'Hotel.*—But as all great events, in which
great perfonages are concerned, are ufhered in
with due decorum, I fhall allot a feparate
gleaning to it.

* * *

LETTER LXI.

TO THE SAME.

" PEUTETRE, Monfieur, que vous vous
" imaginez qu'il va ici comme en Angleterre,
" *ou chaqu'un joue fon rolle comme il veut.* Non!
" nous vivons fous le regne d'un tel Roi, qui
" maintient fon plus bas fujet; ainfi aucun
" Anglois ne doit s'imaginer qu'il peut exercer
" le Rolle de l'Angleterre aux états Pruffiens.
" —Je ne vous ai pas appellé; vous etes venu
" de vous même aupres moi; et vous avez
" loué les chambres; et parceque vous l'avez
" defiré que je mettrois des tappis fur les
" planches, je les ai acheté; le lit demonté
" eft remonté, et puifque vous avez voulu deja
" occuper Dimanche les chambres, je me fuis
                                        " forte

" forte derangé à mes affaires pour les arranger.
" —Pour toutecela jepretend d'être dedommagé,
" puifque vous n'avez pas envie de les occuper ;
" et je vous demande par celle ci, ou, *vous avez*
" *envie de payer le loué pour trois mois, ou non ?* Si
" non, alors je chercherai mon droit à la
" juftice."

" MITSDORFFER."

Cleves, ce 23 *Mars.*

As a Pruffian curiofity, you will accept a
literal tranflation of it, courteous reader, if
peradventure thou art not fufficiently in practice with the French language, to feel the might
and majefty of the fentiments. You, I know,
my dear friend, can relifh them in all their
original bombaft.

TRANSLATION.

" Perhaps, Sir, you imagine you may act·here
" as you do in England, where every one does
" juft as he pleafes. No. We live under the
" government of a king—*Such a King!* who
" fupports the rights of his meaneft fubjects.
" And whofoever dares to fuppofe he may play
" the game he does in Great Britain, within
" the territory of his Pruffian majefty, will find
" himfelf miftaken. It was not at my invita-
" tion you came to my houfe ; it was an act of

F 4

" your

" your own free will ; and you have hired my
" chambers.. .You defired I would cover the
" boards with a carpet; a carpet I have bought,
" and the boards are covered. My bed, too,
" has been taken down in one place and put up
" in another to pleafe you, and I am thereby
" difarranged. For all this, I expect to have
" my. damages. made good, and as you do not
" choofe to occupy the lodgings, I. defire to
" know, whether you choofe to pay for them !
" I fpeak of the three months for which they
" are let to you? If yes, well ; if no, 1 fhall
" feek my right from the laws of the land,
" whereof I have the honour to be a member !"

Boooo!—There's for you! Was ever the
Pope's bull fulminated with more vengeance !

" Myn Heer, faid my landlord, had better
poftpone his journey, till this little, ugly affair is
fettled; .for there is no anfwering to the lengths
this hot-headed man may go ; and to be ftopped
on the road by the officers of juftice would be
difagreeable. Officers of juftice! officers of
nonfenfe! faid I. I. fent for my interpreter,
who, though a native of the place, did not, by
good luck, take the part of his townfman. On
the contrary, he accompanied me, fwearing all

the

the way in High Dutch never to have made any mention of three months, nor any contract whatfoever. He increafed his pace in proportion as he increafed his oaths, and thefe running affidavits prefently brought us to the fcene of action. The landlord was in the very chamber in difpute, which we found, fure enough, fufficiently deranged. Had a fcore of fwine herded in them, they could not have been in a more filthy fituation. Neither curtains, nor mat, nor carpet, nor any furniture, but that of which I had at firft complained. The fury of the interpreter was equal to the difmay of the Pruffian dictator. Our vifit to the latter was fo unexpected, and our detection of him fo unequivocal, that he could not reply to the denunciations of my linguift, who, purfuing his advantages, laid about him like a Draw-canfir. The hoft, at laft, felt himfelf galled, and ventured the retort *uncourteous*: this produced a rejoinder, that again a replication, which ran through the whole vocabulary of angry eloquence; in the heat of which I left the combatants, and with great coolnefs departed for Emeric; but on paffing Cleves fome months after, I fell in company with the very gentleman who occupied thefe memorable apartments, for the ufe of which, his board inclufive, he paid, to a ftiver, *per month*, what had

·been

been demanded of me *per week!* but then, he was a Pruffian and I—an Englifhman !

I cannot write this latter name, without an almoft equal mixture of pride and indignation, pleafure and regret. I grieve that it is rendered lefs refpectable abroad than at home, and that, by the purfe-proud vanity, or diffipated pageantry of individuals, the character of an whole nation fuffers. More than once, in the courfe of thefe Gleanings, have I been forced upon this unwelcome fubject; and I muft now take it up again, becaufe I can no other way, my loved friend, account to you, or to the public, for a multitude of impofitions which lie in referve, which are abfolutely in *waiting,* for my countrymen, the moment they have croffed the Channel, and which, like coftly and troublefome companions, faften themfelves to his purfe-ftrings, till they " leave not a rack behind." For all which, I am forry to fay, *Englifhmen* have nobody to blame but themfelves.

In the firft place they take over with them Englifh ideas of expence into other countries.

Secondly, They take over, alfo, a large cargo of national pride, wifhing to fpread the general received notion of English wealth being greater than that of other countries.

Thirdly, They are in a habit of prodigality at home which is too inveterate in waste, to make economical retrenchments abroad: and, even if they set out on a saving principle, they soon glide into the extravagant passion.

Now, from a co-operation of all these, it is really wonderful to consider how wide the mischief is diffused. A Swifs officer and Prussian gentleman counciled me to let a friend of theirs make my bargains and purchafes, as we were to travel some time in company, and make stops at the same places. I yielded to this good advice, but counteracted its effect by being his associate. It was found out, by some means or another, that I was an Englishman, and that was more than enough. The persons—whether Dutch, Prussians, or Germans—mean not to over-reach you. They intend only to afk up to the character our countrymen have established for riches: They even design sometimes an extortion as a compliment, because it pre-suppofes the pre-eminent wealth of our nation. They argue, too, that while you come so many hundred, or thousand leagues from home, it is not possible you should

want

want money, since, if you did, you would naturally stay at home.

  Thus a foolish ambition of keeping up a false
reputation begins on the other side of the
water, and travels with you to the end both of
water and land. Taking London as the center,
it has gone in as many directions as there are
great post roads, even to the once cheap parts
of the British empire, Yorkshire, Scotland, and
Wales. In every inch of these, you feel the
heavy hand of an English traveller's profusion
forced into your pocket. Those necessaries of
life, which thirty years back might be comfortably procured for the third of their present
purchase at an English market, soon mounted
to the half, then they rose to three parts; and
now, unless you enter into engagements very
advisedly, the difference of English expenditure will scarcely warrant the charge of taking
so long a journey. Shall I be answered, that the
difference in these gradations arises from the difference of the times, refinements, luxuries, &c.?
Certainly these increase the evil: but, even
at this day, as I stated to you in a former letter,
the great articles of life are to be had at more
than an half in half average with the English
market. It will assuredly be granted, that fish,

flesh,

flesh, fowl, eggs, butter, and house-rent, are the *chief* of those articles, and all these are to be had as I have before described. The fair inference is, that where taxation or refinement have levied one impost, national pride and habitual folly have levied twenty. The natives themselves, both in the above countries, and in those more remote, have candour enough to acknowledge this; but *now*, the habit of charge is as strong as the profusion by which it was at first created; and the simplicity and œconomy of a place once destroyed, like a wounded character, never recovers itself. On the contrary, extortion and extravagance erect a sort of temple to Folly on their ruins; and an imposition *taught to others by ourselves*, becomes the custom of a country, till, in the end, foreigners think they have a presumptive right to cheat you. The same spirit that induces us to spoil the places nearer home, enables us to ruin our residences and accommodations abroad. Our profusion traverses the whole continent of Europe; the Alps and Pyrennees sink before it, and wherever, as in Westphalia, from the natural abundance of a country, or the want of traffic, or distance from a public mart, the necessaries of life are *still* to be got at half price, they would, I am convinced,

have

have remained at a third lefs than at prefent, had it not been for Englifh profufion, Englifh pride, and Englifh prejudice.

Under thefe comfortlefs profpects of being impofed upon by our own countrymen's folly, even when *out* of England—for I infift on it, they are the aggreffors—I do not think I can render to my countrymen at this diftance from them—or to you, my friend, whom I fuppofe to be fo near, a greater fervice—than to note the actual rates of living, and the comparative dearnefs or cheapnefs of the feveral countries in which I have refided. This is certainly another very humble office, but a no lefs ufeful one, and either on account of its humility or utility, has been ftrangely mifreprefented or overlooked.

Once more making England a centrical point of travelling, the expenditure will be found to afcend in a feries as you pafs along, *i. c.* the farther removed from the center, the lefs you fpend—fuppofing a lefs influence from examples of Englifh extravagance.

The difference of charge, even to perfect ftrangers,—and making allowances for a *prc-determination*, almoft every where, to over-

teach

reach you to the verge of the laws of the land,—is almoſt incredible. What Engliſh travelling at *home* comes to, I need not ſtate, either in lodgings, at inns, or on the road. Houſeing you ſafe on this ſide of the water, you immediately would perceive the difference, were you diſpoſed to begin your eſtimate ; for, although you may be chagrined at the neceſſity of keeping your purſe in the hand, in your tour through Holland, were you to ſeparate one charge from another, you would, even admitting ſome extortion, find the balance in favour of Dutch impoſition. No, my friend, thrown, without the arms of language, acquaintance, or experience of cuſtoms, on the mercy of the Hollanders, you would laſt longer, that is, you would be leſs *ſpeedily* devoured by the Dutch than by your own countrymen, under like circumſtances. But though your devoration would be more *ſlow*, it would not be leſs *ſure* ; *i. e.* were you not to buy, and dearly buy, knowledge as you go on, and had you no honeſt and diligent way-faring traveller to glean the paths before you.

Leaving you, however, as juſt obſerved, undefended amongſt the Hollanders, you would not ſo ſoon be ſwallowed up as by the Engliſh. The difference of charges is remarkable

markable in going only from one province to another, and when you have left the Dutch boundaries and gained the Pruſſian dominions, you perceive the cheating of one country ſo much more endurable than that of another, that in this inſtance, at leaſt, whatever may be your political principles, you would prefer the deſpotic States to the Republics—and exclaim with poor Lear,

> " The wicked compared with the more wicked
> " Seem beautiful, and not to be the worſt
> " Stands in ſome rank of praiſe."

I believe I have uſed this quotation in ſome former letter, but it becomes appoſite again, and you will excuſe repetition. *How* well it applies at preſent, you ſhall immediately judge. At the beſt inn of Cleves, my charge, for twelve days, was little more than a guinea ſterling; and for which I was accommodated with a very good bed-room, the uſe of the general ſitting-room and an excellent table, adorned with the beſt company, as well reſidents as travellers. At one of the largeſt inns of the Hague, it coſt me preciſely that ſum, a guinea, for *one day's* worſe living, worſe lodging, and worſe attendance. Having mentioned to you the name of the more reaſonable Hague landlord, I truſt your faith in my account will

lead

lead you to choofe the good and to avoid the bad ; and therefore it becomes unneceffary to fpecify the perfon by whom I was thus over-charged. But juftice requires I fhould tell you and the world, that the name of the Cleves landlord is Nyfa.

To prevent the trouble of enquiry, and the vexation of being reduced to contefts at a place of public accommodation, I will take this opportunity to fet down the fixed prices of all the moft reputable table d'hotes (public eating-houfes and hotels) in the provinces of Holland and in Pruffian Weftphalia.

HOLLAND.

	Florins.	Stivers.	Doits.
Breakfaft - -	0	8	0
Dinner - -	1	0	0
Bottle of Rhine, or Bourdeaux wine	1	0	0
Bed - -	0	15	0
Fire, if in your own room, per day	0	12	0

WESTPHALIA.

	Florins.	Stivers.	Doits.
Breakfaft - -	0	5	0
Bed (fire included) -	0	7	0
Dinner - -	0	10	0
Bottle of wine -	0	10	0

In Holland, the train of waiters, shoe-boys, &c. are at the heels of your bill, and interrupt (though not with equal boldness of *authority*) your way to the horse or carriage. In West-phalia, these supernumeraries are all paid by their master, and included in their wages. The above statement then will serve you through both countries from Helveotsluice or the Hague, to the farthest end of the Prussian States: and the variations are unimportant in your route to Berlin on the one hand, and to Vienna on the other.

It should be noted, that the money of Holland is nominally double that of Prussia. I say nominally, because in the *exchange* it makes little to a traveller's advantage; but in pur-chase of the articles of life, it is half in half. Indeed the coin (more especially the silver) is of so base materials, that the circulation is almost wholly confined to Prussia. It is refused currency even on the frontiers of Holland. The Cleves money will not pass even at Nimeguen, where there is a constant reci-procal communication.

It will be proper to mention to you the names and valuation of the Cleves and Prussian coins *.

ccins;* that you may be prepared, and compare them with thofe of Holland.   They fhall be given

* I fhall here, however, make a general obfervation on the fubject of the coins of Pruffia and Germany. The natives (I mean thereby the common tradefmen, who are ever upon the watch for ftrangers) admit that the Dutch money is in effect double the value of theirs, fuch, for inftance, as that forty ftivers Pruffia are given for twenty Holland ; but that it is fair to charge four ftivers for a commodity which may be had in Holland for two; a piece of logic which they juftify on the ground of your ignorance being greater than their cunning. Luckily, however, the price of public boats, and public carriages, are fettled by ordinance, though even this is liable to abufe, and the Seller fometimes paffes a cheat on the Buyer, under the pretended fanction of Government. I had occafion to ftop at an inn of Maifeland Sluice (in Holland) with a good deal of baggage; and I alfo took my dinner, or rather luncheon, being too late for one barge, and too foon for another. When I came to pay the bill, I found fo many extra charges that I fefifted payment till I had afked a few queftions.

Gleaner. What is the meaning of this charge ?
Hotel-Keeper. 'Tis by order of the States-General.
Gleaner. And this ?
Hotel-Keeper. The ordinance is alfo by the States-General.
Gleaner. And this ?
Hotel-Keeper. Is fettled by the States-General.

Gleaner. I can only fay then, that the States-General are aiders and abetters, if not principals, in the moft enormous plunder upon a ftranger's property of any people on earth.

To this remark the Hotel-keeper fmil'd affent, but plunder'd on. I complained of feveral particulars to the Commiffary of

given in the fupplementary pages of this clofing
fheaf, where a number of pickings-up fhall be
thrown into one or two general letters, properly fpeaking, a letter of fcraps on different
fubjects, gathered in different countries;
valuable, perhaps, when made into a collection,
but too minute to ftand aione. I have many of
thefe lieing in flips of paper, on the backs or
edges of letters, in my drawer of memorandas,
which I fill as I empty my pockets after a walk,
a ride, a vifit, &c. &c. and I fhall fet apart a
ftay-at-home-day, to arrange and tranfmit
them. Meantime, we are, juft now, too much
in the heat of bufinefs, in Gleaning the things
of the *firft neceffity* (alas! poor dear human nature,
of what eating and drinking, and other frail
materials, art thou compounded) to amufe ourfelves with affairs lefs folid. If a traveller
wifhes to become refidentiary for a few weeks
or months in any of the pleafant German towns,
and brings with him his family, the beft way
is to make an agreement with a traiteur (a
cook)

the Town who redreffed both my wrongs, and thofe of the Republic, by affuring me every iota was impofition; for which he
fentenced the Landlord to deductions on almoft every article,
and attended me in perfon to fee juftice duly adminiftered. I
certainly enjoyed not a little the confufion of the extortioner,
and was malicious enough to remind him at every refund, that
he paid me back the extorted money *by order of the States
General.*

cook) and live with him, if, as is often the case, he happens to have a good houfe. This, befides the accommodation of having your repaft comfortable and warm, is cheaper by nearly half, as it *includes* the price of a room. I know a gentleman, who fays he is well ferved with breakfafts and dinners, (fuppers are rarely taken abroad) and two good chambers, for twenty-one florins (about one guinea at par) per month, in a very popular part of Pruffian Weftphalia. But even if you take private lodgings, and are only fupplied from a traiteur's with eatables, you gain importantly on England—as thus, *Dinners*, (which imply a fufficiency for fuppers, as you always are entitled to keep what is fent you) are twelve Holland ftivers a-head—about a fhilling Englifh. It is called one portion; it confifts of four covered difhes, which, with bread, cheefe, butter, and fallads (that are always found by yourfelf) contain enough for two meals; as two portions do for four.

I was prefent at a bargain of this kind being made at Cleves, with one of the many publick cooks of that place: he was on the edge of becoming a victim to his ignorance in thefe matters, when an honeft Pruffian who was prefent, with a friendly prefence of mind,

                     obferved

obſerved to the cook—" Certainement Mon-
ſieur eſt un peu Catholique; il ne mange pas
de viande *tous les jours.* I took the hint, and
told the man that when I wanted a double
portion, he ſhould know it in time to make
the neceſſary addition. This reduced the
monthly charge, which had previouſly been
made, to about one pound fifteen ſhillings.

Let me not fail to apprize you, moreover,
that the buying your wine of a merchant, and
of an hotel-keeper, or cook, is, on an average,
difference of more than half in half in Holland,
Pruſſia, and Germany.

At the inns of Holland, you will pay for
table-wine, one florin ten ſtivers (half a crown);
at thoſe of Pruſſia and Germany, from ſixteen
ſtivers to one florin; and at the merchants of
the firſt country, for the ſame wine, eight
ſtivers, and in the two other countries, ſo low
as ſix ſtivers, or ſeven at moſt: and let it not
be forgotten that the eightpenny wine is preciſely the ſame, as to quality, for which (with
duties on foreign ſpirits) you pay in England
from five to ſeven ſhillings a bottle.

There are certain articles ſo incredibly cheap,
even in theſe times of general ſcarcity *every
where,*

where, that I want almoft confidence in my own conviction, or in my truft of your candour, to make juft report of them. In various provincial towns, both in the neighbourhood of the Upper and Lower Rhine, the beft butter is fold, in the month of May, at two-pence per pound, a very fine young fowl, at four and five pence, a duck the fame, butcher's meat at two-pence, and two-pence halfpenny, a full grown hare at eight, nine, or ten-pence, fometimes at ftill lefs, a goofe, or turkey, at ten-pence, when at the deareft, and the fineft Weftphalia ham from three-pence to four-pence per pound. Houfe-rent is in proportion. I leave you, therefore, to judge, how comfortable a family, pinched for neceffaries, and, perhaps, ftruggling betwixt the extremes of pride and poverty in England, may live in the German territories. And yet I ftill cannot help giving Wales the preference for two reafons—firft, becaufe it is nearly as cheap, and in a part of my own country, and does not take money out of the Britifh dominions; and fecondly, becaufe it contains more general beauty than any thing to be met with without taking a long journey, which, with a family, is in itfelf the expenditure of more than could be expected from a twelve-month's favings. As the retreat of an unconnected perfon, or of a

family,

family, refolved to eftablifh in a new country, and, as Dr. Young fays, *fixing would be fixed*, it would be really a faving, without abridgement of comforts, and even luxuries, of thirty or forty per cent. Eggs are frequently fifteen for two-pence, and feldom lefs than ten; and firing is proportionably cheap. Bread, however, is nearly the fame price as in England; I mean fuch as is made from the white flour; but they grow an inferior kind, confiderably darker when baked than our farm-houfe loaves, which is eaten with a farm-houfe appetite, not only by the peafantry, but moft other people. By way of qualifying its bitter and four tafte, the better forts of folks place their butter betwixt a flice of the black and a flice of the white bread, and when they wifh to luxuriate, as on a dainty, or to diftinguifh their hofpitality to a friend, a twopenny loaf of the entire white is brought forth, and cut into as many morfels as there are perfons to be regaled.

It will feem incredible to an Englifh reader, whatever be his fituation, to be told that a German bill of fare confifts of little more than what is appointed for a meagre day, rigidly maintained; infomuch that the Weftphalians, Pruffians, and Germans, in general, may be duly, and truly faid to keep Lent all the year.

I am

I am authorifed by truth to affure you, from long experience of their table, that the yearly expenditure of a large family, in any of the above-named countries, would fcarce exceed, if it could reach, that of an Englifh farmer's houfehold, confifting of an equal number of people, for a fingle month. An enormous difh of potatoes, cabbages, carrots, beans, and other vegetables, forms the bafis of their dinner, which, with all ranks, is taken at twelve o'clock. It is a very great luxury when half a pound of pork, bacon, or butcher's meat is ftuck in the midft of this medley, as the grand center of attraction; and yet this precious morfel is rather for ornament than ufe, rather to be admired and gazed on, like other forbidden fruit, than eaten. A variety of trifles from the garden forms the defert, which is rather tafted than enjoyed, if there happens to be any thing more *recherché*, more valuable, than a nut or an apple; and a fmall plate-full even of thefe become fo " familiar to the eye," that they pall upon the fenfe before you are prefented with a frefh fupply. I proteft to you that I was fo accuftomed to look on a fruit plate and its contents for fuch a length of time, at a table in Weftphalia, that I knew every fpeck and freckle about them, as well as the faces of the family. Indeed I had opportunities

nities to see them so constantly, and closely, that each apple and pear became a *memento mori to the family*.—In the beginning of the week, they came fresh from the tree, with their best look and blooming complexions. A very few of them, alas, were cut off in this the prime of their lives. The rest were brought on the second day, not much altered in their shapes or air. On the third, there was a visible alteration—neverthelefs, the young folks of the family, for there were many children,

> " Sigh'd and look'd, sigh'd and look'd,
> " Sigh'd and look'd, and sigh'd again."

but, alas, sigh'd and look'd, look'd and sigh'd, sigh'd and long'd in vain. It was written in the father's face—ye may not eat: while the indulgent matron cut one into as many quarters as she had sons and daughters, and the next day the father, being in a frolicsome humour, threw an apple and a pear after dinner amongst them, on the floor, where they were as much fought for as Joseph's coat, and produced as much shame to the vanquished, and triumph to the conquerors, as if they were heroes and kings, battling it away for thrones and dominions, perhaps, on the true estimate, as little worthy of conteft. Towards the end of the week, my old friends in the fruit-plate

began

began to drop off one by one ; and though it is amongſt my habits never to eat of thoſe things which the maſter of the houſe diſcovers to me by his manner he conſiders as a rarity; in com- paſſion to theſe poor things, I took off their duſty coats, and thereby prevented a more lingering death.

Some weeks after, I dined at the ſame gen- tleman's houſe, and though, to be ſure, a man would not chooſe to ſwear to an apple, I could all but make oath, that I obſerved, amongſt the re-enforcements of the well remembered fruit- plate, one pippen which was ſo palpable by his marks, that I recogniſed him as an old acquaintance the moment he came in my view —now be it known to you, this was by no means in the ſeaſon of the year, when apples are laid up like honey in the hive for winter pro- viſion, but when they would in England have come freſh from the tree, at every meal. It is ſtrict economy that urges this extreme for- bearance in almoſt every thing that regards, in ſhort, that either ſmells or taſtes like a luxury. And it is impoſed by a very ſtern neceſſity, for Germany and poverty are almoſt ſynonimous terms, and though, in particular inſtances, ſuch a thing as wealth is to be found,

the

the general run of people in all conditions, are reduced to obferve a moft fcrupulous frugality in all things; their income being ufually fuch as to inhibit the leaft article of profufion.

Nor is this œconomy confined to the appetites, it extends to the ornaments of life; I had almoft faid to its vanities, but it may be done in effect to promote thefe. You fhall decide on this, after I have informed you it is the univerfal practife to undrefs after a vifit. A lady, or gentleman, no fooner returns home, than they lay afide their coftly robes, and get into their flippers, nightgowns, yea and night-caps alfo. And appear extremely furprifed to learn it is a general cuftom in England to keep on their out of door dreffes, as they are called in Germany, when they are amongft family friends; nor could I eafily reconcile them to my following the cuftom of my country in this particular, till I had affured them, changing my drefs frequently gave me cold. They call this ftripping practice putting themfelves at their eafe: but it is, in truth, purely done for œconomy.

Frugality is an early part of education in thefe countries, infomuch, that it is common to

observe

obferve a well-bred young lady, in fome of the beft families, wafh up the tea-things, immediately after they are done with, and in the midft of the company, who have been ufing them. At firft, I fuppofed this was a menial office, impofed by a crofs papa, or over-managing mamma; but when I became a refidentiary gleaner, I faw it fo much the fafhion of every family, that I inform you of it as a general rule, not only in Germany, but in Holland alfo.

The natives of thefe places not only eat fparingly, as having little to eat, but they eat feldom—and drink as often as they can. The cuftom of flight breakfafts, vegetable, or rather hodge-podge dinners, and yet flighter, frequently no fuppers, has its beginning in Holland, travels to Weftphalia, like a flender current, narrowing as it goes, with refpect to quantum, and is at its perfection of œconomy in the empire. The only thing in which they yield to profufion, (at their own expence) is in the article of tea and coffee: this they take almoft every hour, but *without fugar*. The women fnuff, and the men fmoke over it. But they ufually drink it out of cups that fcarce hold fo much as an acorn; and though, from the quantity taken, this cuftom gives perpetual

trouble,

trouble, they ftill prefer thefe diminutive machines, which would fcarce ferve a fairy to fip dew drops. To think of a wide Dutch mouth fcrewed up to the dimenfions of fuch a fprite!

It is, I find, very true, that the Englifh are every where looked on to be exceedingly carnivorous; and it is true alfo, that an Englifhman will devour more folid flefh in a day, and pour down his throat more inflammatory liquid, than a Pruffian, German, or Dutchman, in *three* days. An Englifh traveller, however, foon affimilates to the general temperance of the country, the confequence of which is, that inftead of wafting an whole afternoon in an hot room, amidft the fumes of the table; or fleeping to relieve an overloaded ftomach, he feels alert, either for bufinefs, or pleafure, and feems to wonder at this change of himfelf.

I have juft mentioned to you the early dinners on this part of the Continent, but forgot to note to you, that the reafon affigned for it, is exactly the reverfe of what is given out for a four or five o'clock repaft in Great Britain. We eat at mid-day, fays the foreigner, that we may have a long afternoon: We eat in the evening, fays the Englifhman, that we may

have

have a long morning. The cuſtoms of a country ought certainly to give and receive
allowances, but I have found this difference in
the hours productive of great difficulties, between ſome of my countrymen and foreigners;
the firſt inſiſting that as twelve o'clock was too
late for breakfaſt and too ſoon for dinner, it
could be conſidered only as the hour proper
for a luncheon; and the other declaring, that
ſitting down to table at ſuch an unfeaſonable
time was inſupportable: for my own part, I am
bleſt with ſo ſocial an appetite, that it ſeems
made for a ready compliance with the cuſtoms
of all countries. Is it the faſhion of the family
to eat at noon? I ſit down and forget that I
had not been uſed to think about dinner till
nearer night. Does my meal make its appearance with the candles? Be it ſo, I eat heartily,
if I am well; and, if I am ſick, I play with my
knife and fork, to keep thoſe who are better
company. Now this verſatility in my diſpoſition leads me into many pleaſures and content-
ments, which leſs accommodating tempers can
never hope to enjoy. It is peculiarly eſtimable
in travelling: for can it be reaſonably expected,
that without being well paid for it, people will
come into the cuſtoms of a ſtranger, and forego
their own? Will you tell them, it is *polite* to go
to dinner when they are going to ſupper! Or

as an individual are you to derange a family,
who, in turn, could tell you, that the politeness
of their country settles these matters on very
different principles.   Who is to adjust this
knotty point? You fall out with your dinner,
and with each other.   How easily would a little
candour and courtesy place it just where it
should be!—O, good humour! thou least difficult, yet brightest of the social virtues—thou
creator and supporter of every other—where
is the land, the habit, the manners, which
are not reconciled to the heart, by thy assuasive
and smiling power? Inspired by thee, I feel
myself disposed to be happy, and I am so; to
impart it to all with whom I mix in this now
jarring world, and I succeed:—And did the
fond parent know thy value, as I know it, he
would pray that his darling child was rather
filled with thee, than favoured by beauty, genius,
or fortune; for what are these but the miserable
children of conceit, pride, and folly, unpro-
tected and uninspired by thee!

From what has been said on the very necessary, though very much neglected, subject of
eating and drinking, it will, I trust, appear
manifest, that if a traveller will be content
to buy a little experience, which is no where
to be had without paying for, and if he will

not

not be too much in a hurry to make his arrangements; and, while they are adjufting, indulge his heart in a few effufions of that good-humour I have been addreffing, he may be very comfortable to himfelf, and no lefs acceptable to others; but if he will be ftubborn, and inflexibly attached to his own opinions, manners, and cuftoms, and not come into thofe of other people in other countries, he has nothing to do but to live by himfelf, according to his fancy, and—pay accordingly.

But I forget, that all this time while I have been difcuffing the fubjects of the table, I have feated you in the Cleves Wood, and left you in a worfe fituation even than the Germans, without any dinner at all. Rife then, my friend, and, that you may no longer want an opportunity, I put an end to my letter, with the ufual affurances of being affectionately your's.

LETTER LXII.

TO THE SAME.

TAKING it for granted that you will feel yourfelf refrefhed before you fit down to the perufal of another letter, and that all thofe who may become its readers will bring along with them good fpirits and *goodnature*, I will invite your attention to fome further Gleanings on the circle of Weftphalia.

You are not now to learn that Pruffia is a Catholic country, where, however, Proteftantifm, (in the Prefbyterian form) is largely interfperfed. The churches are every where the objects that firft catch the eyes of travellers, for which reafon I fuppofe it is that you meet fo many fteeples and towers, monuments and efcutcheons, in almoft every book of modern travels.

Catholic churches in particular, as being more ornamental, have been fo often defcribed by *publifhing* travellers, that they are, perhaps, the only objects in the wide field of foreign obfervation, which have been meafured with an accuracy that leaves nothing for the gleaner. Open the books of thefe authors at whatever page you may, and it is odds but you fee half a dozen fpires, followed by a long hiftory of their founders, deftroyers, rebuilders, redeftroyers, revolutions, &c. Two churches and a caftle to a leaf is moderate reckoning, and it is well if you get off without a morfel of choice biography, on the quarrels and rogueries, virtues,

and

and vices of the prince, bishops, beggarly
priests, or despotic lords of the castle; for
the Cacoethes *De*-scribendi (if I may be
allowed to sport with the Latinity) is as strong
in some wandering biographers, as in juvenile
poets, when first they fancy themselves in love,
and present you with that picture of their
idols, which imagination has drawn for them.
For myself, and I suppose others may feel
like me on the occasion, I never, without
trembling, observe a travelled author *set in* for
a long story of churches, chapels, chateaus,
and picture galleries, with a determination to
give their " moving accidents" by flood and
fire, during the wear and tear, and traditionary
lying of half a score centuries. And what,
after all, are you presented with, but a meagre
account, into which the mind and memory of
the reader vainly look for something whereon
to rest—something more worthy the human
faculties, than annals of the intriguing abbots,
mischievous priests, and grinding seigniors,
buried under their ruins. I venerate antiquity,
but must have something that comes closer to
the soul, the understanding, or the affections,
than this collection of literary brickwork, and
travelling stone masonry. Peace to the ashes
of the mouldering universe! Unless surviving
virtues, or immortal actions, lie amongst the

ruins, and, like the phœnix, only want an honeſt, helping hand to clear away the earthy ob- ſtructions, to ſpring above them, I would not reſcue an altar, or the canonized bones of a Saint from oblivion. Unembalmed by ſuch virtues, and ſuch actions, the duſt of a monarch, and the duſt of the earth that covers him, is, to me, exactly the ſame thing; and as to the relicks of a worthleſs being, to what good end could they be brought from the tomb, but as a *maukin* to ſhew the villains of the preſent generation, that to ſuch complexion muſt they come at laſt.—In that light only, have I ſometimes, as in the inſtance of a John of Leyden, burſt the ſcarments of the grave, and gleaned the coffin of a ſcoundrel.

Reſpecting church matters, therefore, I ſhall certainly not ſwell the liſt of hiſtorians; but, after I have made one general obſervation, ſhall content myſelf with the relation of a ſingle circumſtance.

It is really a moſt heart-affecting ſatisfaction in a circuit of ſome hundreds of leagues, ſuch as I have taken, over different Catholic countries, to ſee the decent impreſſion that is made on the *peaſantry* (which is ever the moſt numerous body of a ſtate) by religion. Of the

higher

higher ranks, who lose their principles and
their education too often in the pride of philofophy, I shall here say nothing; but the influence of the Catholic faith on the *fubordinate*
ranks is, almoft without an exception, a fober
and fincere attention to the duties it enjoins.
The earneft, yet tempered zeal, with which the
common labourer leaves his bufinefs or his
pleafure, to commune with his Maker, is
amongft the comfortable fights that every traveller muft furely have noticed, and noticing
muft have enjoyed. In the plebeian part of
the community, at leaft, it muft be genuine.
The infidel philofophy of the great is, happily,
above their reach: the hypocritical mummery
or profounder chicane of the yet perhaps more
infidel priefthood (I fpeak of the Catholic
churchmen), is ftill more happily above the
underftanding of the peafant. He can have
no views from intereft, from the world's applaufe, or from the world's difapprobation.
His religion, after education has fettled it in
his mind, becomes one of the ftrongeft habits—
it foon ripens into his moft powerful principles. It is prefently a voluntary offering, and
one of perfect free will, to his God. He accepts
its pains and penalties, and never refifts their
infliction. He is told by his confeffor of a fin,
and he fuffers for it willingly. Neither does

he

he perform its duties fo mechanically as may
be fuppofed—He goes to the church at all
times and feafons: the gates of the temple are
always open, but he is not forced to enter at
the ftated ftroke of the pendulum or chime of
the bell. If his foul feels not the impulfe; if
it prefers the facred moment when the hour of
public worfhip is paft, he can withdraw himfelf from the gaze of the world, and converfe,
as it were, with his Creator face to face: and
in the. Catholic churches, which I have
gleaned even with a fufpicious vigilance, this is
very frequently done, and always with reverence. Strangers, drawn by curiofity only,
may pafs in groupes from all quarters of the
earth, and dreffed in all the different habits of
their country, without feducing the kneeling
Catholic peafant from his duty: his pofture is
unaltered, his prayer unbroken. He rarely
lends an ear to converfation, which is too often
irreverently loud, and not often an eye to their
perfons.

From this exterior decency, it is fair to infer
an internal piety. It is, to be fure, a world
replete with fubtle ftratagem, and falfe ap-
pearances, but if ever there can be fuppofed to
be a principle " unmixed with bafer matter,"
this furely is the moft free from alloy. And if
                                              one

one could felect from the mafs of enormities,
which the prefent governors of France have
committed, and fingle out an act more foul, more
cruel than the reft, I fhould not hefitate to
pronounce their attempt to convert the fimple
heart to EQUALITY of *Atheifm.*

The Augean ftable of the Catholic church, fo
far as it was connected with politics, no doubt
wanted cleanfing, and poffibly fome of its
moft afpiring heads well deferved *Le Glaive de
la Loi*, the fword of juftice, but to my feelings
(and it has arifen out of my obfervation)
better, far better, had the convent and the
cloifter been polluted by the whole chicane
of the priefthood, than that fo many hundreds
of thoufands of blamelefs beings fhould not
only want in future the comfort of a refuge in
mifery, and of a guide in happinefs, but fhould
be taught that the benefits and bleffings of the
paft, derived from this facred fource, were the
trick of a defigning race, and that, for the time
to come, the laws of reafon and nature, that
is infidelity and licentioufnefs, are to fuper-
fede thofe of a Saviour and Redeemer of the
world. Then, by way of proving their profe-
lytifm and faith in the new creed, they are,
inftead of bowing the knee to the crofs, they
are to turn from it in mockery, like the re-

vilers

vilers of old, or to level it with the duft! Glorious revolution, and more glorious revolu-
tionifts! To lay the foundations of a republic
in human blood, and erect a temple to infidelity on the ruins of religion! In the ancient fabric were there defects? Why not
repair them? Muft it fall that a worfe may
be raifed?—but I forget myfelf—a fcourge
was wanted in the land, and ye were perhaps
the proper inftruments to deal deftructions;
for who can punifh iniquity like the wicked?

But I promifed you to clofe with the relation of a circumftance, which I owe to the
Catholic church. Half an hour's walking by
the fide of the Cleves wood brings you to
a little village chapel, whofe bell was ringing
out for evening vefpers juft as I paid it my firft
vifit. Only a few of the congregation were
then gather'd together. I had therefore time
to make an unobtrufive Gleaning. Amongft
the ufual decorations of pictures, paintings,
flowers, and crucifixes, I could not but take
notice of the virgin in a chintz-pattern linen
gown over a full drefs hoop of immenfe
circumference; ornamented with three diftinct
rows of filver croffes, the middle row abundantly the largeft: the crown upon her head
was formed of broken beads, and pieces of
looking-

looking-glafs: the child Jefus held an apple in his hand partly eaten, to exprefs what Eve had fraudulently accepted and fhared with the devil.

I might have yielded up my gravity at the burlefque manner in which this part of facred ftory was caricatured, had not the ridicule, it was fo well calculated to excite, been checked by my obferving an old man and woman; two young men, and two female children, kneel-ing with every mark of devotion round the figures. They are of one houfe faid a perfon, who ftood near me, and, in the fequel, I found that that houfe had to boaft an holy family. The very moment that I looked upon them, the fpirit of mockery died within me; and a much better fpirit came upon me in its ftead. I had no longer eyes to criticife the figures, nor an heart to break a jeft on their abfurdity: As reprefentatives of the bleffed virgin and Redeemer of the world, they fill'd me with awe, and I caught fo much of unaffected holi-nefs from thefe humble fuppliants, as to hold facred the coarfeft imitations and fymbols of things divine.

It happened to be the *jour de pâcque*, on the evening of which feftival there prevails in
Weftphalia

Weſtphalia a cuſtom, that I felt was worth gleaning for you and for the public. You ſhall have it here. The Pruſſian peaſants commemorate the ſolemn event of our Saviour's reſurrection in a ſingular manner. In each village of the circle are to be ſeen three or four large bonfires, which the inhabitants have been preparing at their intervals of daily labour during the preceding week. The fires are lighted about nine at night; about ten, when they are in full blaze, the populace, and indeed people of all diſtinctions, go out of the Cleves gates to view them. I was lucky enough at the moment to be on a viſit to a gentleman, who, at a ſmall diſtance from the weſtern Port, had a ſummer houſe that commanded the country to the extent of twenty leagues. Every quarter or half league has a village, and the whole twenty leagues were illuminated. It was in itſelf an intereſting novelty, but when the *occaſion* was contemplated and combined with it, the heart glow'd like the horizon. In the midſt of the ſcenery roſe the moon. She was at full, but at the moment of riſing ſeem'd another bonfire beginning to kindle and aſcend. She ſoon, however, aſſerted her ſuperiority, and when ſhe had gain'd her proper ſtation in the hemiſphere, I could not help repeating to myſelf a

few

few words, applicable to both.—" Hide your diminifh'd heads", ye feeble works of men's hands: but thou Cynthia art of God. No wonder then at thy luftre! but, even as I pronounced this, I corrected my rafhnefs, my injuftice—and fo are *ye*, ye feeble fires,—added I,—of God alfo; and every humble fpark fhall afcend to heaven !

* * *

LETTER LXIII.

TO THE SAME.

I HAVE already, more than once, in the courfe of this correfpondence, attempted to check the heady current of national preju- dice, which appropriates all that is eftimable in human nature to itfelf, and leaves to the reft of the world only its vices, vanities, and in- fignificancies. I have given many examples of urbanity, that have been the growth of foils lefs celebrated than that of Britain, or than what once was France. I have fhewn it flou- rifhing even in the unwholefome clime of Holland. Let me now offer you an inftance of its blooming power in Weftphalia. In truth it is a flower appropriate to no particular country, but will profper wherever it is duly cultivated.

cultivated. Its natural foil is the human heart, in which it fprings up, and thrives, very foon after that heart begins to beat, and would continue till there is no longer motion, were not paffions and prejudices for ever at work to check its growth or kill it in the bud.

In one of the moft profound receffes of this beautiful country, at the diftance of at leaft forty leagues from a court, thirty from a city, and at leaft ten miles from a market town. I once found urbanity that would have given luftre to them all. I found her in a cottage of clay, at the foot of a Pruffian foreft, under covert of which I was fhaded from obferva-tion. It was on one of the moft lovely even-ings a wanderer like myfelf could have de-fir'd, and according to my emigrant difpo-fition, I had enjoyed it from the uprife even to the down-going of the fun. The fun indeed of that diftinguifh'd day was making a " golden fet" juft as I reach'd the precincts of the wood, where I had not repos'd many minutes, ere I heard the found of a flute, ac-companied by a voice whofe natural fweetnefs excelled it in melody. The notes were indeed affifted by many harmonizing circumftances. You who are a lover of nature, know what a

variety

variety of foothing founds pervade the air at eventide in the fummer.—The pure breath of the zephir, the diftant rivulet, that feems, by its indolent lapfe, and fubdued murmur, to partake of human fenfations,—the drowfy hum of the beetle, which the poet has immortaliz'd, and the general fighing of the leaves, with, perhaps, the horn of the herd-boy, and the lowing of his cattle obedient to his fummons—and above all, thofe founds which imagination herfelf *creates*—all thefe contribute to form that twilight enchantment, which a tender heart, and a benevolent difpofition fo much delights in ; and which, men of the world confider as the day-dreams of madmen.

Had I time to fpare from my cottagers, it would be amufing to run at fome length the parallel betwixt a lover of nature and a man of the world, and to examine the eftimate that each makes of the objects affembled in the laft paffage. To attempt this in abridgement—

1ft. The man of the world, would never be tempted to leave the " chearful haunts of men" without what is called a jolly party : five out of the fix of which probably wifh-

ing

ing themfelves as many different ways before half the day is over, and, at laft, going yawning home thoroughly tired with if not hating one another: for I have fo often obferv'd a party of pleafure to be fo painful a plot upon the members that compofe it, that were I to compile a new Dictionary, in which definitions were honeftly to be given, I fhould under the words *party of pleafure,* inform the reader that it is meant to fignify, *the affociation of a fet of perfons met together with taftes and tempers frequently difcordant, and interefts in oppofition, yet determined to congregate, for the purpofe of teafing one another under the mafk of focial goodfellowfhip; which mafk generally drops, or is torn off in the courfe of a few hours to the difcovery of the whole confpiracy.*—Such is the mere man of the world's party of pleafure: yes, and woman's of the world alfo!

2nd. A man of the world has no conception of the breath or founds *of,*—or *in* the air, in the way that a lover of nature feels and enjoys them. A man of the world indeed obferves that it is curfed hot, and throws up the fafhes, or curfed cold, and pulls down the blinds,—the inflammatory bottles, ten times more burning than the fun-beams, are ftill on the table,—yet, at the fafhionable hour he

goes

goes forth—where?—To the *public* walks.—
For what purpofe?—To fee the *public*.—But
goes he not into the beautiful woods?—Yes,
into the *public* parts of them, where he has
a chance to fee the world he loves fo well.—
And is he never led by his fancy or his feelings into the fequefter'd parts where nature
modeftly and humbly difplays her genius and
graces? No, my friend, ladies and gentlemen
of the world ufually avoid thefe bye-road
beauties, unlefs carried thither by fome paffion
that fhuns the day.—And as to clay-built
cottages, woodland inhabitants, ruftic fongs,
and lazy waterfalls, they are pafs'd by as fit
only for country Corydons, or fhepherdeffes
bemus'd. Far different is the attractive
fcenery of a world's man and woman—the
broad and beaten track amidft the crufh and
clatter of coaches, which are fo wedg'd
together that they move as if in funeral
proceffion,—walks fo cramm'd that you cannot pafs without difficulty,—a clufter of gla-
ring lamps ftuck upon trees, to the blufh of
the moon beam,—the fun himfelf fhut out to
make way for a parcel of artificial lights,
brought into an unwholefome room crouded
with company and card tables,—a kind of
elegant peft-houfe where people infect one
another by common confent, and are fuffo-
cated

cated on principles of politenefs.—Thefe are
the appreciated fcenes of men and women of
the world!—And I ought not to fail obferving,
that, amongft thefe well-bred broil'd and
roafted, who fit with the perfeverance of an
hatching hen, as if nail'd to the fides of the
card table,—there are always a certain number
of fentimental miffes, who affect to have fouls
fuperior to fuch wafte of time, and build up
a fort of reputation on never touching a card,
but when politenefs, or a dowager mamma,
infifts on her making up the fet.—Thefe dam-
fels fidget, or glide about the rooms, and
ogle their fair images in the pier glaffes, till
pick'd up by ftray batchelors, or cut out
married men, or fong-tranfcribing young
ftriplings, who get into prattling parties, or
file off into corners for a touch of the pathe-
ticks, or conftruct the horn work of a future
fiege in a whifper'd tête a tête. Moft of thefe
light troops affure you of their deteftation of
the town, but yet run their pretty faces into
one or other of its hot-houfes every night,
and go through a fummer campaign amidft
more fire and fmoke, than would melt down
the conftitution of the whole body of alder-
men. Mean time there is another fet difpers'd
here and there infidioufly laying a mine to
blow up reputations, and while the game of
the

the other parties goes on, these engineers
prepare a very notable masked battery, and
play off their artillery, as if only in a mock
action, at your wife or daughter, till they
almost surrender at discretion before your
face. The play amongst the card veterans,
becomes too intense for observing on any
stratagems but their own : the card passions are
all at work, breaking the unlucky chairs of
some, biting the lips, gnashing the teeth, flap-
ping the foreheads, or stamping the feet of
others, and while the *honours* are lost by one,
and the *odd trick* gained by another, the
mistress of the house slaves in hospitality, and
struggles through the elegant mob, with more
toil and difficulty, than a landlady at an election
dinner!

" But somewhat too much of this." Let us
fly from these artificial beings, to the children
of nature and the heart. Suffer me to re-
conduct you to the simple, yet ever-blooming
paths, from which these world-warped tribes
have too long led us astray.

Allow me to place you once more within
sight of the flute and voice I mentioned to you
before, and listen to the magic that ensued.
The wood notes, wild as they were, charmed

me. I rofe and advanced. A few paces brought me within fight of a cottage door, which was wide open. The fong and mufic proceeded, mingled with dancing, of which I could rather hear the happy ftep, than perceive the enlivening figure. But I was prefently obferved, and actually as fair a maid, accompanied by as blooming a youth as Arcadia ever fancied, tripped forward without quitting hands to invite me into their dwelling. You are here prepared for

     " The white wafh'd wall, the nicely fanded floor,
     " The decent clock that click'd behind the door, &c."

All thefe, and more were to be feen, but the infides of cottages in all countries have been fo many thoufand times furnifhed and un-furnifhed, either by real tour-makers, or thofe who, like the Virtuofo in the comedy, only travel in books, then publifh their *travels through other people's books*, (all which, you know, may be very commodioufly done at home, without ftirring out of their elbow-chairs) and, moreover, *book-cottages* are all fo much alike for neatnefs, accommodation, arrangement, and furniture, that I could rather wifh you would upon this, as upon a former occafion, make choice of the defcription you like beft, out of the whole collection of voyages and travels

that

that may be in your library, and assure yourself, that whatever comes nearest to a simplicity, which does not exclude convenience,
will give you a just idea of my Westphalian
cot.

As the first day of the Carme was solemnizing
while I was at the village chapel, so that on
which I entered this woodland habitation was
the last of that festival; and this peasant family
were then celebrating it. Religion, therefore,
no less than hospitality, and both under guid-
ance of sincerity, invited me to assist at the
felicity. Every simple delicacy of fruit and
flower, was in an instant placed before me.
Their discourse was so provincial, that probably a German citizen of Cleves, might have
found a difficulty to decypher it. But the
language of bounty, like that of love is
universal :

" All heads can reach it, and all hearts conceive."

It is the volume of nature ; one of its fairest
pages was spread open. Had I run I could
have read it; and, believe me, my generous
friend, it exhibited instruction well worth the
observance of those who live in prouder dwell-
ings. I found here no broad, coarse ridicule
at my ignorance ; none at my intrusion. I was
a stranger within the gate, but I received the

 welcome

welcome of a friend. I difcovered no wifh to know from whence I came, or, whither I was going, fave a fhort expreffed affurance, that when I, myfelf, found it proper for me to depart, I might be fure of being put into the right way. A very old man and woman, a labourer, who was the mufician, the youth and maiden whom I have before mentioned, and three more couple of lads and laffes, formed the affembly. Soon after my entrance, every body found fomething to do for me expref-five of good-will. The aged man gave up his rufh arm chair, and infifted on my occupying it; the matron, his wife, contributed a cufhion from a wicker one that ftood oppofite; the eldeft daughter, ftill in a dancing ftep, (the carriage of the lighteft articles difputed by her attendant youth, in his dancing meafures alfo) brought to the table and fpread on it a cloth, white even as her apparent innocency. Another prefented me with a bowl of new milk, another with fruits, another came bounding in with flowers, moiftened by the evening dew-drop. Bread, butter, and flices of ham, were added to the banquet, and when I had nothing left to be done for me, my entertainers did not ftand, like many, even Britifh ruftics, fo taken by furprize, to ftare me out of appetite, and with wide opened mouths, as if they could

themfelves

themfelves fwallow all that they had fet before me; but wifhing me good appetite refumed their feftivities. Never was the banquet of a monarch more harmonious—feldom fo difinterefledly; but all at once I miffed the mufician, and one of the dancers fupplied his place, the old man nodded time with his head, then beat it with his ftick, and the matron accompanied with her foot. Time flew infenfibly—the fun was in an other hemifphere—the moon fet—the ftars became clouded, and the combining influence of thefe feveral circumftances forced on me the confideration, then firft remembered, that I was a benighted gleaner, feveral leagues from the town, whence . I had wandered by innumerable crofs paths, juft as fancy had carried me. The good people read my embarraffment, and chafed it away by frefh dances, fongs, and mufic; in the midft of which, up rofe the veteran, and with an air of gallantry giving his hand to the aged dame, who had literally been his partner for eight and fifty years, hobbled an alamande, with much more agility than could have been expected. He then run into a dance, which they call *Schleifern,* confifting fimply in two perfons of either fex, taking hold of each other's drefs behind, and moving in a circle to flow mufic: a way-loft man, in a ftormy night

 upon

upon an heath, would have forgot his condition
while this dance was performing, had he re-
flected on the occasion of it, which was a
genuine effusion of hospitality to man, and
gratitude to God. The young folks became
almost wild with pleasure, and struck into
many artless gaities, till they encircled the old
ones in a kind of spontaneous dance which
gradually contracted the circle, so that in the
end they had the aged couple closed within
their arms. Every one present formed a part
of the love-knot, and had share of the embrace.
It was one of the prettiest impromptu's of
gaity and affection I ever beheld; and I repeat,
that a traveller who had unknown leagues at
midnight to measure back without a guide,
must have forgot his fears. When the frolic
was over, the good veteran led his ancient
dame back to her chair, with the same courtesy
and natural grace he had conducted her from
it, and as she sat down, there was a transitory
glow in her cheeks, which exercise and felicity
had called into them. It was a momentary
renovation of her youthful days, in which she
must have been extremely handsome; for time
that had robbed her of the colourings, had
committed less violent ravage on the proportions of her beauty. Her husband looked at
her with affection, and then at the company

with

with fome little elevation of felf-love, at the feats he had performed.

Before thefe animating trifles (of great figure in domeftic happinefs) had time to grow cold, the original mufician, whom I told you was the labourer, returned introducing an old foldier, who faluted me, at firft fight, in excellent French, which almoft in the next inftant, he tranflated into very interpretable, though ungrammatical Englifh. He loft no time in telling me, that the cottager had fetched him from an houfe where he had been paffing part of the Carme, above a league's diftance, for no other reafon than to conduct me back to the place from whence I came; promifing me at the fame time, faid the foldier, a fuitable reward for my trouble, but that I fhall not accept of, feeing I have the honour, Sir, to be your countryman.

Confider, my friend, awhile, the unbought, nay, unfollicited hofpitality of this groupe of poor peafants—take a retrofpect of their behaviour—finifh the picture by fuppofing you fee the old man and his wife, *thanking me* for the pleafure they had in entertaining me: fail not to paint on the canvafs the old foldier, offering himfelf to me as a voluntary guide,

in cafe I fhould perfift in refufing the bed,
which both the aged and the young would have
yielded to me; then, on fetting out, under
favour of the rifing moon, let your imagination give form and figure to the whole groupe
of youths and maidens, attending me part of
the way, ftill dancing, while the honeft minftrel
labourer compleated the midnight ferenade!
And the whole was performed with fo much
fport, glee, and goodwill, to the founds of
which a thoufand woodland echoes refponded,
that the verieft mifanthrope would have been
converted into a lover of mankind. I do proteft to you, I never felt my pulfes vibrate with
more enthufiafm. It was with difficulty I
forced upon the mufical labourer, a fmall prefent, or rather payment, for fetching the foldier;
and when all but the laft left me, a fentiment of
regret ftruck my bofom, and grew more and
more comfortlefs, as the found of their retreating footfteps and voices diminifhed on my ear,
and when even on ftanding a moment to liften—
a paufe to which my grateful heart impelled
me—they could be heard no more, the fenfation fwelled almoft into tears.

The foldier feemed to feel a fort of fympathy, and amufed the way with the adventures
of his life. They did not, however, begin to in-

tereft

tereft me fo foon as they might have done, had they been related at any other feafon. He told me, however, that he had lived fo many years out of his native country, that he had almoft forgot his mother tongue, as you may perceive, Sir, faid he, by my bad Englifh. He added, that he had ferved his late Pruffian Majefty, the grand Frederick, almoft feven and thirty years, and had the honour to have been fhot in almoft every battle, and part of the human body; but was ftill as heart-whole, and care-free, as any man in the circle of Weftphalia. The Grand Frederick, Sir, continued he, has fettled upon me a little penfion, and given me a fnug apartment in the Chateau of Cleves, where, fhould your honour deign to come, I have always a glafs of good Rhenifh, to offer an Englifhman, aye, and any other honeft man; and where, if your honour pleafes, we will drink the kings of England and Pruffia, (for they now happen to be good friends, you know) in a bumper, before we get into bed! Thus ended my little jubilee, to the infinite content of my heart; and, I truft of your's: At leaft, I can wifh you no greater good than that each of your future days may be crowned like this; and that your after flumbers may be as fweet!

LETTER LXIV.

TO THE SAME.

THE weekly vifitation of the begging friars, and Sunday affemblies, are amongft the things which fhould be recommended to the notice of thofe who go into Weftphalia, being both really curious in their kind.

In regard to the firft, it is an invariable rule for one or other of the mendicant brothers to make the tour of the town in, or near which, his convent is fituated. Sanctioned by the cuftom of his country, he gains admittance into every houfe, whether public or private, and is " happy to catch you juft at dinner-time." He moves round the table with his little box, into which every one puts, or appears to put, fomething, but evidently more as a thing of courfe than charity. He neither fpeaks, nor is fpoken to: he glides almoft unheard, and unfeen, behind your chair, and having finifhed his collections, which are probably fcanty enough, he bows off as he bowed on.

The

The fecond circumftance, viz. the Sunday evening card route, is full as fingular, but by no means fo filent. It is compofed of thirty and forty (frequently more) of the moft re-fpectable perfons of the town, who, after the devotions of the fabbath, which they perform with great exactnefs, almoft, indeed, to rigour, affemble at the beft inn, and pafs the evening partly over a pack of cards, and partly over a good fupper. The laft time I was at the city of Cleves, where I have now in fancy fet you down, I was an eye-witnefs to this fupplement to the Sunday duties, there being, at that time, no lefs than feven tables, well furnifhed with preparations for the nocturnal affociation. Tra-vellers of any decent appearance are always welcome. There is never any thing like a debauch, and the company feparate about twelve. The fingularity of all this confifts only in its oppofition to our *modes* of doing the fame thing in Great Britain; and we may truly fay the matter is more elegantly conducted in London. Would it not be thought very odd for the nobility and gentry of both fexes, and of the firft character, to meet at a tavern in that great city, where, the moment a lady made her appearance, a ftove full of hot coals was placed under her petticoats, and, on the en-

trance

trance of each man of fashion, an immenfe pipe with a fpitting box?

How often, in the traverfe of different countries, has a traveller occafion to exclaim, with the poet,

"I fee full plainly cuftom forms us all!"

And, in truth, it requires the ftrongeft power of our habits to reconcile us to fome things that will rife up in our way as we journey along.

Amongft other *preparations*, with which my zeal has armed you, let me not omit to befeech that you will make up your mind to the *dirty* doings of Weftphalian Pruffia, and, indeed, in certain cafes, of the whole Germanic empire. I have, in a former letter, invited your obfervation to a comparative view of the countries of Holland and Pruffia, in refpect of the gradual relief which the eye receives from the fatiguing uniformity of the one to the rifing diverfities of the other; but this is not the only matter that awaits your attention, O ye readers of this hiftory, and ye fojourners in this land. Would ye fee placed before you one of the moft ftriking contrafts in the world, behold it in the general neatnefs of the Hollander, and almoft univerfal filth of the Pruffian and German.

It

It is impoffible for an Englifhman, whofe eyes are, by no means, unaccuftomed to the decencies of life, in his own country, to withhold the tribute of his admiration on the peculiar niceties of the towns, within and without, from his firft landing in Holland to his taking leave of its Seven Provinces. The doorways, the paffages, the windows, the inner apartments, the kitchen, the very lumberrooms (where, by the bye, every ftick, board, and other unoccupied thing, is laid in a picturefque manner, as if by the hand of fymmetry) the warehoufes, where induftry is for ever at hard, and very often at dirty work ; the very out-houfes, which frequently connect with the general fitting-room, and in which, perhaps, twenty cows are ftalled on the one fide, and as many horfes ftabled on the other, and in which all forts of domeftic fowls, nay, where not feldom the very pigs are nourifhed; each and all of thefe places are kept in fuch order, difpofed in fuch arrangement, and with fuch uniform cleanlinefs, that, whether it proceeds from the neceffity of the climate, in regard to the influence which its humidity otherwife might have upon the health, or whether from a principle, or only an habit of neatnefs, it is certainly a charming cuftom,

" More honour'd in the obfervance than the breach."

3   But

But the offenſive reverſe is forced upon you, almoſt immediately on your quitting the con- fines of the Stadtholder. The diſguſting con- traſt will ſtrike you in *almoſt every particular*, ſo that if you pleaſe to re-peruſe the liſt of the items above ſtated, taking their oppoſite, that is, reading dirty for clean, as you go on, you will have before you a picture of Dutch nicety and Pruſſian naſtineſs.

And the remark is to be extended to perſons as well as things. Notwithſtanding the inceſ- ſant toil, which an unremitting attention to neatneſs in a flat, foggy country, muſt occaſion, there is, in the midſt of their labours, an air of *propreté*. The common ſervants, even in their drudgery, are always to be ſeen with clean ſtockings, which are always ſhewn to the middle of the leg, ſlippers, which, notwithſtanding the violent motion of the mop and pail, hang on the foot as if by magic, and head dreſſes which are oftener ſeen without hat or bonnet, be the weather what it may. Whereas, in the neighbouring countries, the houſes are more *mal propre* than the ſtables of Holland, and the Sunday apparel of the common people (females more eſpecially) is worſe got up, and worſe put on, than the Saturday night working- dreſſes of the Dutch peaſantry.

In

In your perufal of this and every other
fimilar account, I muft once again warn you
that I confine myfelf principally to the inns,
hotels, and other public places, to which a
traveller muft, of neceffity, firft repair, or to
thofe private lodgings, which, if he makes any
ftop, are ufually his fecond movement. But
it may be received as a general rule, that if
all thefe places are in one country neat, inviting
and regular, and in another utterly different,
it is fair and candid to draw this inference, that
dirt is the general characteriftic of the one
country, and cleanlinefs, of the other. Certain
it is I have feen regularity, elegance, and
delicacy, in the circle of Weftphalia; and I
have alfo witneffed the reverfe of thefe in
Holland: but thefe can be confidered only as
exceptions to the general rule.

No human being is more aware than yourfelf,
my dear friend, that there are certain *decencies* in
civil fociety, which are always very charming,
and in certain cafes, not a little embarraffing;
but without the adroit performance of which
human nature, in fome of its higheft luxuries,
no lefs than in feveral of its loweft neceffities,
is but a very dirty piece of bufinefs. Amongft
thefe decencies is one, concerning which an
Englifh traveller not yet affimilated to the man-

ners

ners of other countries, and retaining, and ever wishing to retain a respect for the decorums of his own, is at a loss how to write; particularly when those writings will, probably, come under the eyes of his delicate countrywomen. Yet, a little adventure on this *ticklish* subject met me on the way, so extremely characteristic of the manners of, at least, one half of the civilized globe, and so extremely *un-character-istic* of one comfortable corner of the earth, where the *personal delicacies*, if not the Graces, have taken up their abode, that I cannot in fair description help going over this *trembling ground* to give you its Gleanings. Now Yorick would have made no difficulty on this occasion. He could, you know, reconcile his readers to whatever matter he thought proper to set before them; but as I, by no means, possess the magic of that illustrious traveller, I do not feel my-self entitled to the indulgences which such magic claims, and shall, therefore, not presume to take the same liberties.

In a certain fair district then, within and but just within the circle of Westphalia, there stands a pleasant and very considerable town, situated on the banks of the Lower Rhine, y'clept Emerick. Its extreme beauty excited in me a first sight wish to make a stop of
some

some weeks; and being arrived just at that period of life, when the comfort of a good night's rest in a good bed is considered as one of the necessaries of life, in however tumultuary a manner one passes the day, I preferred private to public lodgings: and, accordingly, after due refreshment, went out in search of them. My broken German dialect stood me in good stead on this occasion. I soon saw a lodging bill; and knocked at the door, but the master and mistrefs of it being from home, I had to blunder out my meaning to four domestics, who I fancy babbled a jargon lefs intelligible than my own; though no country could appropriate it, it was a mixture of all, but the proportions of the compound went more to Dutch, Cleves-land, and German, than to any other language. In this patois they gave me to underftand as well as they could, that the heads of the houfe being abfent, nothing could be done till their return on the morrow. I was, by convention with a party of acquaintance, to fleep that night at the diftance of two leagues, and left the houfe without any favourable prepoffeffions, refolving to take a future opportunity to look for other lodgings. But judge of my furprize when the lord of this unpromifing habitation made his appearance in my chamber, before I had rifen, the next morning, to affure me he

was in defpair at my difappointment in not feeing his apartments, which he protefted to God
were the moft pleafant, moft airy, and moft
beautiful of any in the Weftphalian circle, and
he verily believed in the German territory.
Then enfued the following queftion and anfwer
converfation, which I will endeavour to render
intelligible without a *fays I*, or *fays he*, to the
irkfome repetition of which I have as mortal
an objection as Marmontel himfelf: Would I
could as happily prove it expletive! Are thefe
apartments well furnifhed?—Delightfully in
every part of them.—Then I wifh my little
temporary menage to be fometimes at home:
is this poffible?—Every earthly convenience,
Sir.—Perhaps, then, I might now and then
dine *en famille*?—Nothing fo eafy.--You have,
no doubt, a proper table?—I only wifh you
would do me the honour to come and judge for
yourfelf: I honour the Englifh, and live very
much in the Englifh fafhion: ROST BIF on the
table every Sunday.—It were needlefs then to
afk if you can give me a good bed?—The beft
and fofteft in the circle—that's all.—Indeed,
then they need not be better.—No, truly, and
I have had fuch lodgers to lie upon them; No
lefs than the flower of the nobility of all
nations—Le Comte de A—, la Comteffe de
B—, Madame la Ducheffe de C—, the duke

of

of D—, the earl of E—, bishop F—, baroness
G—, and a string of the first titles, all the way
to Z.

As the man ran through these illustrious ini-
tials, in alphabetical order, I beg'd to know
if he was indulging himself in a laugh upon
that stale trick of travellers, the assuming
false titles while they were making the grand
tour,—and, if so, the satire was well enough
directed against such a pettifogging ambition,
which, however, was pretty well punish'd already, as these fictitious *grandeurs* are generally charg'd in every bill upon the road.—
Laugh! no, I never was more serious as to
the whole alphabet of great folks having at
different times occupied my apartments,
although they did not happen to come into
them in the exact Dictionary form, and order
aforesaid: And as to a travelling title, while
a lady or gentleman pays up to the price of
nobility, there is no question but she, or he,
are right noble, and honourable.

Although I now perceived there was a
spice of the wag in mine host, I began to
think there might be some part of his house,
which did not at first strike the view, and
which might spurn all sort of connexion with

K 2

the

the miserable shop at the door of which I had
entered : In short, I now fear'd that instead of
finding the mansion too bad, I should find it
for a quiet, observing, and unobserv'd Gleaner
too good. With that kind of alteration of
air and tone therefore, which an honest and
well-temper'd man glides into, when he sup-
poses he has undervalued any thing by an
overhasty judgment, I informed the master,
that I was apprehensive his rooms would be
too spacious and splendid for my purpose,—
that I was by no means any one of the superb
personages of his alphabet, but simply an
Englishman in pursuit of health, and the pure
air and water which so greatly contribute to
them ; but for which I could not afford to pay
too dear a price.

By no means too dear, you will have them,
sir, in a manner for nothing—and as for
air and water, I say nothing—vous verrez—
I wont say any thing—not a syllable—perdie,
vous verrez—you will see.—I do not suppose
there is such air in the heavens, nor such
water under them—vous verrez—that's all.

Then you may expect me at Emerick the
next morning.—I kept my word. Mine host
was standing in expectation at his door; and
scarce

ſcarce gave me time to ſpeak, before he ran with me through the ſhop before commemorated, and which after all was the only way of entrance. Then he took me into a poor, white-waſh'd, brick bottom'd, rough pav'd back room, with one window, opening to the Rhine, but ſo loaded with iron bars without, and ſo guarded by a net work of ruſty wire, that you could only get a peep at the river *au traverſe*. Then recommenc'd the Dialogue, there's an apartment for you ſir,—there's a ſalle ſuperbe à manger, ou pour voir le monde,—yes, there's a noble dining-room, or to receive company.

Not allowing me a moment's time to reply, he daſh'd with me into a ſort of kitchen at the back of this ſuperbe Salle, and throwing open a door at one end of it, bade me take care of my head, which was a very neceſſary caution, the doorway making it convenient to ſave that head from being broke by doubling the reſt of the body. He mounted a ladder, and taking my hand, hawl'd me after him. Up we both went as abſolute a perpendicular, of near forty ſtairs, as ever led to the main-maſt head of a firſt rate man of war. I do aſſure you, the ſtrong wing of a pigeon would have required a little breathing as it aſcended.

                              My

My landlord allow'd of none, but kept exclaiming—now, now we shall come to a charmante Kamer,—a charming chamber.—At the
end of our clambering we reach'd a room that
had neither bed, chair, or glass; I was about
to exprefs my furprize at this, when, anxious
to fhew me all his lions, my hurry fcurry guide
hurried me to a *very little apartment indeed*, the
door of which he was proceeding to open with
his accuftomed rapidity, when a voice from
within exclaimed in a tranquilliz'd tone.—
Arrête un petit moment s'il vous plait Monfieur. Stop a moment, fir, if you pleafe: To
which courteous requeft, the landlord, recognizing the voice, and bowing towards the
door, replied, Ne vous derangez pas Mademoifelle: Pray Mifs dont difturb yourfelf,—and
while the young lady fettles this little affair,
we may look about us fir, quoth he,—there you
fee good fir is the Rhine again, and you have
it alfo, as you fhall prefently fee in the room
adjoining. What do you think of my water
now fir? And as for air, can any thing be
better contrived?—do but obferve the delectable fituation of this fame—ah fa—continued
he, addreffing the late occupier of the very
little apartment, who now made her appearance,—ah fa—now you fhall judge of the
agrémens of my lodgings,—be fo good to ftep
in

in fir,—there's neatnefs,—marble pavement—
fides of beft Dutch tileing,—and obferve ftill
the delicious Rhine rolling under you.

Here he pointed to another outlet, where, I
muft confefs, I fhould never have thought of
looking for a profpect;—But the mafter of the
manfion abfolutely piqued himfelf upon it.—
There fir, what do you think of that!—In
your very bed chamber—almoft within reach
of your bed, Monfieur,—there's comfort,—
there's recommendation!—Affurément bien
commode, faid the young lady, joining in the
converfation with all the eafe in the world.—
Indeed fhe had left the door open on her
coming out, purely with a defign to affift
the great character her friend and relation,
as I afterwards underftood he was, had
given it.—The man concluded his eulogy by
again intreating to know what I thought of
it? Hereupon, I obferved to him, that though
I could not fay they fettle thefe matters *better*
in Weftphalia than in England, yet they do
fettle them in the former place much more at
their *eafe*.

The lady had juft left the room, fo that my
anfwer was addreffed only to my officious groom
of the chamber, who was extremely furprifed,

K 4

when

when I told him that the little adventure of the little lady in the little apartment could never gain credit, were I to relate it in my country; nay, could never have happened in any decent part of the kingdom of England, except by an accident, which would have covered even a girl of ten years old with confusion, and made a female of maturer age ashamed to lift her eye to the discoverer, if he happened to be a man, for some days after: I added, that the sense of decency was so nice in my country, that very serious illnesses had sometimes been incurred from the dread of some such exposure. . Ma foi, cela est bien bisarre: i'faith that's whimsical enough, said the man.—He then shewed off the rest of his house in the same inflated style of panegyric. And pray where are the superb beds? They may be had fir in a month, and I might have the beautiful salle below, and the charming chamber above, and the delicious apartment thereunto belonging, for so very trifling a sum as seven hundred florins a year, and my diet for seven hundred more. The enormity of the demand, being no less a sum than would purchase the fee-simple of the whole house, shop, and little apartment into the bargain, brought our discourse to a short conclusion. I could not but feel it as an insult levell'd at his

opinion

opinion of Englifh folly, and left his houfe with telling him, I was forry we had taken up fo much of each other's time to fo little purpofe. He feemed to think fo too, and dropping his vivacity and his courtefy at once, fuffer'd me to depart even without a bow. My friend, I beg pardon; and your's my good Reader: I dare fay you are *nice*, but I prefume alfo, you are *wife*;—the delicacies of your country,—the graceful decency of its manners and cuftoms, deferve to be appreciated; but, inafmuch as they are brought into comparifon and contraft with the difgufting freedoms of other nations, they will be yet more valued, and appear more amiable.

In truth, people of both fexes, on this fide the water, have fcarce an idea of thofe decencies, which by habit, if not by principle, difcover themfelves even in the loweft domefticks of Great Britain. Throughout Holland, Pruffia, and the Empire, even more than in France, the men and women difplay almoft *oftentatioufly* thofe objects which we conceal with the greateft care. As if proud of the natural defects that are confidered as humiliating with us, you will fee them carrying to and fro, in open day, and as a fort of pageantry of *difplay*, all the arcana of the bedchamber;

chamber; whether you are in ficknefs or in health it is the fame thing, and I have remarked that the fervants who prefide over thefe fhews (in England they would be *myfteries*, and difpofed of as if by magic)—the fervants, I fay, generally choofe to exhibit their machines at breakfaft, by paffing from one room to another, not fo much as fuppofing it *poffible* your delicacy can be diftreffed about the matter. Our fenfe of propriety on this occafion paffes for *mauvaife honte*. May it never be exchanged for either confident impudence, or habitual grofsnefs, which, though lefs culpable, is not lefs offenfive. In a word, may that *fhamefacednefs*, which the holy writers have ufed to fignify one of the moft lovely virtues in oppofition to the boldeft vice, ever continue to be reckoned amongft the prejudices of Britifh education! A prayer in which I am fure your own modeft nature, and chaftened manners, will heartily join your affectionate friend.

LETTER LXV.

TO THE SAME.

IN our first sheaf I collected for you a Gleaning of the village superstitions of Wales. I will now offer you those of Germany, especially in the country of Juliers, Le Mark, &c. bordering on Westphalia. The country people of those places have the most solemn faith in sorceries and witches, who though in their proper shape are only a pack of very old women, can assume any form, either bestial or human; but are, it seems, most fond of appearing in the character of cats. Some of this witchery is carried to such excess, that many people in the country of Juliers will on no consideration intermarry with a person, who may be supposed of having a sorcerer's blood in his veins; nay, the most advantageous matches have been refused, and the attractions of love itself been resisted, rather than a daughter should go to the arms of a man who has ever had a witch in his family, and the geneological tree was never more cautiously examined, and traced by a birth-proud noble to escape the disgrace of pollution, than it is to avoid an alliance with a sorcerer or sorceress. If there

can be found in the history of twenty generations, only twigs sufficient to make up one
hereditary besom, or broomstic, on which the
witch by descent might horse two of her fingers;
not only the shuddering parent, but the trembling lover; would consider it as strong a bar to
his marriage, as if his mistress had been taken
in inceft.

They believe also in loup-garou's, or men-
wolves; a gentleman of the first character here
for learning and integrity, but who, unhappily
for his country, is now no more, (Mr. Bauman,
of the Privy Council of Cleves, and first pastor
of the reformed church,) related to me the
story of a man at Cologne who assumed the
character of a loup-garou, and who lived by
the pillage of whatever in that character he
could lay his hands on for many years, infomuch that he had amassed great wealth, as well
in money as valuable moveables; but he was at
last assaulted and taken, by a country man who
swore he defied the devil and all his works, and
who had been long marked with a general op-
probium for this daring disbelief of evil spirits.
This man was encountered by the loup-garou,
on the day he was known to have sold a quantity of corn at the Cologne market, and to have
received the money; but so far was he from

tamely

tamely yielding up his honeſt profits to either
man or beaſt, that inſtead of flying with terror
before the wolf-man, or dropping his money-
bag; he held the ſaid bag at the extent of
his arm, which was a powerful one, and felled
the thief to the earth, with that very gold and
ſilver which he would have purloined.   When
he ſomewhat recovered the blow, our heroic
farmer threw him like a ſtunned calf over his
horſe, even in his wolves cloathing, and delivered him over to the magiſtrate, who, after
the due courſe of law, ordered him to be
hanged in his loup-garou dreſs, in the public
market-place of Cologne.   One would have
thought this difaſter would have opened the
eyes of ſuperſtition; but, alas, eyes hath ſhe,
and feeth not! Neither are her votaries to be
driven from the ſteadfaſt faith that was in them
by the detection of a ſingle impoſtor.   On the
contrary the Colognians believe, at leaſt they
have a tradition at this day, that the real loup-
garou, being angry with the man that was
hanged, got into him, and in order to be
revenged, put it into the head of the farmer,
that he might be taken up as a thief, and come
to an untimely end; but that the inſtant the
halter was round the pretender's neck, the
ſpirit of the real wolf-man ſlipped out of him
again, and enjoyed his triumph, to think how
                                      cleverly

cleverly he had brought his enemy to the gal-
lows. Thus the very circumſtances that ought
to weaken ſuperſtition give it ſtrength.

Their credulity embraces alſo ſeveral other
imaginary beings, particularly of the fairy
tribe. Theſe, however, differ from our's in
ſome of their manners and cuſtoms. They are
of the ſame ſpecies, but inhabitants of a different country, you know. The moſt popular
of the fairies of Germany are ſuppoſed to be
little men and women, who inhabit the iron
and copper mines, and are, in general, very
gracious and obliging. For inſtance, they will
come in the night time into houſes, and when
a maid ſervant happens to be on good terms
with them, that is when ſhe believes in their
power with all her might, they will clean her
plates and diſhes after an entertainment ; put
her rooms in order, and even give her an idea
of it in her ſleep, ſo that as a fairy was never
known in this country to fib, though with us
they are ſomewhat given to lying, ſhe indulges
herſelf with a nap extraordinary ; and is ſure to
find all her work done to her hands when ſhe
comes down. They come alſo into ſhops,
warehouſes, &c. with the ſame induſtrious and
good natured intention. The taylor riſes and
finds the half finiſhed ſuit ready to take home ;
the

the cobler his shoes, &c. Neverthelefs, when ill-treated, thefe powerful little fpirits are cruelly vindictive, and will hide, mangle, and deftroy every thing before them: inftead of affifting the artifan, they will pull his work to pieces, inftead of befriending the poor maid fervant, they will trepan her with fair promifes, that thus cajoled, they may tempt her to lie in bed that fhe may get a good fcolding. In fine, thofe perfons who take any delight in knowing our neighbours are on the whole upon a level with ourfelves, may pleafe themfelves with the thought, that if foreigners have all the virtues, they have likewife all the weakneffes of human nature.

I fhould not forget under the article fuperftition, to mention that in the pretty country of Skuytz, fouthward of Weftphalia, they have an idea that cats are to be reconciled to a new refidence only by coercive meafures. In purfuance of which notion, a widow woman, at whofe houfe I lodged, imprifoned a poor cat three nights and days in a dark room, to the entire deftruction of my reft, and almoft to the cat's infanity, in order to make her in love with her new houfe. Now in England, you know, where cats are not a whit more remarkable for an amiable difpofition, we fhould have

ftroked

ſtroked the poor animal till ſhe purred approbation: we ſhould have permitted her to feed
and ſleep the firſt night by our fire-ſide, and ſo
hoſpitably treated her, that at the breakfaſt
table next morning, ſhe would have found herſelf one of the family.

Not that I would have you ſuppoſe I am an
advocate for the feline race, except on general
principles of juſtice and mercy. A dog is
often an *example* to his maſter, and a proper
object of his love, honour, imitation, and good
faith. But a cat I take to be (with very rare
exceptions indeed) both a traitor and a ſyco-
phant. She is won to you only by fawnings,
and if you puniſh her on ever ſo juſt a cauſe, ſhe
either ſtrikes immediately, or owes you a
grudge, the unexecuted malice of which ſhe
can hold till an opportunity of vengeance
occurs. Even when you imagine you have
gained her affections, ſhe will deſert you, like
a faithleſs lover, and elope from your arms.

Perhaps, you may not think this the proper
moment to introduce an anecdote of one of
theſe inſidious creatures. You may ſuſpect me
of imitating the Grimalkin diſpoſition by ſitting down in malice. Were I about to become
an accuſer it might be ſo: but what I have now

to

to mention exhibits no charge, though it will report an unlucky event.

In this very town of Cleves, which with its environs will detain us some time longer, I was residing with a Pruffian family, during the time of the fair; which I shall pass over, having nothing remarkable to distinguish it from other annual meetings, where people assemble to stare at, cheat each other, and divert themselves, and to spend the year's savings in buying thofe bargains which would have been probably better bought at home. One day after dinner, as the defert was just brought on the table, the travelling German musicians, who commonly ply the houfes at thefe times, presented themselves and were suffered to play, and just as they were making their bows for the money they received for their harmony, a bird-catcher who had rendered himself famous for educating and calling forth the talents of the feathered race, made his appearance, and was well received by our party, which was numerous and benevolent. The musicians, who had heard of this bird-catcher's fame, begged permiffion to ftay; and the mafter of the houfe who had a great fhare of good-nature, indulged their curiofity: a curiofity, indeed, which every body participated; for all that we have heard or feen of learned pigs, affes, dogs, and horfes was faid to be extinguifhed in the wonderful wifdom, which blazed in the genius of this birdcatcher's canary. The canary was produced, and the owner harangued him in the following manner, placing him upon his forefinger. Bijou (jewel) you are now in the prefence of perfons of great fagacity and honour: take heed you do not deceive the expectations they have conceived of you from the world's report: you have got laurels: beware their withering. In a word, deport yourfelf like the bijou (the jewel) of canary birds, as you certainly are.

All this time the bird feemed to liften, and, indeed, placed himfelf in the true attitude of attention, by floping his head to the ear of the man, and then diftinctly nodding twice when his mafter left off fpeaking; and if ever nods were intelligible and promiffory, thefe were two of them.

That's good, fays the mafter, pulling off his hat to the bird. Now, then, let us fee if you are a canary of honour. Give us a tune:—The canary fung. Pfhaw, that's too harfh: 'tis the note of a raven with a hoarfenefs upon
him:

him: fomething pathetic. The canary whiftled
as if its little throat was changed to a lute.
Fafter, fays the man.—Slower—very well—
but what a plague is this foot about, and this
little head.—No wonder you are out, Mr.
Bijou, when you forget your time. That's a
jewel.—*Bravo, bravo,* my little man.

All that he was ordered or reminded of did
he do to admiration. His head and foot beat
time—humoured the variations both of tone
and movement; and, " the found was a juft
echo to the fenfe," according to the ftricteft
laws of poetical, and (as it *ought* to be) of
mufical compofition—*Bravo! bravo!* re-echoed
from all parts of the dining-room.—The
muficians fwore the canary was a greater
mafter of mufic than any of their band. And
do you not fhew your fenfe of this civility, Sir,
cries the birdcatcher, with an angry air. The
canary bowed moft refpectfully, to the great
delight of the company. His next achieve-
ment was going through martial exercife with
a ftraw gun, after which, my poor bijou, fays
his owner, thou haft had hard work, and muft be
a little weary: a few performances more, and
thou fhalt repofe. Shew the ladies how to
make a curtfey.

The bird here croſſed his taper legs, and ſunk and roſe with an eaſe and grace that would have put half our ſubſcription aſſembly belles to the bluſh—That's my fine bird—and now a bow, head and foot correſponding. Here the ſtriplings for ten miles round London might have bluſhed alſo. Let us finiſh with an hornpipe, my brave little fellow—that's it—keep it up, keep it up.

The activity, glee, ſpirit, and accuracy with which this laſt order was obeyed, wound up the applauſe, (in which all the muſicians joined, as well with their inſtruments as their clappings) to the higheſt pitch of admiration. Bijou, himſelf, ſeemed to feel the ſacred thirſt of fame, and ſhook his little plumes, and carolled an *Io pæan* that ſounded like the conſcious notes of victory.

Thou haſt done all my biddings bravely, ſaid the maſter, careſſing his feathered ſervant; now then, take a nap, while I take thy place. Hereupon the canary went into a counterfeit ſlumber, ſo like the effect of the poppied god, firſt ſhutting one eye, then the other, then nodding, then dropping ſo much on one ſide, that the hands of ſeveral of the company were ſtretched out to ſave him from falling, and juſt

as

as thofe hands approached his feathers, fuddenly recovering and dropping as much on the other; at length the fleep feemed to fix him in a fteady pofture; whereupon the man took him from his finger, and laid him flat upon the table, where the man affured us he would remain in a good found fleep, while he himfelf had the honour to do his beft to fill up the interval. Accordingly, after drinking a glafs of wine, (in the progrefs of taking off which he was interrupted by the canary bird fpringing fuddenly up to affert his right to a fhare, really putting his little bill into the glafs, and then laying himfelf down to fleep again) the owner called him a faucy fellow, and began to fhew off his own independent powers of entertaining. The *forte* of thefe lay chiefly in balancing with a tobacco pipe, while he fmoked with another, and feveral of the pofitions were fo difficult to be preferved, yet maintained with fuch dexterity, that the general attention was fixed upon him. But while he was thus exhibiting, an huge black cat, who had been no doubt on the watch, from fome unobferved corner fprung upon the table, feized the poor canary in its mouth, and rufhed out of the window in defpite of oppofition. Though the dining room was emptied in an inftant, it was a vain purfuit; the life of the bird was gone, and its

L 3   mangled

mangled body was brought in by the unfortunate owner in such dismay, accompanied by
such looks and language, as must have awaked
pity in a misanthrope. He spread him half-
length over the table, and mourned his canary-
bird with the most undissembled sorrow.
Well may I grieve for thee, poor little thing;
well may I grieve: more than four years hast
thou fed from my hand, drank from my lip, and
slept in my bosom. I owe to thee my support,
my health, my strength, and my happiness;
without thee what will become of me. Thou
it was who ensured my welcome in the
best company. It was thy genius only
made me welcome. But thy death is a just
punishment for my vanity: had I relied only
on thy happy powers, all had been well,
and thou hadst been perch'd on my finger,
or lulled in my breast at this moment! but
trusting to my own talents, and glorifying myself in them, a judgment has fallen upon me,
and thou art dead and mangled on this table.
Accursed be the hour I entered this house!
and more accursed the detestable monster that
killed thee! Accursed be *myself*, for I contributed. I ought not to have taken away my
eyes when thine were closed in frolic. O, bijou,
my dearest only bijou, would I were dead also!

As

As near as the spirit of his disordered mind can be transfused, such was the language and sentiment of the forlorn birdcatcher; whose despairing motion and frantic air no words can paint. He took from his pocket a little green bag of faded velvet, and taking out of it some wool and cotton, that were the wrapping of whistles, bird calls, and other instruments of his trade, (all of which he threw on the table, "as in scorn,") and making a couch, placed the mutilated limbs and ravaged feathers of his canary upon it, and renewed his lamentations.

These were now much softened, as is ever the case, when the rage of grief yields to its tenderness: when it is too much overpowered by the effect to advert to the cause. It is needless to observe to you, that every one of the company sympathised with him. But none more than the band of *musicians*, who, being engaged in a profession that naturally keeps the sensibilities more or less in exercise, felt the distress of the poor bird-man with peculiar force. It was really a banquet to see these people gathering themselves into a knot, and after whispering, wiping their eyes, and blowing their noses, depute one from amongst them to be the medium of conveying into the pocket

of

of the bird-man, the very contribution they had juft before received for their own efforts. The poor fellow perceiving them, took from the pocket the little parcel they had rolled up, and brought out with it, by an unlucky accident, another little bag, at the fight of which he was extremely agitated; for it contained the canary feed, the food of the "dear loft companion of his art." There is no giving language to the effect of this trifling circumftance upon the poor fellow; he threw down the contribution money that he brought from his pocket along with it, not with an ungrateful but with a defperate hand. He opened the bag, which was faftened with red tape, and taking out fome of the feed put it to the very bill of the lifelefs bird, exclaiming—No, poor bijou, no—thou can'ft not peck any more out of this hand, that has been thy feeding place fo many years—thou can'ft remember how happy we both were when I bought this bag full for thee. Had it been filled with gold thou had'ft deferved it. It fhall be *filled*,—and with gold, faid the mafter of the houfe, if I could afford it.

The good man rofe from his feat, which had long been uneafy to him, and gently taking the bag, put into it fome filver; faying, as he handed

handed it to his neareft neighbour, who will refufe to follow my example; it is not a fub-fcription for mere charity, it is a tribute to one of the rareft things in the whole world ; namely, to real feeling, in this fophiftical, pretending, parading age. If ever the paffion of love and gratitude was in the heart of man, it is in the heart of that unhappy fellow, and whether the object that calls out fuch feelings be bird, beaft, fifh, or man, it is alike, virtue and —— ought *to be rewarded*—faid his next neighbour, putting into the bag his quota. It is fuper-fluous to tell you that after the feed had been taken wholly away, and put very delicately out of the poor man's fight, every body moft chearfully contributed to make up a purfe, to repair (as much as money could), the bird-man's lofs. The laft perfon applied to, was a very beautiful German young lady, who as fhe placed her bounty into the bag, clofed it im-mediately after, and blufhed. As there are all forts of blufhes, (at leaft one to every action of our lives, that is worth any characteriftic feeling, fuppofing the actor can feel at all) Sufpicion would have thought this young lady, who was fo anxious to conceal her gift, gave little or nothing; but candour who reafons in a different manner, would fuppofe what was really the cafe—that it was a blufh not of

avarice

avarice and deception, but of benevolence graced by modesty. Curiosity, however, caught the bag, opened it, and turned out its contents, amongst which was a *golden ducat*, that by its date and brightness had been hoarded. Ah ha, said curiosity, who does this belong to, I wonder? Guilt and innocence, avarice and benignity, are alike honest in one point; since they all in the moment of attack, by some means or another, discover what they wish to conceal. There was not in the then large company a single person, who could not have exclaimed to this young lady, with assurance of the truth—*Thou art the woman!* There was no denying the fact; it was written on every feature of her enchanting face. She struggled, however, with the accusation almost to tears, but they were such tears, as would have given lustre to the finest eyes in the world, for they gave lustre to her's, and would have added effulgence to a ray of the sun.

Well then, if no body else will own this neglected ducat, cried the master of the house, who was uncle to the lady abovementioned, I will: whereupon he took it from the heap, and exchanged it for two others, which enriched the collection.

While the business of the heart was thus carrying on, the poor birdman, who was the

occasion

occasion and object of it, was at first divided by contrary emotions of pain and pleasure: his eye sometimes directed to the maffacred canary, and sometimes to the company: at length generofity proved the stronger emotion, and grief ebbed away. He had loft a bird, but he had gained the goodwill of many human beings. That bird, it is true, was his pride and fupport, but this was not the crifis any longer to bewail its fate. He accepted the contribution-purfe, by one means or another filled like the fack of Benjamin, even to the brim, and bowed but fpoke not; then folding up the corpfe of the canary in its wool and cotton fhroud, departed with one of thofe looks, that the moment it is feen is felt and underftood, but for which, being too powerful for defcription, no language has yet been provided. On going out he beckoned the muficians to follow. They did fo, ftriking a few chords that would have graced the funeral of Juliet. My very foul purfued the founds, and fo did my feet. I hafted to the outer door, and faw the bird-man contending about returning the money, which the *founders* of the benevolence (for fuch were the muficians) had fubfcribed.

I have

I have nothing to add to this Gleaning, but a piece of information that belongs to it; the very next morning I was a witnefs to two traits of the heart of the mafter of the manfion where thefe tranfactions had paft.. A nobler minded man lived not—Alas, he is no more. On my coming down to breakfaft the day after, I faw the footman departing with the *cat who killed the bird*; not, faid the gentleman, to put her to death for an act that was natural to her; but to put her where I know fhe will be out of my fight, for I never could look at her again without being reminded of the moft uncomfortable part of yefterday's adventure: poor bijou! I have not a doubt but all we have done atones but fcantily for the lofs of fuch a friend. Juft as he faid this, the niece, whofe perfon and mind I have already gleaned for you, came into the breakfaft room: And now, faid the old gentleman, to finifh this bufinefs. Look ye, Henrietta, I gave you this new ducat to lay out at the fair in any manner you liked beft: and though I think the way in which you difpofed of it the very beft you could have chofen (nay no more blufhing) I think it never ought to go out of our family; for do you know that I have taken it into my old fuperftitious head that tho bleffing of the Giver of *all* good will ftay with us while fuch a ducat remains amongft us. I

therefore

therefore bought it back cheaply with two others. Age is fuperftitious, you know, my dear. Indulge me then love, and take care of it while I live, after which it fhall be your's— and in the meantime, that you may not lofe your fairing, in this little purfe are ten others, that, though not fo diftinguifhed by what, to my old heart, is more precious than the gold of Ophir, may ferve well enough the common purpofes of life.

Much of this was fpoken with tender diffi- culty, and the gift was received with more: but fhe loved the hand which in the firft in- ftance had enabled her to be generous too well not to reward it. Was not this, indeed, an illuftration of the virtue of the man of Rofs, who

" Did good, yet *blufh'd* to find it fame."

To apologize to you for this ftory, as I have faid on former occafions, would be to infult you and myfelf. I rather expect your thanks.
Adieu.

LETTER LXVI.

TO THE SAME.

AND you tell me I am not difappointed. I *have* your thanks. Under ſuch encouragements, I reſume the pen with alacrity. It is inconſiſtent with the plan of this correſpondence to ſet down a formal liſt of roads or routes, or to preſent a meagre catalogue of cities, towns, and villages. When you are at a centrical place, as Cleves, for inſtance, you can ſcarce take an unpleaſant courſe in ſuch a Duchy, and if you are diſpoſed to make the tour of Weſt-phalia, on a plan of pleaſure, or health, it is nearly immaterial whether from this its capital, you verge towards the South, or to the Weſt, the Eaſt, or the North; ſo abundant are the beauties on every ſide. But, previous to a more extenſive excurſion, there are in reſerve for the deliberate traveller a great variety of rural beauties, which lie entirely out of the ordinary track, and which are, therefore, generally paſt, not only unſeen, but unheard of. To ſome of theſe I ſhall direct you, becauſe they deſerve your attention, and will, probably, never otherwiſe have it. A ſtranger no ſooner gains

Cleves,

Cleves, than he fets off for Duffeldorf, Maef-
tricht, Aix la Chapelle, or Spa; and all the
fweet fide fcenery, and enchanting villages behind are left neglected, becaufe they do not
happen to lie in the broad high road of a large
town: and to drive from one large town to
another feems to be one of the grand refolutions
of modern travel. For this reafon I prefume
it is, that a real lover of the ftill fmall voice of
nature may refide in an out-of-the-way village,
in any part of the Dutch, Pruffian, or German
dominions, and never fo much as hear it mentioned, even amongft the *traditions* of the place,
that an Englifh traveller had fojourned therein
for a fingle day. Hence (to fpeak only of the
hundreds of delicioufly-fequeftered fpots, that
are fituated in the neighbourhood of Arnheim,
and of Nimeguen, one way, and of Cleves and
Emeric another) you may as well look for the
Emperor of Morocco as for an elegant foreigner, or any refident foreigner at all, except
here and there a ftraggling family, whom neceffity hath driven into retreat.   But whether
obferved or not by the duft-loving eyes of
vanity and fafhion, nature goes filently and
bloomingly on. I would recommend *you*, my
friend, and all other of her genuine admirers,
to feek her in the agreeable country of Kuyh,
in the little principality of Boxmeer, and in
                                          the

the enchanting bounds of Pruffian Guelderland. All of thefe, indeed, poffefs beauties, that to be won, muft be woo'd ; for they are feveral leagues out of the common, or, if you pleafe, of the *fafhionable* track : but then they are in the direct road to nature, and their paths are peace.

I performed the whole tour of Pruffian Guel-derland on foot, and I know not the period of my life that has been fo truely paftoral. I ftopped at every town and village, and verily think I fhould have been welcome at every houfe. You are convinced of the general fer-tility of the foil by the abundant fleeces of the fheep, and of the falubrity of the air by the florid countenances of the people. Though the country muft, in a general view, be called level, it is furnifhed with great variety. Long, meandring green lanes, pleafant interfperfed thickets (principally of fir and oak) Arcadian-looking cottages, all in the beft repair; vene-rable caftles, an infinity of towers, fteeples, fpires, convents, and ancient abbeys; meadow-grounds, often compacted into little verdant enclofures, often expanded into fpacious fields; the whole fertilized by delicious ftreams, fed by their parent flood, the Maife, which, were it near my natal banks, would become a rival

to the Thames—all these attracting objects
diversify the view. It must be owned that a
league of uniformly dreary heath ground frequently intervenes; but even this is relieved
by herds, flocks, and shepherds; and, by the
power of contrast, the sterility becomes a not
uninteresting object in a traveller's picture.

For the inhabitants, I scruple not to propose
them, in addition to my former observations,
amongst the models of imitation for the good
people of England, in point of pleasantry, and
useful courtesy. I should be worse than un-
generous, I should be ungrateful, were I to
refuse them their merits on this head. In the
course of one day's Gleaning, as if destiny had
planned it on purpose to shew me some speci-
mens of real urbanity, amongst a set of persons
who had certainly never studied it as an art of
politeness, but cultivated it as a gift of nature,
I was blest with the happy faculty of losing my
way frequently. As I passed along from a little
village called Geysteren, to another named
Venrai, a shepherd, perceiving me long before
I saw him, came running to assure me that I
was out of all tracks, and then enquiring my
destination, attended me on my way, till it was
too direct for any one, but a man who deviates
by design, to miss. His sheep-dog quarrelled

with my little fpaniel, and the fhepherd, de-
firous to teach him fome of his own good
manners, held him by the collar, and harangued him on the fubject of rudenefs to
ftrangers; during which eloquence he growled
yet more, as crofs creatures generally do when
forced to hear good advice. By that happy
knack of getting into a *wrong* road with which
I am gifted, I was obliged to afk for the *right*
juft at fun-fetting. I faw a peafant at his door.
Pray, friend, is this the way to Venrai?—" This
is the firft houfe that belongs to quite a different town, fir. You are a mile further to the
left than you ought to be." Off fet my peafant
without faying another word, and did not ftop
till we had gained the firft houfe of the hamlet
I had enquired for. " You muft now go *right
out*, fir," faid the guide, and, before I had time
to thank or reward him, he was out of fight.

Earlier in the day I had enquired of an
ancient woman, on her way to the church, the
road to a little village called *Wel*, on the banks
of the Maife. She informed me, but fufpecting
I might not underftand her, fhe ftood, unafked,
till I had taken the right path. The good
woman then went away fatisfied that fhe had
done me a fervice. By a fort of characteriftic
fatality, I made the fecond turning the reverfe
of

of my information. " To the right about, fir,"
quoth the old woman, who efpied me from
another place, where fhe had made a ftand.
You, my friend, who know my methods, will
not wonder to hear that I followed the impulfe
which led me to run acrofs the fields, purely to
take hold of her hand, and give her the thanks
of my heart. By an impulfe no lefs genuine,
and, perhaps, more generous, fhe went back
to my ground with me, and would not leave
me till fhe had made, *as one would have thought,*
another miftake impoffible.

Yet I contrived it. The bewitching ftory
of Marmontel's fhepherdefs of the Alps, which
I read to relieve a long walk over a heath, conducted me, juft at the termination of the faid
heath, and of the faid ftory, into a farmer's
yard. Being Sabbath-day, the farmer was
regaling himfelf with folded arms, and a fhort
pipe in his mouth. Suppofing I had bufinefs
with him, he conducted me into his houfe,
which was furely kept by the goddefs of *Propreté* (neatnefs) if fuch a divinity there be.
I explained, and apologifed. He fmiled, and
thanked me.—" But you muft be weary, fir;
repofe, and refrefh." In an inftant, as if by
magic, the table was fpread, and fo white a
cloth; bread, butter, and milk fo good, and

a wel-a welcome fo cordial, that I muft beg of you, if ever you make the tour of Pruffian Guelder- land, to attempt wandering, by happy negli- gence, or, if that fails you, by well-timed con- trivance, into a farmer's yard; no matter where, as this man is but a fpecimen of his countrymen.

Nor were thefe examples of urbanity all: at noon of the fame day, I was refcued from the moft imminent danger, by a good natured fellow, who informed me I was making the beft of my way into a quagmire. Nor is this courtefy confined to the peafantry. It extends to all claffes. At no ungleanable diftance from my proper path, I was attracted by a magni- ficent caftle, and, relying on the courteous, general character of the country, I entered its venerable and awe-infpiring gate. The family were at Liege. The domeftic chaplain only remained at home. He was faying grace, and croffing himfelf, juft as I entered his apart- ment.—Pardon the *ill-tim'd* vifit of a curious Englifh ftranger—was my opening fpeech. " *Well-tim'd*, I hope it will prove, as I am fure it is welcome," was his reply, rifing from his feat, and placing me in it. I had already, in my kind of running way, taken refrefhments at half a dozen cottages; an apple at one, a

cake

cake at another, a cordial at a third, and fo
on; but the good chaplain "fo gaily prefs'd
and fmil'd," as he fet a clean cover, napkin,
filver fork, and fpoon, before me, I could not
but accept the invitation. After our repaft,
learning the object of my vifit, he made with
me the tour of the chateau, which, had it been
infpected by a critic in paintings, pictures,
and an amateur of Gothic architecture, would
have been the journey of a day. In our way
back to his room, we paffed into a very noble
garden, with the fruits and flowers of which he
loaded my pockets and hands; and when, after
a parting glafs of wine, I left the apartment
in which I had firft feen him—" Remember,
fir, this has been parfon's fare; the next vifit
you make, the owners of the caftle, whom I
fo faintly reprefent, and who are to be here
to-night, will do you more honour." The name
of this fine caftle is *Wel*, on the Weft fide of a
very picturefque · little Pruffian village, upon
the banks, and almoft upon the brims of the
Rhine, that majeftic river, which, you know,
common geography tells you, nd truly tells,
rifes from two fprings in the Alps, and runs
North to the lake of Conftance, then Weft to
Bafil, afterwards North between Swabia and
Alface, then paffing through the Palatinate,

M 3   the

the Electorate, and the Duchy of Cleves, at
laft enters the Netherlands, five miles below
Cleves, where it becomes broad and rapid.
The direct courfe of this noble river is above
500 miles; it is generally one quarter, and,
in fome places, half a mile broad, and from
one and a half to feven fathoms in depth. It is
navigable to Bafil in Switzerland, which is
four hundred miles, by long boats with round
bottoms, which commonly go at the rate of
four miles an hour, and, in thefe, paffengers
are conveyed at the eafy rate of one ftiver (one
penny) for five miles: but the navigation of
the Rhine, like that of the Danube, is interrupted by nine cataracts, the principal of which
is at Shaffhaufan, in Switzerland, where the
whole river falls from an height of 75 feet.
But what is there in the whole of this defcription, my friend, that fills the imagination, or
warms the heart, like the philanthropy of the
chaplain of the caftle? The fimple ftream
of good will, that flowed from his bounty to
me, indicated a foul, whofe " genial current"
had it not been checked by more obftructions
than the cataracts of the Danube, or the Rhine,
would have fertilized and enriched more than
thofe mighty waters. I have purfued the courfe
of both thefe rivers, for many a beautiful league.

I have

I have gazed, with all the fondnefs of a real lover of nature, and, with fomething of a poet's eye, on their numerous objects. I have painted, with an ardent pencil, fome of their landfcapes; I have often wondered and admired, but never yet did I fee, or feel, on their bofoms, or on their banks, unlefs proceeding from fimilar fources—the fources of philanthropy—any thing fo touching as the little fcenery of an hour, in and about the Chateau of Wel, fo true it is that

"An honeft man's the *noblef* work of God."

But, alas, fortune, according to her caprices, is either the lavifh fountain that feeds the ftream of human benevolence, or the ftupendous and immoveable cataract, that contracts its courfe, and circumfcribes its power. Of our Pruffian prieft, I have only further to fay, that every look, word, and action, proved

"Large was his bounty, and his foul fincere;

And I have not a doubt that

"Heav'n has as large a recompenfe beftow'd,

in the teftimony of his own confcience.

Friends he ought to have in abundance, but he has gained one more, while there is the breath of life in the Gleaner. Nay, I am willing to extend the date of my gratitude towards him beyond the grave; for if any thing that hath been done in this fublunary fphere is worthy to be remembered in another, it is furely the fair deeds, and authors of a generofity, that is free from being polluted by the droffy materials of the prefent world. If fo, what a claim has the unbought, and unfullied act of this blamelefs prieft on the memory of your friend, when his powers of recollection fhall be immortal. Since the day on which I received the bounty I have not feen the benefactor, but I often pleafe myfelf by reflecting that my fenfe of his goodnefs will be amongft the facred pleafures that I may reafonably hope fhall not " quit me when I die."

We muft not take leave of the Rhine till I have mentioned the amufement in referve for you, on the borders of that Imperial river. The continual commerce and paffage of people over the different ferrys of that, as well as its neighbour, the Maife, is very diverting; and, though you fometimes feem in a country where, if one of the villages was emptied of its inhabitants, they would fcarcely fill a boat, you will perceive multitudes almoft every half hour during the Summer, pouring in fhoals to the ftrand. I was much

entertained

entertained in a ramble I made to the pretty village of Elton, which is in the neighbourhood of Cleves, and one of the moſt diſtinguiſhed beauties of the Duchy, part ſtanding upon an almoſt Cambrian-looking mountain, and part in a delightful valley. It is ſituate on the other ſide of the Lower Rhine, on paſſing which, I found myſelf in the Pont-Volant (Flying-bridge-boat) with, at leaſt, an hundred people, the greater part of whom were ſinging hymns, pſalms, and Ave-Mary's, in chorus. Never did I behold ſuch a collection of ſorrowful countenances, nor hear ſuch a concert of ſolemn cries: and I ſhould have been juſtified in ſuppoſing the whole party to be mad, had I not been told they were only penitential. They were Pruſſian peaſants come from their pilgrimage to Kaveler, a village, (where I may uſe the word *millions*, in ſpeaking of the numbers) which yearly receives the homage of the German people, of all ranks and ſexes. It is the Mecca of this quarter of the globe. The groupe in queſtion were juſt come from a confeſſion of their ſins, and were filled with compunction, or with conſcious abſolution; and as the firſt or laſt of theſe operated, they were ſunk to the duſt with ſhame, or treading in air with joy. On their landing, they formed themſelves into two

bands,

bands, singing in procession, and with their hats off. I gleaned them all the way from Elton in the vale to Elton on the Hill, and never beheld so moving a curiosity. Nevertheless, a small circumstance happened, that, for a moment, disconcerted the gravity of their progress. In ascending the steep, one of the penitents made a false step, and came down in so unlucky a way, that Religion herself must have smiled, as, indeed, she did, in the persons of those her sternest, and perhaps truest votaries: for there is a certain spark of waggery in human nature that can no more help the force of ridicule, on the sight of a ludicrous object, than hunger can resist appeasing appetite, when the means are in its power. And this fall was ludicrous enough, being, indeed, an exposure of what has, by proscription, and by habit, been long considered as the most ridiculous part of human nature: at least the one that has been most subject and obnoxious to ridicule. The poor penitent, indeed, would, I believe, have laught herself, but that she looked on her fall as a judgement, and so contented herself with doubling her Ave-Marias, and continuing the procession with more zeal than ever.

I will not trouble you with the long list of religious miracles believed to be wrought by the

the Virgin in favour of the good Catholics that refort to Kaveler.   However great thefe may be, the prefent race of French certainly have no faith in them; but on the contrary, when the armies of the Republic took poffeffion of this place, the plunder was not only carried to the holy altars, but to the facred figure itfelf. The fhrine was ftripped of all its long collected treafures, and, as fcarce any votary goes empty handed, thefe were immenfe: befides which, a rigorous contribution was levied on the inhabitants; an exorbitant fupply of ftockings, boots, fhoes, blankets, mufkets, &c. for the army was infifted on; the image of the Virgin was facrilegioufly polluted, and that of the Saviour of the world very narrowly efcaped the mock ceremony of the guillotine; the modern Ifraelites, however, repeated their unhallowed practice, which I think I have before mentioned fomewhere, of placing the red cap of licentioufnefs on its head, and writing on its fide (as refolving to refufe even the Son of God his *title*) Voïla, notre *Ci-devant* Seigneur.— Behold he who was *formerly* our Lord.   His facred head was ranfomed at no fmall coft. When this place was retaken by the Auftrians, the vifits of congratulation and condolence drew together an almoft incalculable multitude of fupplicants, from every quarter of the Ger-

man

man Empire. Perhaps, the devotion on that occasion must go into some excesses; but I leave you to judge whether the extreme of penitence or of plunder, is the evil most to be palliated.

The day succeeding this I strolled some leagues farther into the country, and being overtaken by one of those passing showers, which in spring time collect, drop, and disperse almost in the same instant, I took shelter in a road-side hut, in which I caught the labourers just sitting themselves down to dinner. There were thirteen persons, including the maid servant, who having set the food on the table, took her chair amongst them. Their repast consisted of nothing but one very large dish of potatoes, for which they returned God, both before and after eating, as much, possibly more thanks than he receives from many of his creatures, on whom he bestows the richest delicacies of his creation. It was truly a picture, and a very beautiful one, drawn by the faithful hand of nature, of social happiness and religious decency, (for which the peasantry of Germany are remarkable) amidst the heavy duties and toils of life. I have only given you a single specimen of a universal and invariable practice.

With

With refpect to government, all kings and high authorities will have, at leaft, an equal number of enemies and friends. Of the former, the prefent Pruffian monarch has his fhare; and yet, as far, at leaft, as the interior regulation of his kingdom is concerned, there feems very little juft caufe of complaint. Where a ftanding army is enormous and perpetual, there muft be proportionate levies on fome part of the people, to fupport that divifion of the citizens that take up arms in protection of the reft. Yet, I know not the part of the earth, where more liberty of fpeech or action is indulged than in the Pruffian territories. Political fubjects are, indeed, forbidden, but this, as ufual, only gives edge to the defire of doing what is inhibited: accordingly the monarch is *cut up* and *carved* at every public table in Pruffia, with as much freedom of abufe as even a modern patriot could well long for. The eafe with which the *little* folks appear to live, notwithftanding the exaction of royal rights, might be envied by the *great* folks of *any* nation. Their houfes, and cottages are actually overftocked, *crouded* with furniture; and although there is little or no fotting in the common public houfes, each ordinary beer-houfe, I am convinced, contains double the quantity of pots, glaffes, china, &c. which

would

would be neceffary to equip an Englifh kitchen. In fhort, the only mifery-ftruck houfes to be feen in Pruffia, or generally fpeaking in the German empire, are thofe of the nobility and gentry in *declining* circumftances. In their abodes, indeed, your generous heart would in vain feek for the comforts and accommodations of the peafantry. Difmantled caftles, chateaus in decay without, and nearly empty within, tawdry beds, time or moth-eaten tapeftry, rufty armories, broken pillars, and every fign of high birth in low circumftances, are exhibited to your aching fight. Yet the labour and difficulty with which the proprietors of thefe fragments endeavour to conceal thefe diftreffes is wonderful. To fuch as have feeling hearts it is even pitiable. They keep up the family carriage, the family train of domeftics, and the family liveries, which are overloaded with ornament, and almoft ftarve themfelves to feed their vanity. Hence on a going out day, the magnificence of which is the œconomy, the almoft famine of a month, a paffing fpectator would miftake gaiety for happinefs, and grandeur as only a fuperfluity of wealth. But never could it more truly be faid, that " all which glitters is not gold." All this inconvenience and indigence arifes from the cruel neceffity they are under to preferve the *ways* of men of

family

family without the *means*. A Pruffian gentleman may not, confiftently with anceftral
dignity, enter into any fort of profitable
commerce to eke out a flender patrimony: for
trade though it might enrich the pocket is
thought very much to impoverifh the blood;
on which account thefe martyrs to family
honours go half naked and more than half un-
fed. And while the proprietors of a few
miferable and mortgage-eaten acres are ftarving
upon their inherited pittance, and are right
honourably in want of the neceffaries of life,
the plebeians, who are not forbid to make their
blood ftill poorer in order to preferve its purity,
may carry on all the gainful arts without any
other lofs than the chance of being ftarved
upon principles of good-breeding.

The little Signiory of Boxmeer, about feven
leagues from Cleves, and five from Nimeguen,
has claim to much of your attention. It is
fingularly fituated: it is only a fhort mile
diftant from a part of Holland. You have but
to ferry acrofs the Maife, and you are in Pruffia.
On the other fide of a fmall hamlet, you are in
the dominions of the Emperor. To the right
and left about a league you are in two other
diftinct Signiories, and in itfelf it is a principality fo abfolute, that life and death is in the

power

power of the reigning Prince, (who is of the illuftrious houfe of Hollenzollen) and whofe difpofition makes his defpotic power a mere fhadow of authority; for he is the parent of the people, and they enjoy all the privileges of an happy Republic. Yet even in this little well governed ftate, there are patriots who have been once vifited and plundered by the French; yet who are ftill wifhing the return of thofe ravages. How unaccountable!

The Boxmeer farmers cultivate a moft beau-ful feed they call *fparcette*, which yields two crops in the feafon, and the after one is gene-rally the beft. The verdure is more exquifite than any thing I have ever feen: it refembles in figure our wheat when very young, but furpaffes it abundantly in colour. The cows prefer it to grafs, and return for it moft excellent butter.

There are two Carmelite Convents in Box-meer, one of which is for women. This latter I gleaned: (the other has nothing glean-worthy.) At the gate of the Convent for the men, I met a gentleman with whom I had been formerly acquainted: he appeared very penfive, and begged I would defer my vifit to the Convent till the next day, and take my coffee at his houfe.

houfe. I attended him. On our way to his villa, he told me that the object of his vifit at the Convent was to converfe with the fuperior on the fubject of his niece, who was to enter upon her noviciate the next day. You remember Fanchette, perhaps, Sir, the handfome girl whom on your former vifit to this village, you ufed to call the Boxmeer Bloffom. Her fifter if you recollect had buried herfelf alive; for you know my opinion on the fubject—fome little time before you left us—and to-morrow fhe finifhes her career, by taking the veil. So that I fhall lofe both my domeftic comforts for ever without any hope of feeing them again; and you know how dear their company was to me, efpecially fince my fon continues a profligate, and has deferted me—I was both affected and furprifed at this intelligence; for the Boxmeer Bloffom was frefh in my remembrance, and I recollect the regret with which I faw her fifter purfue the fancy fhe had taken on enclofing herfelf. This latter, indeed, was fomewhat of a penfive caft, and had if I may fo fay, a bias to feclufion, with the fuppofed incitement of a tender difappointment: but the former was gay by nature, even to excentricity, and was addreffed by the man of her heart, with the fanction of her uncle, who was both able and willing to unite fortune with love.

On entering the uncle's houfe, we were told by a fervant that Fanchette was gone on a circuit to her neighbours to pay them her eternal adieus, but left word that fhe fhould return to make her uncle's coffee. She performed her promife with fo.much exactnefs that as the words *uncle's coffee* were pronounced, fhe was almoft in the act of pouring it out. Her air had loft none of its pleafantry, her features none of their beauty: fhe was ftill the Bloffom of Boxmeer.

I will relieve you again from the irkfome iteration of fays I, fays he, and fays fhe, by giving you our chat in dialogue.

Uncle. I began to fear, Fanchette, that you would have been feduced from my coffee table on this, alas, laft evening, by fome of your young companions.

Niece. O fie! how could you think fo! though every body afked me, and on refufal, would have accompanied me here, but there was fo much weeping and wailing about nothing that I really begged of them to ftay at home.

Gleaner. Nothing do you call it, my Bloffom, to know one of their friends is going out of the world to-morrow morning.

Niece.

Niece. Ah ha, Sir, so you are come back. Why, really by all your regrets, one would think I was already at the point of death, and going to be buried.—It is as vain, I suppose, to tell you as I have told others, that I am going to be happier than I have yet ever been.

Uncle. But is it not both death and burial?

Gleaner. I ask the same question?

Niece. And I make just the same answer that I have already done to hundreds; but as you are resolved to have it so, my death let it be. I hope, however, Sir, you will do me the honour to assist at my funeral? I will present you with a ticket of admission to the ceremony. And in the mean time, as I have a great deal to do, as you must consider all my worldly affairs are to be settled to night, we must make haste and get the coffee over.

Gleaner. What is yet omitted then? I shall be sorry to lose your company.

Niece. That's very obliging, but you know that when I am to be buried in a few hours it takes some little time to prepare one's self.

Soon after this she made her exit, but in a few minutes came back to beg I would indulge

her

her with a moment's converfation in the garden.
—I remember you perfectly, faid fhe, and feel
uncomfortable that you fhould imagine I treat
lightly the act I am about to do: but, befides
that, from my very inmoft foul, I look upon as
a feftival, what my friends call a funeral, I love
my uncle moft dearly, though he continues to
oppofe my happinefs in the only point wherein
it confifts, and as I cannot refift his tears,
though I can his arguments, I have no other
way but an apparent unconcern. Comfort
him, therefore, as the laft favour I intreat of
you; perfuade him to reconcile himfelf to my
felicity—and God preferve you.

She hereupon gave me her hand, and waving
it fo as to forbid reply, went fmiling out of the
garden and fought her chamber.

The next morning fhe rofe the fecond in the
houfe. As I am ufually the firft of every
family, go where I will, from a long-indulged
habit of " enjoying the cool, the fragrant
hour," we had another [fhort *tête-à-tête*, in
which fhe informed me fhe had juft come from
taking an everlafting leave of a featherbed,
fheets, and fhift, which were to be exchanged
for very oppofite pieces of furniture. The
ceremony of throwing away her drefs cap, and

all

all its *plumery*, as a sign of her renouncing the vanities of the world, was still to be performed, as had previously been settled.

Her deportment was more aweful than on the former day, but her attempered air, and sober step, took nothing from her personal attractions.

I soon lost sight of her, on a promise to attend her in her last moments. She said the necessity, as well as the time of assumed vivacity was now past, but that she felt a wish I should gratify my curiosity, and again recommended her good uncle to my care, observing, that, though he was too fond of the world, he was one of the worthiest persons in it. She then departed for the convent, which, indeed, almost joined to her uncle's house, and I found that the ceremony would begin in two hours.

You will perceive that I had an interest in becoming witness to a scene like this; and I feel, while I write, that you are not without a wish to receive a faithful Gleaning of it. Depend upon it then in my next.   In the interval, and always, your wishes are mine.

LETTER LXVII.

TO THE SAME.

JUST as I was entering into reflections on the subject of my last, and had brought
myself to believe, that every individual ought
to be the architect of his, or her own happiness, seeing the ideas about it were as different
as mens minds, features and understandings,
the bereaved uncle came down stairs in deep
mourning.   The idea of an interment had
settled itself in his soul, and he indulged it.
I could perceive he had been weeping, and that
it was not only the " customary suit of solemn
black" which he had put on.   He took me by
the hand, after more than an hour's pause;
during which, he either rocked himself up
and down in his chair,—cover'd his face with
his hand,—or sighed heavily.

It is amongst the solemn maxims of my
life, never to reason with a man in this kind
of situation.   One may as well talk of sobriety
to an intoxicated person, as of patience and
resignation, or the folly of grieving, to a
mind overborne by sorrow.   The Convent-bell
arous'd him, and still holding my hand, (his
own

own trembling as he fpoke)—Hark! the poor
Fanchette's funeral-bell tolls!—we muft be
going! I obeyed in filence. A great multitude were waiting in the antichamber of the
convent: but by favor, and by intereft, (both
which have their effect, even in the temples
devoted to thofe who have *renounced* the *world*,)
we were immediately admitted into the gallery, and obtained feats that commanded the
chapel, wherein the ceremony was to be performed. Indeed our places were directly in
front of the very part where the fifters were to
take their ftation.

Only two of the Novices were in the Chapel,
and thofe were ftrewing the floor with frefh-
gathered flowers, and ever-greens; and at
that end of the apartment where the chief
objects of the day were to be difplayed, was a
large piece of green carpeting. Soon after
thefe preliminary preparations, which have all
their effect on the mind, as tending to inflate
curiofity, the ceremonies of the entrance,
(which were not a little impofing likewife,)
began. Firft came in the fuperior of the
convent, then the nuns, according to their
order, and then the two fifters, who were
conducted by two fifters, to a little altar in the
centre of the room, feparated from the gal-

N 4

lery,

lery, only by a flight and open partition.
Ifabel, fo was the elder fifter named, was
placed on the right, and Fanchette on the left.
We had a complete view of both. Each
had a lighted taper in her hand, and their head-
dreffes were diftinguifhed, by the blue hood,
and the white. There was enough of family
fimilitude left in their features to difcover their
relationfhip: It had been much ftronger, but
the refemblance was, in great meafure, diminifhed by their oppofite fituations in life.
Ifabel had now been twelve months in a manner *out of the world,* and in the practife of all
the aufterities of the Carmelite order; and,
though thefe are not fo rigid as fome others,
the regulations they prefcribe are more than
fufficient to take out of the cheek that bloom,
which human fociety, nature, and the heart,
fo liberally beftow upon youth: befides which,
Ifabel had fomething of a conftitutional pale,
correfponding to the penfive colour of her
mind,—if I may fo exprefs myfelf. Fanchette, on the contrary, although fhe had
yielded to a fentiment that determined her to
devote herfelf, had too recently taken her *leave*
of the world, and of the gay and frefhning
air it breathes—(in the country at leaft,)—and
was, moreover, by difpofition, fo impaffion'd,
that the contraft betwixt her and Ifabel was the

6

more

more ftriking. The eyes of both were extremely dark, but although thofe of Ifabel were (from the extinguifhed complexion of her cheeks,) more deep, and perhaps more interefting, than Fanchette's, they were of a more fubdued and dying luftre: Fanchette's, were "as the radiance of the rifen day", and her fifter's, as the parting beam of a fun, prematurely clouded, even at noon.

On their reaching the altar, the fuperior of the men's convent addreffed the two fifters, in an exhortation replete with unaffected eloquence, and to which they gave the moft fix'd attention. This done, Ifabel, who was to take the veil, arofe, and between two of the fifters, came forward to make her profeffion; which, though in Latin, was delivered with the moft admirable articulation, and claffical propriety, kneeling before the Prieft. Then followed the prayers appointed for the occafion.

The Prieft having laid the proper dreffes of the order on a table before him, afforted them. Meantime, the fuperior took off the white, or noviciate veil, and enrobed Ifabel in black, but over this under veftment was placed the white cloth cloak, and the neck and head drefs

of

of black linen.   A broad belt and the beads
were then fettled.   The Prieft dipp'd a brufh in
holy water, with which he fprinkled the Devo-
tee: and   during   this ceremony,   the moft
folemn airs were   played on the organ,   in
which the profeffed join'd, apparently with her
whole foul.   She was reconducted to her feat,
where fhe remained at her devotions, while
her fifter underwent the ceremonies of the
Noviciate.   Thefe differ little from the other,
except that fhe was invefted with the white
head cloth inftead of the black.

But, previous to the affumption of thefe,
fhe delivered a box to the Prieft, from which
were taken the richeft ornaments fhe had made
ufe of while in the world.   The holy Father
threw them on the floor with an air of difdain,
and with yet greater indignation Fanchette
trampled them under her feet, as objects
unworthy her future attention.   In a former
part of the ceremonials, while her fifter was
putting on the eternal veil, I obferved that the
before animated countenance of Fanchette
became fuddenly pallid, but while fhe was
renouncing thefe her worldly ornaments, the
blood fallied into her charming face, as if to
give in a more powerful evidence of her entire
difavowal of all the pomps and vanities of
life.

life. And now fucceeded feveral grand, and truly fpirit-ftirring choruffes, of Priefts, Nuns, and of the congregation. High mafs was next performed in the body of the convent below. This pageant, with all its prieftly ornaments, tingling of bells, and the feducing apparatus of incenfe and of facrifice, are fo well known, and have been fo well defcribed by various authors, that I fhall pafs on to more new and interefting objects. Amongft thefe your heart will diftinguifh the two fincere and forrow-ftruck lovers of thefe beauteous victims. Both were prefent; the one in the vain hope of prevailing on Fanchette, even while at the altar, to change her cruel refolution; the other to attempt this alfo, or at worft to enjoy the afflicting luxury of *feeing* this Ifabel tear herfelf from his hope for ever; not, as I was informed, without a faint idea of the poffibility that the fudden fight of *him* whom fhe had once fondly loved, might change her vow, in thefe the laft moments of her power, to confecrate it to love inftead of religion. Thefe young men were both of refpectable connexions, of decent fortunes, and of blamelefs characters: the name of Ifabel's lover was Bernard, and that of Fanchette, Lacrew.

They

They had both placed themselves so as perfectly to see; but only one of them to be seen by the beloved object. Lacrew relied upon an open attack, and, therefore, kept constantly in view of the fair citadel; Bernard conceived more hope from an ambuscade, and, therefore, by way of masked battery, entrenched himself behind a pillar on one side of the gallery, from whence he could make a sortie at the moment he judged most favourable. His motive for thus attempting to carry the place by surprise was strong; he had been extremely ill, and Isabel, to whom a report had been made of it, had reason to suppose *herself* the cause, particularly as his sickness increased from the day, that, (in reply to his strongest urgency, to spare his life while yet in her power,) she had *refused*, but, confessed to a confidential friend, that, though she felt more emotion at the account of his distress than she *ought* to do, she could not suffer him to work her from her pious purpose. But the person who carried this account to him, conveyed it, in the *usual way of secrets*, to another confidential friend, who deposited it, in *solemn trust also*, to a third, who, with the *like sacred injunctions*, communicated it to Bernard himself; and although this report, at the time that it indicated some remains of

feeling

feeling for him, denoted her refolution to feclude herfelf for ever from his fight, by an act, which, as before obferved, would put it beyond her power to make him happy, he conceived from it, (what cannot lovers imagine?) that, fince fhe was thus arous'd to fome fenfibility of his fufferings, only at a *defcription* of them, how would it be called forth at the unexpected *fight* of a once beloved and now agonized object; whom fhe had every reafon to fuppofe in his fick chamber, at the diftance of thirty leagues? he refided at the fartheft part of the country of Juliers, and fhe had every reafon to imagine he was unable to leave his room. And fo indeed, except to accomplifh an atchievement of *defperation*, he was.

But thofe who have ever felt the influence of the faireft hope, in the moment almoft of fuch defperation, will not wonder that the poor Bernard, in oppofition to the advice of his medical, and other friends, and even of his own weaknefs at other times, now found himfelf ftrong enough to leave an apartment; wherein he had, in a manner, been bed-ridden feveral weeks, and to throw himfelf not only into the open air, but into an open poft-wag-gon, as they here call the public-ftage, and which,

which, (being without windows, and undefended from wind or weather, and very abfurd-
ly conftructed,) is a *difeafe in itfelf*.　He gain'd
the village of the convent, it feems, late in
the evening that preceded the morning, " big
with the fate" of his heart: yet, that heart
prompted him to take a moonlight view of the
outfide of the convent, which contained his
treafure.　He appear'd not to have fuffer'd from
thefe exertions, or, at leaft, the fuffrance and
agitation *within* abforb'd every external difafter for the moment;　fo true is the remark of
our great mafter of human nature, that,

 " —————When the Mind's free,
 " The Body's delicate".————

and this unhappy lover might juftly exclaim
with old Lear in the ftorm,

 " The tempeft in *my* mind
 " Doth from my fenfes take all feeling elfe
 " Save what beats there :
 " For where the greater malady is fix'd,
 " The leffer is fcarce felt.

Lacrew, who lived in the village, and was
almoft a next door neighbour, had lefs occafion
for ftratagem ;　and having had almoft daily
denials from his miftrefs, was more reconciled
even to the lofs of her ; not without a mental
refource, however, that he firmly believed a
          woman

woman of her difpofition, would foon ficken of a monaftic life, and that long before her year of trial had paft, fhe would return to the world, and of courfe to him ; for fhe profeffed to love him better than any thing *in* that world: yet fhe fancied fomething yet dearer to her *out* of it.

Her lover, indeed, expected, as he afterwards acknowledged to me and the uncle, that fhe would, even during the ceremonies of initiation, find fomething in them too formidable for the gaiety of her character, efpecially if he placed himfelf full in her view. In this, however, he was miftaken. His miftrefs had him almoft the whole time under her eye, but feldom looked towards him, and when fhe did, fhe withdrew herfelf with an hafte and refolution, that confounded and chagrined her admirer.

The fifters having gone through the accuftomed ceremonies, rofe from their kneeling attitude, and retiring fome paces back, each threw herfelf with a determined earneftnefs, but not in the mockery of tragic violence, at full length upon the carpet, and on their faces, and, had this falling fcene been in rehearfal actually on the ftage, by the moft expert tumblers, and pofture mafters and
miftreffes

miſtreſſes of the Theatre for ſix weeks, it
could not have been more adroitly perform'd.
Thus humbled to the ground, they imprinted
on it an audible kiſs to expreſs their lowlineſs
of ſpirit; and to ſignify they had renounced
the lofty follies of the world, to whoſe pomps
and vanities they were henceforth dead: the
better to carry on which idea, two of the nuns,
the one in her noviciate, the other in her
veil'd ſtate, toll'd the paſſing-bell, even while
the bodies of the ſiſters, thus ſymbolically
buried alive, were cover'd with a pall, as if
the breath of life was really gone from them.

It was at this intereſting and awful moment,
that the lover of Iſabel broke from his con-
cealment, and ſhewed to the aſtoniſhed ſpec-
tators a countenance, in which was painted
every paſſion of the heart in deſpair: but he
did not ſpeak.

The burial-ſervice was chanted to the notes
of the organ, which, aſſiſted by the vocal
powers of the prieſts, nuns, &c. might be truly
ſaid to enter the ſpirit and elevate the ſoul.
It was impoſſible for an Engliſh auditor, whom
the Gods have made ſomewhat poetical, not to
apply to the occaſion the beautiful deſcription
                                                  of

of Pope; and for an inftant, not to adopt the
doctrine it inculcates:

> " O grace ferene! O virtue heavenly fair !
> " Divine oblivion of low-thoughted care !
> " Frefh blooming hope, gay daughter of the Sky !
> " And faith, our early immortality,
> " Enter each mild, each amiable gueft,
> " Receive, and wrap me in eternal reft !

The whole congregation were indeed extre: ly
affected at this part of the ceremony. I was
touch'd even to tears. As the veil'd Ifabel
rofe, her eye fettled for an inftant on Bernard,
who had preffed forward by this time through
the croud, and ftood with his face directly
parallel to his miftrefs, who might be almoft
faid to rife from the dead. Confidering circumftances, he muft to *her* appear in nearly
the fame fituation, and the fenfation might
have been fomething like what we may fuppofe
affected William, when Margaret's ghoft ftood
at his feet.

And now it was Ifabel difcovered that
human nature was not yet extinct in her, and
that all the imagination of Pope was converted
into truths which fhook her frame, and agonized her heart.

> " What means this tumult in a veftal's veins,
> " Why rove my thoughts beyond this laft retreat,

" Why feels my heart its long forgotten heat?
" Yet, yet I love !"

Thefe queftions, and this anfwer, certainly fucceeded each other in her bofom in the language of nature, though not expreffed in numbers.

It was plain to fee—

" She had not yet forgot herfelf to ftone".

Bernard was quick-fighted enough, in the midft of his grief, to perceive this, and attempted to turn it to his advantage. Abelard himfelf, could not with more addrefs have " oppofed himfelf to heaven", or more dexteroufly affifted " rebel nature to hold out half her heart". Though from what followed, you will fee Bernard had not, like the above-mentioned lover, the power,

" To teach her 'twas no fin to love".

it was manifeft, neverthelefs,

" Back through the paths of pleafing fenfe fhe run".

and it is no lefs certain, for the inftant, that

" Not on the crofs her eyes were fix'd"

but on *him*.

Yet though thus affailed by the unexpected view of, as *fhe* thought, an expiring lover, and

and at a time when every principle, and every feeling of her soul had furmounted trials, which required every *affiſtance* from furrounding objects, rather than to find amongſt them, wherewithal to *diſtreſs* her, (in, perhaps, the only vulnerable part—her pity for the miſery, of which ſhe might well ſuppoſe herſelf the occaſion,)—although, I ſay, theſe ſtrong events, might, for a ſhort time,

> " Blot out each bright idea of the ſkies".

far from indulging in the oblivious draughts of paſſion, or reiterating the looſe imagery of Eloiſa, or avowing with her that

> " From the full choir when loud Hoſannas riſe,
> " And ſwell the pomp of dreadful ſacrifice,
> " Love found an altar for forbidden fires".

The tranſitory terror, tenderneſs, alarm, or ſorrow, which ſhe felt at the ſight of poor Bernard, at ſuch a time, in ſuch a place, might well claim abſolution, if not aſſent, from the power who had juſt received her vows.

> " Devotion's ſelf might ſteal a thought from heaven,
> " One human tear might drop, and be forgiven!"

She did not long, however, ſuffer the once dear object of her love, to " diſpute her heart", which, aſſuredly, a life paſt in chaſtity and innocence, long before ſhe dedicated it to her God, had rendered more acceptable than that whoſe

fuppofed effufions, the poet has fo enchant-
ingly poured forth.

After fhe had gazed about half a minute,
in which fhort fpace more was painted in the
face, that at any former period of my life I
had feen, though the work of hours, fhe clos'd
her fine and humid eyes with a fortitude, which
might have induced the angels to fanction
the momentary and human fympathy, which
had bathed them with tears, but fhe was unable
to reprefs one gentle figh, the weight of which
was felt by my whole heart as it iffued from
her very lovely lips. Whether it was the figh
tender, or penitential, the figh of regret for
the fufferings of her lover, or of felf-reproach
for having allowed it to efcape,—it was the
moft graceful, moft penetrating I have ever
known. It will heave for ever in my memory,
and Ifabel's face was, (on her rifing from the
ground) fo near me, that I ftood within the
very breath of it. Had I not frequently feen
that the gayeft minds and manners take, with
occafion, a more firm and folemn caft, than
thofe from whofe general gravity one *expects*
the moft fix'd and unmoved conduct, I fhould
have been furprifed at the unaltered mein of
Fanchette, who, though more airy, more
lately an inhabitant of the world, and who

" warm

" warm in youth, had bid that world farewell."

(her approved lover ſtill before her, exhibiting himſelf in the moſt pity-moving attitudes,) Fanchette relaxed nothing of her attention to the buſineſs or duty of the day. On the contrary, her look to Iſabel denoted all the admonitory council, which the moral echoes, or, as the Poet calls them, *more* than echoes

" talk'd along the walls."

Eloiſa could never have heard, or fancy that ſhe heard, the hollow ſound from the ſhrine, more diſtinctly than I thought I perceived the *ſenſe* of that ſound in the charming features of this lovely girl:

" Come ſiſter come, they ſaid or ſeem'd to ſay
Thy place is here, ſad ſiſter, come away.
Once like thyſelf, I trembled, wept, and pray'd,
Love's victim then, tho' now a ſainted maid.
But all is calm in our eternal ſleep,
Here grief forgets to groan, and love to weep,
Ev'n ſuperſtition loſes ev'ry fear,
For God, not man, abſolves our frailties here."

How applicable to the occaſion! Nor was it long ere Iſabel, as if theſe verſes had actually been recited, illuſtrated thoſe which follow them, in the celebrated epiſtle of the lovers of Paraclete,

" I come, I come, prepare your roſeate bowers,
" Celeſtial palms and ever-blooming flowers.
" How happy is the blameleſs veſtal's lot, &c.

Not

Not fo the lovers:—Bernard, after a long ftruggle with his heart, exclaimed, in fad and broken accents—Ah God!—Ah God! and ran out of the convent; nor was it long ere his example was followed by Lacrew.

The ceremonies, thus interrupted, were foon refumed. The fifter-votaries were re-conducted to their chairs, where both joined in the prayers moft devoutly.

And now the holy wafers were given, and the folemnities of the Catholic church in the facrament began. Thefe ended, the fifters rofe, kiffed the robes of the prieft, bowed themfelves before the Crucifix, embraced each other; then the fuperior, the nuns, noviciates, and penfioners, all of whom were received with fmiles, that feraphs feemed to have affifted, while a dozen handfome girls, refidents for a convent education, ftrewed flowers over them, as they advanced to the laft ceremony, namely, that of *crowning*, emblematic of *that crown of glory*, with which we are affured the good are to be diftinguifhed in the world to come.

By way of fupplementary matter, it is to be noted, that the ceremony was performed on the birth-day of the veiled fifter, a circumftance

that

that gave it additional folemnity. The reft
of this aweful day was paft, agreeable to cuftom,
in all manner of innocent feftivity; by way of
teftifying that fo far from feeling any regret
for having renounced the world, the fenfations
were in unifon with the ceremonies; and, indeed (had it not been for the affair of the heart
in the cafes of the two lucklefs lovers) I fhould
believe that cuftom and example had their
ufual effect, in conjunction with zeal and
imagination, to make a monaftic life preferable
to every other, in the eftimate of the inhabitants of the convent. What confirms me the
rather in this is, that the year following, being
at the felf-fame monaftery, I beheld the felf-
fame Fanchette, after her twelve probationary
months' refidence, volunteer the fame fort of
ceremony, and with the fame apparent fatisfaction, and, though fhe had loft fome of thofe
complexional rofes, which feem to bloom beft
in the world, fhe had gained more of thofe
lillies, which never fail to grow in the cheeks
of a nun, either from feclufion, or feverity, or
a mixture of both. There was an air of peculiar content in Fanchette, at this *confirmation*
of the choice fhe had made in the beginning
of the former year; nor was there lefs fatisfaction in the countenance of Ifabel: in fhort,
the moft fcrutinizing eye might have affured

the

the heart, thefe two fifters, in changing their
plan of life, had only varied, not diminifhed,
their happinefs.

On bidding them (as probably it will prove)
an everlafting adieu, at this fecond vifit to their
convent, I borrowed once more an applicable
paffage from our great poet, and I cannot but
believe every line found its echo in the minds
of the beautiful devotees. Nor do I think,
fince the epiftle of Eloifa was written, there
can have happened fuch an exact illuftration of
its beft, and moft interefting fentiments; fince,
in the fifter nuns, were demonftrated all the
fpirit, the foftnefs, and the beauty of Abelard's
miftrefs, without any of her cupidity, fenfu-
ality, and libertinifm; and the exquifite apoftrophe which follows was the work only of
fancy in Eloifa, but of feeling in Ifabel and
Fanchette.

> " How happy is the blamelefs veftal's lot,
> " The world forgetting, by the world forgot;
> " Eternal funfhine of the fpotlefs mind,
> " Each pray'r accepted, and each wifh refign'd;
> " Labour and reft that equal periods keep,
> " Obedient flumbers that can wake and weep,
> " Defires compos'd, affections ever even,
> " Tears that delight, and fighs that waft to heav'n.
> " Grace fhines around her with fereneft beams,
> " And whifp'ring angels prompt her golden dreams.
> " For

“ For her th' unfading rofe of Eden blooms,
“ And wings of feraphs fhed divine perfumes.
“ For her the fpoufe prepares the bridal ring,
“ For her white virgins hymeneals fing.
“ To founds of heav'nly harps fhe dies away,
“ And melts in vifions of eternal day."

Since my firft idea of poetical excellence, my fenfes and my heart have attefted the beauty of this paffage, and, indeed, of the whole poem; but never has it been fo impreffive as fince the above-defcribed incidents.

Amidft the whole, however, of the fafcination, I could not but notice a fmall fpice of worldly vanity, in certain parts of the ceremony, fuch as one of the *poor lowly* brothers being appointed to place the embroidered robes of the *High* Prieft over the *backs of the chairs*, to give them a more graceful flow, as the wearer fat down. I obferved, alfo, methought, fomething of earthly pageantry lurking in the *caution* with which the female veil, whether white or black, was *fixed before*, and *folded behind*; as well as in the attention to graceful pofture, with which the profeffed threw herfelf on the carpet; for, though, as I before faid, it did not partake of the nature of a theatrical exhibition, it had the air of having been a little ftudied, becaufe it was impoffible

not

not to see that some care had been taken that the vestal garment might preserve an interesting negligence: but when we consider that the same kind of regard to attitude and position was betrayed by the dying Pompey, we may certainly allow it to two fine young women, who gave up, *for ever*, the conquests of their charms, at a period of life, when victory most solicited them. And, after all, their attentions to external finery were but the *ashes of human vanity*—a few remaining sparks, that just shewed themselves, and were then extinguished for ever.

The cost of the festival is always defrayed by the nun, or novice, and the friends, relations, and a few chosen priests from the neighbouring convent, composed the guests. To this eating and drinking scene, a little masquerade, in which all the nuns are allowed to assume borrowed characters, ensues. This done, the guests retire, such I mean as are not of the convent. The religious withdraw to their cells, and the next morning re-commence those duties, which know no recess throughout the revolving year, till a similar occasion produces a similar jubilee.

It

It was a fad and forrowful day for the uncle of thefe fifters ; he endured not to remain in an houfe ftripped of its chief ornaments and affociates, and which had the further *défagré-ment* of ftanding, as before noted, in full view of the convent, which he confidered as at once the prifon and the tomb of his relations. In a few weeks, therefore, he removed to another part of the country, where he ftill bears about

" A difcontented and repining fpirit."

But fuch an effect might naturally enough arife from fuch a caufe. Far, very far from both be the bofom of my friend!

LETTER LXVII.

TO THE SAME.

ADJOINING the little figniories of Boxmeer, is the pleafant country of Cuych*, a fmall, but productive territory, once in the poffeffion of Spain, but now a part of what is called

* Herman de Cuych gave name to this country in 1058. John, the fon of Wennemaer yielded it, long after, in exchange of other territories, to William of Guelderland ; but, at length, the Dukes of Burgundy becoming proprietors, they united it

to

called the Generality, a country subject to the Prince of Orange, and an object worth gleaning. It may be about the size of Hertfordshire, and is, like that, replete with unpretending graces. You would feel its resemblance to England, even more closely than the other parts of Westphalia—the same pleasant pathways, meandring through cornfields—the same soft pasturage—modest risings—humble and flowery hedge-rows—the woods and copses filled with the same kind of birds—the river Meuse no less fertilising than the Thames, nor less beautiful—the same sort of whited cottages, moss and houseleek growing over the thatch.

If a footpath and river-bank traveller is disposed, occasionally, to survey this country, he will find a thousand beautiful scenes, which crouds had never yet to boast.

It is extremely pleasant to trace, as one journeys on, these similitudes and dissimilitudes of one's native land; here recognising, in certain objects, our old acquaintance; there paying, in others, our first salutation to entire

to Brabant. After this again, it was given as a pledge to the Count of Buren, whose only daughter and heiress married William of Orange, in 1551. Thus it was that the charming Cuych country became annexed to the possessions of the Prince Staltholders.

strangers;

ftrangers; and whether thefe happen to be of
the vegetable or animal world, a tree, a flower,
a wood, a meadow, a ftream, a river, a flock,
an herd, a cottage, or its inhabitants, the generous heart extends to greet whatever has delighted him at home, or entertained him
abroad.

In turning over a little corner in my travelling writing-cafe, I find a fmall bundle of
papers, fuperfcribed materials for a *fcrap letter*,
which is to confift of various minute Gleanings,
too infignificant to ftand alone, but which, collected and tied together, may be of fome value.
After the *long* ears of corn have been gathered,
you have feen the patient Gleaners return
from the field, with a few hands-full, not of
ftem or fubftance to be bound with the reft
of the fheaves, and yet too good to be loft.

To thefe minutiæ, therefore, I fhall confecrate the remainder of the prefent letter, defiring you will indulge them with the favour by
which you have diftinguifhed the reft.

In Holland, Weftphalia, Germany, and
their dependencies, it is cuftomary for the
common tradefmen and fervants to drop their
fabots, flippers, or fhoes, at the threfhold of
the

the apartment, where their employers, masters,
or mistresses, are sitting, and pad along, with a
trembling sort of circumspection, as if in fear
of leaving a plebeian mark of their footsteps
behind them. And at every word you speak,
their hats, whether in the house, or the open
air, are so painfully doffed, and pinched by
their veneration, or their custom, that I have
a thousand times smilingly put their hats on
their heads, and requested they would consider
a good rub of their shoes at the door-way was a
sufficient passport to any room wherein they
might be introduced to me: but the habit or
civility is inveterate, and I verily believe they
would pay the same homage to the empty
apartments, had they occasion to enter them,
in absence of their supposed superiours. I repeat that I am no advocate for indiscriminate
familiarities, nor for Republican rudenesses,
but I love the poor, at least as well as the rich,
and I feel myself, as an individual of a majestic
species, humbled in *their* degradation. I
would have them subordinate, because I think
society demands its classes, but I cannot endure
they should be servile : and, after all, it is often
affected, for sometimes I have, at a second or
third Gleaning of these bowing, bare-headed
and footed gentlemen and ladies, found, heard,
or seen them as saucy, proud and vain-glorious,

as

as if they knew how to defcend from their heights only to promote their interefts, in the hope of over-reaching you in a miferable fous or ftiver.

In each of the above countries you will be obliged, as before obferved, to have one man to drefs the hair on your head, my good reader, and another, (if peradventure thou art of the bearded fex), to fcrape it from thy face. But the laft mentioned perfonage, whom they call furgeon, is every where fo infufferably vain, formal, and *mal adroit*, that a penny barber in England does his bufinefs ten times better, and twenty times more expeditioufly. The Continental fhaver, whether Dutch, Weftphalian, or German, is one quarter of an hour bringing his inftruments of furgery out of his pocket and arranging them; another in the apparatus of wipeing, whetting, fetting, and proving upon his hand, before he puts the razor on your chin; another in the operation, and at leaft the fourth quarter in putting his furgical matters up again, and all this you muft go through patiently or worfe will follow; every refiftance cofts you a drop of blood, remonftrance is not even liftened to, and a requeft of hafte is a flice from your chin, or a gafh in your throat. I have had more reafon to bewail a nervous

complaint

complaint that fhakes my hand, fince I came into thefe countries than ever.   I certainly mangle myfelf delicioufly whenever I attempt to atchieve this daily labour myfelf; but I yield to the pedantry of thefe executioners, only becaufe I confider being murdered by the hand of another is better than fhedding my own blood; as it is lefs heinous, you know, to fuffer affaffination than to commit fuicide.

Serioufly, it is a moft provoking and clumfy operation abroad, and I have as often wifhed myfelf beardlefs, as I might once have wifhed the contrary.   And as to any *confideration* that the head or face, thefe furgeon-barbers have in hand, is human, a butcher, who might chufe to fhave the chops of a bullock, before he flaughtered it, would be more gentle.   Your barber-furgeon pinches you by the nofe with as little remorfe as a farrier draws the nippers round the noftrils of an horfe! he fqueezes your head as if he was binding up your brains, after a contufion; and holds back your neck, as if he was going to cut your throat, which, indeed, he generally does, in proof of his great powers of pharmacy.   In a word, bleffed are thofe ladies who happen to have no beards, and happy thofe ladies or gentlemen, who when they travel can operate upon themfelves!

In

In almoſt every great road town upon the German Continent you will find an Engliſh ſhop, where you may be ſupplied with Engliſh manufacture. There is a very excellent one at the Hague, kept by Mr. M'Queen, which may almoſt be termed an *univerſal warehouſe of Britiſh commodities.* It is true you pay ſome-what high for theſe, but you are to conſider firſt their ſuperior excellence; ſecondly, the hazard, loſs, and expence of their tranſportation; and, thirdly, it ſhould be noted, that as the Dutch and German cuſtomers buy almoſt every thing *for life*; that is, make an expenſive article laſt as long as *they laſt themſelves*, and pay bills about once in ten years, (when they condeſcend to pay at all; for no tradeſman dare ſend in his bill *undemanded*) if articles were not highly rated, an Engliſh trader abroad muſt ſtarve.

It is obſervable, that the inns abroad kept by Engliſhmen, or people who ſpeak our language, are dearer than thoſe kept by natives, about fifty per cent. and it is remarkable, alſo, that the Engliſh landlords over-reach their countrymen more than a ſtranger. See you avoid them. There are at leaſt ſix Scotchmen, and three Iriſhmen, to one trader Engliſh born, diſperſed over foreign lands: *the firſt thrive*, the *second live*, the third *barely exist*. Can you account for this? The *truth* of the remark reaches from one end of the Continent to the other, with scarce an exception. I think I have found out the reason, but it might seem invidious, and a prejudice to mention it.

There subsists in some parts of Holland a curious circumstance respecting divorces—an husband who is desirous to obtain repossession of either an eloped, parted, or wandering wife, is to send a written summons to her, inviting her company to bed and board; if she refuses, he is to go in a boat on the river Meuse, to any distance he pleases, then he is to call the said wife three several times, and if he receives no answer, or if she does not appear, he is to come back, as fresh and fair a batchelor as before he purchased the wedding ring; and is at liberty to choose another mate, whose hand he may accept after the publication of the banns and marriage ceremony. The truth of this almost incredible story, is too general to be disputed by any body but those who cannot believe what they have never seen. And yet there are numbers of my dear countrymen who will suppose it a Gleaning of the author's imagination. To which I shall only reply, that in the small town of the Brielle in Holland,

there

there are not lefs than half a dozen couples who have been thus re-married.

But as a celebrated traveller (Lady W. Montague) juftly obferves, we travellers are in very hard circumftances. If we fay nothing but what has been faid before us, we are dull, and we have obferved nothing: If we tell any thing new we are laughed at as fabulous and romantic, not allowing for change of company, or of cuftoms that happen every twenty years in every country; or remain fixed for ever, though, perhaps, not before noticed. The ceremonies attending vifitings, and burial condolences, deferve mention. In Pruffian Weftphalia, a letter is fent by the furvivor informing the friends of the deceafed that fuch a relation has departed this life; but it is the etiquette *not to reply*. Your fympathy is taken for granted; and thus, the affair is not only conveniently fhortened, but a great deal of trouble is faved to both parties.

With refpect to vifits, it is the eftablifhed punctilio for new comers to make the firft advances to refidents, exactly inverting the etiquette of England; and the reafon affigned for this practice is, that new fettlers may have the privilege of declining company fhould

they

they not wifh for fociety, or of extending or narrowing it fhould they defire acquaintance; your vifit being always returned immediately, and if you do not vifit in the courfe of the firft month, it is prefumed you prefer folitude.

Perhaps this may be an improvement on the plan of England, where every one has free liberty to gratify curiofity, often at the expence of real courtefy, for numbers go once for a well-bred ftare, drink their difh of tea, and fhew they have had enough of you, by never cultivating you unlefs you happen exactly to fuit their tafte, which is often the refult of their fingularity, or caprice. Whereas, in thefe countries, you have leifure for previous enquiry; you can felect your acquaintance, and if it is not of the beft kind the place affords, it muft be your own fault.

. Another inconvenience attending your not being fortified with the language of the country, whether Dutch or German, is the impofition you are liable to, efpecially on leaving a town or houfe, where you may have had any running accounts. The people you have dealt with pretend to underftand *you* fully when you *make* your bargain; but when you come to collect your bills, they proteft that you have miftaken *them*; and this errour is always to their advantage.

vantage.   For inſtance, you agree with a ſurgeon-barber at ſo much per month to ſhave you, and with a ſhoe-boy to clean your boots, &c.   You reaſonably conclude the price ſettled between you includes every thing : but at the end of the month you are charged ſo much for putting ſoap on the face, and ſo much for taking it off; ſo much for rubbing away the duſt from your ſhoes, and ſo much again for blacking them.   Let it be clearly ſtated, there-fore, that, in your country, ſhaving and ſhoe cleaning mean what they expreſs.

The price of timber in Weſtphalia, and the countries that environ it, is amongſt the things calculated to ſurpriſe an Engliſh traveller.   A noble fir of between thirty and forty years growth, is thought rather dear at ſix florins, about ten ſhillings Engliſh : and an oak of more than half a century, is rated at about twelve, or at the moſt fifteen ſhillings.   Inferior wood in proportion.   The birch tree is here found in abundance, and contributes much to the beauty of the country, drooping with an air of poetical melancholy, almoſt with as much elegant ſadneſs as the weeping willow. The natives of Weſtphalia tell you, that the juice is good to drink, the foliage good to ſee, and the branches good to burn : they ſeem no leſs ſenſible than ourſelves, alſo, that the twigs

P 3   have

have other virtues chiefly adapted for the use
of nurseries and schools.

Simple curiosity is alike in all countries.
You remember the account I sent you in my
first sheaf of the astonishment of an whole
family of Cambrian rustics, at the sight of a
shining steel watch-chain.   I found a companion for this picture of *wonderment* in the
surprise of some Westphalia cottagers, who
surveyed a common bamboo stick with as much
attention and awe, as if it was a wand of
enchantment; and feeling the knots with a
trembling hand, as if there was magic in every
joint.

You will be pleased to hear the *universal* reputation which is enjoyed by the manufactures
of your country.   I think I slightly glanced at
this subject before.   Whatever is English becomes every where abroad an object of admiration.   I have witnessed this in various
instances, but in none more than in the
rhapsody which the sight of three pair of English shoes produced in an honest cobler of a
little town in Prussia.

These articles, neat as imported from London, lay upon my table just-unpacked, as this
child

child of nature entered my room to receive orders for a trifling repair in my boots. He incontinently caught up one of the fhoes, and for fome minutes was too much abforbed in wonder to fpeak. He turned the fhoe about in filent admiration; felt the fole, which his *look* denoted was of the beft leather poffible—examined the ftitching, the form, the elegance, the folidity, the fimplicity, the lightnefs, the ftraps, the quarters, fitted it to his hand; as he did which he fhewed figns of the moft perfect approbation—then by way of comparifon, held it down to his own fhoe, and *as* he did fo, gave teftimony of the moft ineffable contempt, even for his own performance, which was, perhaps, the higheft compliment that could be paid to the performance of another. His features, and action, had actually all the force of Hamlet's parallel of the old Fortinbras his father, and the ufurper:

" Look but on this picture and on this, &c. !"

His phifiognomy teftified that *his* work was no more to compare to the Britifh Crifpin's

" Than he to Hercules!"

It was long before he could attend indeed to any thing refpecting himfelf, and after his rhapfody fubfided a little, he feemed to under-

take

take even the cobbling art of taking up a few loose ftitches in an *Englifh boot* with reluct-ance.

Nor does our country triumph in this handy-craft fame without the beft-founded preten-fions, fince in every article of workmanfhip we caft them at a diftance that rather gives the fenfation of defpair than energy. Doors, win-dows, their ornaments, their neceffaries, their comforts, their finifhing, their application, their fitnefs, their buildings, their elegance, all yield the palm to the fuperior arts of the Britifh artificer. And if there is a general rule without an exception, I am, from very long and diligent fcrutiny, inclined to think it lies in the unrivalled excellence of our manu-factures in the comforts and conveniences of life.

You have heard numberlefs anecdotes of the late Pruffian monarch. A ftronger idea of his infatiable military ambition cannot be well given, than in his exclaiming to one of his officers while furveying the profpect from his chateau at Cleves; " very fine, to be fure, noble woods, pretty gardens, fair towns, well-filled rivers, and all that, but I can never think it a good profpect while any part of the objects it includes is the property of another fovereign!"

I will

I will juft note to you, that amongft the pictures of this chateau, is a very fine one of Jefus and the virgin, and on the reverfe, a full length portrait of the painter himfelf, fufpended in the middle of the room to fhew at once the genius and the vanity of the man!

Of the German Theatre I have little to obferve, farther than that it excels in *paffion.* You muft have often noted the defect of the Englifh actors, (I fpeak generally) when not immediately in difcourfe or action in the fcene. They feem to think that their character comes to a paufe at the end of every fpeech, and they wait for the cue words to refume it: thefe are no fooner given, than they kindle in a moment. They wait the match and go off like a cracker. Then all is dead and inert, till the other perfonages have fettled the bufi-nefs in hand, whether an affair of love, hate, hope, or defpair; nor does the paffive character they are fpeaking to, ever interrupt the pro-grefs of thefe paffions, or fhew any fenfibility thereof, except by ftepping a pace back, or a pace forward; by a ftamp of the foot, a thump of the breaft, or a fmack of the forehead.—But on the Theatre Allemande all is life, vigour, and ardency: yet rarely overftepping the modefty of nature; and the bye play is fo fkill-

fully

fully managed, that where the poet himself sleeps, the vigilance of the actor guarantees his nap, without any diminution of his poetical fame.

I am aware that this is the cafe, fometimes, in the Britifh theatre, but it is more rare; and commonly fpeaking, Homer himfelf could not there nod, had Homer been a dramatift, without fome of the performers flumbering with him, and caufing the audience to flumber alfo.

High however, as they eftimate the manufactures of Great Britain, the untravelled Pruffians and Germans appear to have but a very confined idea of its extent: for, in the firft place, many of them imagine, that it is rather neceffity, than choice; rather policy, than curiofity, which takes fuch numbers out of England. They believe the population is too great for the place; that *our* little country being overftocked, the fuperflux wander about the earth in fearch of *more room.* Almoft every perfon tells you he knows an Englifhman!— that is to fay, in the courfe of his life, every man has met with one of the Britifh wanderers, or, fome folitary family refident abroad. The Germans immediately prefume

this

this perfon, or family, muft be known alfo to *you.* If you anfwer in the negative, they won-der, which certainly implies a contracted idea of Great Britain as a territory, however they may think of it as a nation.

The Germans bring up their children with great tendernefs, but in a manner to prevent the effects of effeminacy, or the ordinary ail-ments proceeding therefrom; I have feen the fons and daughters of gentlemen run through the dews of the morning without fhoes, ftock-ings, or any under garments, but fhirts and fhifts: chacing each other round the court yards, gardens, &c. in this *almoft* natural ftate, after a night of inceffant rain. About noon, when there feems the lefs real neceffity to wrap up, they begin to *put on*, juft in the proportion as other children *throw off*, but they all look as healthy as if they were educated in the way of England. The mothers of Great Britain will fhudder at this relation, yet, could the cuftom be reconciled with decency, which furely were eafy, it might deferve adoption. Colds and coughs, which are not only bad dif-orders in themfelves, but the parents of worfe in England, are rarely heard of along the continent of Germany: And after you have turned your back on Holland, the gout begins to

lofe

lofe his excruciating power, till, in advancing further north, he is, in a meafure, fubdued; at leaft, a victim bound hand and foot by this tyrant, who hourly brings fo many of my compatriots to the rack, is rarely feen. Muft we not impute this general exemption from one of the fharpeft pangs to which our frailty is heir, to early expofure of the body and limbs to all the fkiey influences?

I think I have not yet mentioned the mode of ferving at table in Holland, and Pruffia. Vegetables are eaten firft, no perfon offers to begin till all are helped; meat comes next, this is cut into very thin flices in a plate, and paffing round the table, every one receives, or declines. If a fecond, third, fourth, or fifth fort of meat is on the board, there are as many plates-full fent round it,—the fervant watches your glafs, filling it when empty: the bread is cut into exceeding thin flices, and no healths are drank except at parting.

An elegant Englifh family fettled in Holland, has lately given a *Dutch drum* or route, of which the lady of the houfe has favored me with a defcription: As it is well told, and a curiofity in itfelf, I will here prefent you with a Gleaning; and in her own words.

" Dear

" Dear Mr. Gleaner,

" At your defire, I am fitting down to give you a defcription of what is called in this country, a *contre vifite*. That I might accommodate to the cuftoms of the place, I invited the afliftance of a good natured Dutch neighbour, who helped me through all the ceremonials : And being no lefs a perfonage than the Burgomafter's wife, fhe was wholly competent to the bufinefs. I fhall write in way of general direction, as to what is to be done, &c. &c.

" Two of the largeft rooms in the houfe are always appropriated to the occafion: the better if they communicate, as is indeed ufual abroad, but that is not material. Card tables are to be fet in the four corners of each room; the middle being kept perfectly clear,—the place of honor is always determined to be on the right hand fide of the pier glafs. From each fide of this glafs you are to place two rows of chairs, with a fquare box called a ftove, at the foot of each chair; and, if in winter, you are to take care thefe ftoves are well fupplied with burning turf, or rather with the live afhes of turf; and, if in fummer, the fire is to be omitted, as a Dutch woman is too much in the habit of canting up her legs on thefe abominable little footftools to fit

comfortably

comfortably without them, and in the cold weather, she could neither ufe her hands, or arms, without fmoke-drying her feet.—By the gentlemen's feats you place fpitting boxes; and, as if thefe would not hold enough, a dozen or two of fpitting pots are to be fet on the fide tables, or to grace the corner of the card equipage: feveral flates and pencils are alfo to be provided. All the plate you can mufter is to be crouded on the grand fideboard, and at leaft an hundred tobacco pipes, with tafteful devices wrapp'd about them, not forgetting half a dozen pound boxes of tobacco, with a fuitable fervice of ftoppers.

" Thefe preparations being fettled, you are ready to receive the company, who begin to appear at your Dutch drum about *five in the afternoon!* The *reigning* burgomafter's wife enters firft. You are to receive her at the door, after a good run to meet her, (by way of teftifying your joy) with a dead ftop, and you are to take care that your curtfey is at leaft as profound as hers; the better if a little deeper. And if you would adopt the fafhion of this country, you fhould revive one of your boarding fchool finkings at the commencement of a minuet, or one of your fchool reverences to your governefs on leaving the room. You are

to

to take her by the hand, you are to fay you are extremely honoured by the vifit, and then *kifs her three times!* Then lead her to the right hand fide of the glafs,—order a burning, red-hot ftove to be put under her petticoats,—(the genteeler if you condefcend to place it your-felf,)—and then receive the reft of the company, *ftoveing* them and *kiffing* in the fame manner; more carefully however *placing* them according to their *rank in the town or village*, than if they were fo many Britifh peer-effes to be fettled by the High Steward, at the trial of a fifter peerefs for high Treafon. When all the chairs are filled, you may order refrefhments.

" In the firft place, tea is to be prefented three times round the room. This over, the card tables are to be arranged, the ftoves refrefhed, the pipes lighted, and the fpitting boxes begin to work. You are to prefent *four kings* to the burgomafter's wife, and the three you mean to play at her table. To the next lady, in her rank, you prefent the *queens*: But make a memorandum, that, when once feated, nobody ftirs from her table till the party breaks up at ten o'clock, fo that you are fixed as a ftatue for almoft five hours. The refrefhments are to be handed about every *quarter of an hour*, but

to

to vary, as to the collations. One quarter gives coffee, another wine, another liquors, another orgeat, and at every time the company eat and drink with unabated appetite ; and thofe who offer the moft good things of this world, are made the moft honorable mention of, in the annals of *contre vifitifm*. The ceremonies of taking leave are like thofe of entrance.

" It is to be obferved, that when you give one of their vifits it is not from your own invitation : the reigning burgomafter fends you word, if convenient, he will come to you fuch a day. If you accept the challenge, you are to fend off your cards, in which you invite *the town* to meet him ; who very obligingly obey the fummons, whether they ever faw you before or no ; or whether they fhall ever fee you again.

" All the fmoking party keep their own room; but leave fuch a ftrong fenfe of their orgies behind them, that it is neceffary your houfe, (if your nofe is not a native of Holland,) fhould perform a quarantine of a month before it can be purified.

" A *contre-vifite* feldom includes fupper, but when a fupper is to be given in Holland, it
always

always comprehends cards and tea, with the immenfe et cetera of about eight times coffee, as many cakes, wines, jellies, &c. &c. &c. and fuppofing thefe to begin at half paft five, and fupper to be on table at half paft ten, though the intermediate hours are fully employed in eating and drinking, it does not in the leaft prevent the fupper being devoured, as King Richard voracioufly fays, " marrow, bones and all", for though in general life, at *home*, the Dutch eat but little of folid food, they pay it off *abroad* with moft incontinent rapacity. Indeed, they feem, · like certain wild beafts in training for the grand gorging day, when they are to be turned out upon criminals, to referve themfelves for thefe great public occafions: and a Dutch fupper, at the end of five hours ftuffing, might very well furnifh out one of our Lord Mayor's feafts, and fatisfy all the manfion-houfe monfters on any one of the important days,

" Big with the fate of Turkeys, and of Geefe!"

By way of fpecimen, I fhall conclude with a Dutch Bill of fare, of which I made a N. B. in my pocket-book, immediately on getting home from the laft cramming-bout to which I had the honour of being invited. I fhall only premiſe that we were only 14 perſons at table. Mem.—It was a ſupper.

TOP.

	A very large fillet of veal *bak'd*, and forc'd-meat balls.	
Stew'd Endiff.	An immenſe ſallad.	Peas boiled in the ſhell.
	A forc'd pike, of 25lb. weight.	
	Pan full of ſtew'd Pears.	
Plumb pudding.	Yard wide pye, of all meats, birds, and beaſts.	Half-yard ſweet pye.
	Pan full of apples.	
Near a peck of boiled potatoes.	Another monſter of a pike, four ſauce, 20lb. ditto.	Vaſt diſh of Sorrel.
	Sallad bowl of different pickles.	
	Whole quarter of ſheepiſh lamb, roaſted,	

BOTTOM.

N. B. Nothing left but the large bones and plates.

To which pleaſant, but faithful deſcription, I ſhall only aſk with the Poet,

" Is this a ſupper, this a genial room?
" No, it's a temple and a hecatomb!"
" Treated, careſs'd and tir'd, I take my leave."

There are difperfed over the provinces of Holland, of Pruffia, and of Germany, various towns, bourgs, and villages, which amongft other privileges poffefs that of affording pro-tection to fugitives for debt: and there are fome which offer an afylum even for crimes. Of thefe Vianne, Cleves, and Neuweid, may be mentioned amongft others. They are either free towns, or independent feigneuries. The former have ufually taken their rife from the exigence of the ftate, which has often made the Prince a borrower of the people. The Emperors frequently wanting fupplies of money to carry on their wars, or for other occafions, have hir'd large fums of great trading towns, and paid the debt in certain extra grants, privileges, and immunities, making them independent of the governors of the provinces or diftricts where thofe towns ftood, or in their neighbourhood. Accordingly fuch places remain free; exercifing all kinds of fovereign power, with the right of enacting laws, con-ftituting authorities, courts of juftice, and coining, as well as of offering a fanctuary to ftrangers, debtors, &c. &c.—I am forry to in-form you, that this latter privilege is not feldom made a revenue of the town, or the feigneur, or a perquifite of office. But it muft

 be

be owned the fee is not large,—a guinea or two for inftance per perfon, which makes your perfon facred beyond limitation, provided neverthelefs you conform peaceably to the laws of the land where you eftablifh your refidence, which it is certainly not only decent but eafy to do, as they are no way rigorous in them-felves, and the protected places are for the moft part fituated in a fine country.

Vianne, for inftance, is built on the banks of a fine river, on the confine of the beautiful province of Utrecht, nearly half way betwixt Rotterdam and Nimeguen. It remains pof-feffed of all rights of Seignieurfhip independent of Holland. It is fuppofed to be the Fanum Dianæ, of which Ptolemy makes mention.

The towns and villages of the Dutchy of Cleves already live in my defcription, and I truft in the reader's memory. And fhould mis-fortune find it neceffary to take refuge in either of thefe he will pafs his days or years of exile amidft the beauty and health of nature.

With refpect to Neuwied, independent of giving

" The poor, and the unhappy,
" A privilege to enter."

it

it has claims on our attention, being one of the most agreeable towns and placed in one of the most charming countries of Europe. The account of it is sufficiently popular, but the best Gleaning of it is by the author of the journey, or rather voyage of the Rhine, a work I have already commended.

"It is in this town, says he, that the writer of these pages—a victim of French despotism, has found refuge, honour, and happiness; after having been despoiled of 1,400,000 livres, and driven from a country that was dear to him. It is in this free and sacred land he at length is permitted to reside in peace with his rescued family. And here, also, it is, that he announces a virtuous Prince, and a gentle race, to philosophers, men of letters and of humanity—to peaceable citizens, and to ingenious artists—to honest labourers, and to the worthy of all descriptions, who like him may be expelled from the scenes of rapine and desolation."

The gratitude of this author for the protection he received, has not seduced him into effusions of praise, which exceed the truth. The sweet sejour of Neuweid merits all he has said of it. It is situated on the borders of the

Q 3   Rhine,

Rhine, betwixt Bonne and Coblentz. The country is agreeable, the inhabitants sociable, and the air wholesome. Vines and orchards surround it. Hills and vallies smile on every side. The water is particularly excellent, the corn good and abundant. Butcher's meat in all its variety, and a no less plenty of vegetables, fruit, fish, fowl, and game. Lodgings are reasonable, and elegant. The prime of every commodity from the famous fairs of Bonne, Coblentz, Mayence, and Franckfort, as well as from Holland, are to be had at Neuweid, as they can come by water to your very door. And to crown the whole the reigning prince is a man of politeness, urbanity, genius, peace, and benevolence. He is descended from one of the most honourable and ancient houses, and what is better, he is in every sense of the term an HONEST MAN! Of the prince, of his family, and of his palace of Mount-Repose, (two leagues from Neuweid) a thousand fine things have been said by the ingenious writer abovementioned, but after what I have just termed him, would not all these go to an anti-climax:

" An honest man's the noblest work of God."

Amongst the objectionable things which an English traveller will find in Prussia, Westphalia,

phalia, and through all the Catholic countries, is the frequency of holy-days, feasts, fasts, and fairs.

I would have every creature adore his Creator, according to the customs of his country, and resort to the places of worship as often as his piety inclines. But I cannot fail to regret that the church should exact an observance of mere ceremonies which trench on the duties of social life, being convinced that a performance of these is a part of religion. It is the result of reiterated observation that enables me to assure you nearly the half of a servant's and labourer's time is taken up in the churches, and very frequently made the pretext for a neglect of necessary business, and, indeed, promotes idleness. I have always noted that the most church going people in this country are the worst domestics, the most supine, and the most superstitious. How it happens I know not, but religion in this country seldom works the blood into enthusiasm: the being righteous overmuch in Germany more commonly produces a moody torpid stupidity. Methodists and other fanatic sectaries are rare. These bodies amongst us produce, you know, ebullitions of zeal that ferment to distraction. It is

in England a raging madnefs; in the German
dominions a gloomy melancholy; and with
refpect to fociety, the latter is the evil moft to
be lamented. The firft is a violent fit, and
paffes foon away, and though the returns of
the paroxifm are quick, the intervals admit of
fome activity in fecular affairs. But the German malady after fending a man from his
honeft employments, his mafter and his family,
two or three days in the week without counting
Sunday, continues him in a kind of religious
apathy all the reft of the year.   On the holy-
days it is with great difficulty a cook will drefs
dinner, or a chambermaid tofs up the beds.
If you want bread it muft be made and baked
the day before: to put an hand in the oven
would be facrilege, and to fetch a pail of
water an offence laid up amongft others for
next confeffion.   The confequence of all this
is, that after they have run in and out of the
church till they are weary, you will fee them
in lazy circles ftand about the ftreets with
folded arms and gapeing mouths, or fleeping
in their houfes, kitchens, &c.   At intervals,
however, they wake to the recollection of the
Saint in whofe honour the fête is inftituted,
and renew their afpirations.   It is common to
hear them break forth in the midft of any ordinary

dinary occupation, even during the few days their religion fuffers them to work, into an hymn or fpiritual fong. I once paft fome months in an houfe where a peafant fervant to his other bufineffes, added that of a barber; and under whofe razor, (being in a fmall country place), I came almoft every day. He had been ufed on my firft employing him only to reap the chins of the ruftics, and any thing that could cut ftubble would anfwer that purpofe; for, befides that it is the general practice for the gentry of Germany to fhave only once a-week, a German chin after it *has* been fhaved would turn the edge of a Dutch razor. When the man, therefore, came upon a face that called for daily fcraping, and found it had been ufed to gentle ufage, he looked upon it as fo arduous an undertaking, that he called in all the might of his religion to ftrengthen his arm, and incontinently retired into a little chapel adjoining the houfe, both before and after the operation; firft for going through his job with judgment, and then in thankfgiving, for having performed it without cutting my throat. On these occafions he always fung two ftaves of the fame pfalm, and with fo much violence of lungs that one would think he imagined heaven would be deaf to his

prayers,

prayers. Indeed I often thought fo too, for, notwithftanding his bawling, if my chin and throat came off with no more than half a dozen flafhes, the blood gufhing at each, I reckoned it a morning of efcape. But this fellow would fometime-burft forth into a mufical howl at mealtime, with the meat in his mouth; and yet, having a few acres of ground now and then to reap and mow; alfo, if too much fun, or rain, or froft, or fnow, thinned his crops, he would be as full of growl againft the good God of feafons; as if he were—a French Republican!

Fairs, or what they call Kermiffes, are very proper fupplements to their fafts and holy-days: not that thofe are more numerous than in England, but becaufe it is the cuftom for the fervants to vifit every kermis, at whatever diftance, where fhe or they have a friend, or relation: and as each kermis lafts a week, and as it is thought very hard if the permiffion is not given for at leaft a couple of days at each, you may guefs in what a fituation families are left betwixt one practice and another. If by accident you call on a friend, and ftay dinner, the cook is gone to the kermis, or to the church, or elfe it is a faft-day, and fhe can do

nothing,

nothing, but drink coffee *eight or ten times,* and go to the kirk.

Yet a kermis, particularly a village one, is worth seeing. It is an annual affociation of all the fcattered parts of a man's family and friends. I attended one in Weftphalia, on a principle of that general curiofity which carries me every where. But having no village connexions while at Cleves, I wandered about a little place in the neighbourhood during kermis time. The firft joyful groupe which I faw gathered together arrefted my ftep. I ftood leaning on the gate of a large farm yard, at the farther end of which I obferved a number of perfons fitting round a table, and others dancing, and almoft every body finging. The firft glympfe of a ftranger brings an invitation, efpecially on public occafions. This urbanity is almoft univerfal in Weftphalia. I followed a courteous introducer who led me to the mafter and miftrefs of the houfe. Their teftimonies of welcome came fo faft upon me, that had I eat and drank of half the different good things which were fet before me, I muft have been *killed with kindnefs* on the fpot. I foon underftood that I was at the houfe of a farmer, whofe happy family from great grandfather to

grand

grand-child, were amongſt the gueſts : and all theſe different characters on the ſtage of human life, were dancing on a graſs plat behind the great barn, and all ſuch as were or had·been married, arrayed in their bridal dreſſes. One of the brothers' wives introduced a ſuckling of two months to the great-grand-father, who was enjoying health, in the ſight of four and thirty relations, and in the 87th year of his age! It was a *banquet* for a good natured ſpectator to ſee the joy with which the old man danced the little creature on his knee, then preſented him to the other parts of his family, according to ſeniority, that the young-ling might have a *kermiſs-kiſs* from all his kindred. But the pretty mother! How I wiſh that you had ſeen the mother during this tranſaction :—not on account of her prettineſs, but becauſe the fineſt bluſhes that ever circu-lated from the heart into the countenance, and the ſofteſt tears that maternal fondneſs ever brought into the face of a lovely young woman, would then have been enjoyed by my friend! and it was her firſt child! and it had been a match of love ; and the babe, according to its parents, wiſh was a ſon, and according to family wiſhes alſo, it bore the name of its great-grand-ſire, and was thought, by affection (who

takes

takes likenesses you know in a moment) to
inherit the hue of the eyes and some of the
features. The attitude, half bending over it, in
its circuit, as it passed from the arms of one
relation to those of another, was a subject for
painting, and might have been highly finished;
but the extacy in which, at the end of the cere—
mony, she received, and the kisses with which
she covered it, were beyond the reach of human
pencil, and required all the powers of nature
who works in colours " dipt in heaven."
After this every body drank health, and many
more happy *family fêtes* to the old man ; who,
in return, pledged a bumper of Rhenish to the
company; one of the sons assured me that the
veteran's maladies were slight, and always cured
by a visit to one or other of his family. His
medical son *prescribed* this affectionate remedy:
thus when his own home became a little
folitary, the good old man went to another:
and as all the family live within a short distance
from the ancient manfion of this their fore-
father, there is a cure within reach for every
diforder: he gets rid of a cold at the house of
one child, of a *fever* at that of another, of a
touch of the rhumatifm at a third's, and at a
fourth's of an head-ach. Upon getting a little
more into the private hiftory of the houfe,

(from

(from a gueſt who was my next hand neighbour, and juſt animated enough with wine to
become a benevolent hiſtorian) I found that
the grand children were worthy of the ſire; for
that all the brothers, of which there were nine,
had entered into a ſocial domeſtic compact,
the particular articles of which had been committed to writing; that in the courſe of affairs,
they were mutually to ſerve each other, either
with a ſum of money, or any other aſſiſtance,
ſuited to the nature and neceſſity of the caſe.
And as if Providence intended to try the virtue
and ſincerity of each, all the brothers in turn
wanted and *found* a friend in the good offices of
each other.—Ah, my friend, we have not got
all the ſimplicity, happineſs, and virtue to ourſelves: and God forbid we ever ſhould have.
How bleſſed to ſhare them, as they *are* ſhared,
with all the human race!

I have gleaned various inſtances of their
being diſperſed over theſe diviſions of the
globe. I have ſhewn to you the natural affections blooming in Holland, Cambria, and
Weſtphalia. Permit me now to preſent to
you one more example, of which I was an eye
witneſs in the firſt mentioned country.

In

In a trip from the Hague to Rotterdam, and from thence to Haarlem, I was juft in time for the after-dinner boat to get a place in the cabin, and to fee an aged mother and her daughter give and receive the farewel looks, expreffions, and embraces, to and from fome friends and relatives. Never did I fee the feelings of the heart fhine with more lucid brightnefs while each was in view of the other; nor defcend in more tender tears when they could behold each other no longer. As the boat moved on, the groupe on fhore followed as long as they could at the edges of the canal, and the party in the cabin thruft their heads out of the door to catch the kind looks and fayings, till the horfe being hooked to the fchuyt, they could no longer keep pace with us. The fucceeding moments were paffed in deep fighs on the part of the mother, and tears on that of the daughter, neither of whom took any more notice of me, nor of any other perfon in the cabin, than of the cufhions they fat on. A perfon in the corner told me thefe people would, perhaps, never fee each other again for fome years, as the mother and daughter were going to fettle in North Holland.

I was prepared to hear him fay North America at leaft: but to people *untravelled*, a
feparatio n

feparation of fifty miles is an immeafurable
diftance.   And the fympathy of divided affection extends the fpace to infinity! The filence
was long, and I honoured them for it; had
there been a cranny in their hearts for the entrance of common place curiofity, or for converfation with a ftranger, I fhould have deemed
it a robbery of what was due to their abfent
friends. I perceived the daughter to ftrain her
longing eyes towards the only opening at which
there might be a *poffibility* of catching a parting
glympfe of her relations, and I difcovered at
the fame time, that I intercepted her. fight—
would to heaven that ftranger did not fit betwixt me and my friends, was the fentiment
written in every line of her face: but as fhe
continued to look, I gave her all the chances
fhe could expect by moving my pofition. No
fooner had I done fo than fhe exclaimed—I fee
poor Catherine's cloak, and the fkirt of Sally's
gown, through the window! The glow of that
friendfhip which is fo delicioufly animating
in the days of our youth, flufhed her cheeks; but
it was fweetly blended alfo with the gratitude,
which, at that period of our lives, gives fuch a
colouring and grace to the complexion; after
this fhe farther won my regard by fuch a penfive caft of the head, and direction of the eyes,

as

as plainly indicated her heart was returning to the Hague, with her friends, and she took little or no notice of any thing, or any body else, during the rest of the voyage.

I have slightly mentioned to you somewhere the love of ornament amongst the Dutch, as inconsistent with the weight, not to say heaviness, of their appearance. I think this over-finery is to be discovered principally in their liveries, which are often gaudy and rich, *some-times* elegant. It is exhibited also in their furniture, barges, chimneys, china, and mills. It even shews itself in certain indescribable places, yet, generally speaking, all these things are so out of keeping with their own figures and fashions—such, for instance, as their deep brown or blue suits of Dutch homespun or Prussian, their unyielding features, immense breeches, preposterous petticoats, stupendous hip-pads, and measured pace—that they seem as little of a piece as if the said homespun jerkins, &c. were to be trimmed with gold and silver foils and fringes.

As to the *waterfaring men* (fresh or salt) they are *be-buttoned* from top to toe, each button, not excepting those of the waistband, a third part larger than an English crown-piece, and always of solid silver. One whimsical fellow, who was master of a fishing-smack, used to exhibit himself with a suit of coarse blue bays, or serge, the coat buttons of which were Zealand rix-dollars (a piece of silver the size of our crown) the waistcoat was buttoned with florins, the trowzers with schellings (larger than our shilling) the waistband and flaps with pieces of thirty stivers (half-a-crown), his check shirt with dublikys (silver two-pences), and his shoes were fastened by twenty-eight stiver pieces, cut into clasps, and a gilder for the button of his hat; which hat was, in itself, a curiosity, being folded into three corners, in the way that grocers make up their penny-worths, into long bags of white-brown paper, which, you know, are,

" Small by degrees, and *whimsically* less."

Indeed even the *higher* class of Hollanders are too full of button, wearing four where an Englishman would content himself with one, and placing them so close that it is quite a labour to fasten and loose them.

I have praised the Dutch neatness; it is *worthy* of praise; but occasionally carried to excess.

excefs. It now and then goes into caricature. You have always the fear of the pail and scrubbing brushes before your eyes. On the grand cleaning day, which here is Friday, the maid servants are to be seen puddling below, ankle-deep, and spouting above at the windows as if they were playing off an engine to extinguish a conflagration; although the great end proposed, is only to wash away the duft that may have gathered on the fashes, in the courfe of the week. An Englifh traveller who comes from the comfort of a dry room, or whofe ftate of health would fuffer from damps, muft reconcile to this *défagrement* as well as he can; as he will, from an intention of civility, be fhewn into an apartment juft wafhed, he had better double his defenfe, by an additional pair of focks, or ftockings; for the Dutch landlord would deem it rude to take his gueft into a room that has not been laid under water fince the laft company went out of it, and were you to argue againft the thing, he would fet you down as a dirty traveller, who did not know how to behave yourfelf in a clean country.

Through every part of Holland, the natives are great obfervers of fymmetry. Is a brufh,

for

for example, part of the furniture of a room, it will be found hanging up, equidistant with another of the same size, shape, and fashion, to answer it.

> " Cup faces cup, each saucer has its brother,
> " And half the cup-board just reflects the other."

This matter is also spoken to in former Gleanings.

But with respect to the modes of *dressing*, it is out of my memory whether I have before mentioned a great and general resemblance betwixt the Welch and German peasantry. At least eighty out of every hundred of the latter are habited in the dark blue, or deep brown of the former, and have a number of customs in common, which is the less to be wondered at, when we consider the mixture of the two nations, when the Saxons, sometimes by treachery, sometimes by invitation, and some-- times by invasion, became masters or partners of Cambria. But so many ages having passed away since the Saxon heptarchy, and even since the expulsion of the Germans, whether friends or enemies, from the principality of Wales, it was curious enough for a traveller, who had just been gleaning that country, to find such a

general

general refemblance in the drefs, air, habits, and even features of a people fo remote, and with which, modernly fpeaking, they had not, nor ever could have, the flighteft intercourfe.

" They who came over out of Germany into " Wales (fays Caradoc) to aid the Britons " againft their enemies, the Picts and Scots, " were partly Saxons, Angles, and Juthes; " from the firft of which came the people of " Effex, Suffex, Middlefex, and the Weft " Saxons; from the Angles, the Eaft Angles " and the Mercians, and they that inhabited the " North fide of the Humber; from the Juthes, " the Kentifh men, and they who fettled in the " Ifle of Wight."

Thus the Englifh nation and its appendages, like the Englifh language, appears to be a compound of every other country, and, particularly, of Germany. From fettlements, marriages, defcents, &c. it is reafonable that there fhould be preferved fome family cuftoms and family features. A likenefs of countenance may be traced, indeed, through all claffes of the Empires of Germany and Great Britain: and the former being certainly (taken as an whole) a brave, ingenious, and generous

nation,

nation, I was pleafed to trace the fimilitude, and admit the original alliance. Time has worn out the refentments; but whatever brings to memory a bond of connexion, and of amity, though formed between individuals or countries three thoufand years ago, has a charm for the heart. Had I but the hem of a garment in my poffeffion, that had been worn by the greateft foe of my family on the day of reconciliation, or at the moment that he came to my anceftor (whom he had injured) to avow, and to repent of, the wrong, and to promife future loving-kindnefs,—that fragment of the drefs fhould have a place in my wardrobe, and be held as a memorial.

With regard to the ancient Germans, were we to take a comparative view of them, and of the ancient Britons, we fhould find a fimilitude in the features of their minds as well as manners, efpecially in the grand articles of war and religion. The heroes, fages, and priefts of one country, had their counterparts in the other; had Cambria her Druids, Bards, and Chiefs, that devoted themfelves to wounds and death, for the fake of God and their country, conformably to the facrifice, the chivalry, and worfhip of the times, the Germanic

manic nations had holy, brave, and wife men who correfponded to thefe characters, and afford additional evidence of their having borrowed manners, maxims, and fuperftitions, from one another.

In order to throw luftre on the parallel, I will pick a little hiftorical Gleaning of what I remember. We venerate the traditionary independence which animated the ancient Welch. The ancient Germans cultured the fame fpirit. The Roman hiftorian reports them to refpect only thofe duties, which they impofed on themfelves. The nobleft youths blufhed not to be numbered among the faithful companions of fome renowned chiefs, to whom they devoted their arms and fervice. A noble emulation prevailed amongft the companions to obtain the firft place in the efteem of their chief; amongft the chiefs to acquire the greateft number of valiant companions. The glory of fuch diftinguifhed heroes diffufed itfelf beyond the narrow limits of their own tribe. In the hour of danger it was fhameful for the chief to be furpaffed in valour by his companions; fhameful for the companions not to equal the valour of their chief. To furvive his fall in battle was indelible infamy. To protect his

perfon,

perſon, and to adorn his glory with the trophies of their own exploits, were the moſt ſacred of their duties. The chiefs combated for the victory, the companions for the chief. The nobleſt warriours, whenever their native country was ſunk in the lazineſs of peace, maintained their numerous bands in ſome diſtant ſcene of action, to exerciſe their reſtleſs ſpirit, and to acquire renown by voluntary dangers. Gifts, worthy of ſoldiers, the war-like ſteed, the bloody and ever victorious lance, were the rewards which the companions claimed from the liberality of their chief. The rude plenty of his hoſpitable board was the only pay that *he* could beſtow, or *they* would accept. War, and the free-will offerings of his friends ſupplied this munificence.

But, to uſe the language of Biſhop Hurd on another occaſion, and apply them to this, leſt you ſhould think my love of antiquity has operated like enchantment, in regard to the ancient German chiefs and companions, I muſt deſire you to conſider the courage and conduct of the modern ones, who have ſo long, and ſo nobly, and almoſt without a day's receſs, re-pelled the hordes of France, when almoſt *her whole population has been forced into the field.*
Can

Can we difcover, in times paft, a braver, a more faithful, or a more perfevering body of men, than thofe fubjects of Auftria, who are, at this very moment, under command of Beaulieu, Clairfait, and Cobourg?' Each of whom might certainly hold a place in the temple of Victory as diftinguifhed as any general that Rome had to boaft. Nor could the boldeft of the race of Cadwallader be difhonoured by an alliance with the fublime progenitors of thefe illuftrious defcendents.

It is painful to obferve that the religious zeal of the old Germans was as wild, favage, and *fatal*, as that of the ancient Britons, and, that the fanatic minifters of the one anfwered to the Druids of the other. Both were alike able to perfuade, that, " by fome ridiculous arts of divination, they could difcover the will of the fuperior beings; and both taught that human facrifices were the moft precious and acceptable offerings to their altars. The Germanic, like the Druidical temples, were in dark and ancient groves, confecrated by the reverence of fucceeding generations. " Their " fecret gloom, the imagined refidence of an " invifible power (fays Gibbon) by prefenting " no diftinct object of fear, or worfhip, impreffed

" pressed the mind with a still deeper sense of
" religious horror." I am sorry to discover a yet
stricter similitude between the Priests of Germany, and the Druids of Wales : the former
no less than the latter, we are informed, had
been taught by experience the use of every
artifice that could preserve and fortify impres-
sions so well suited to their own interest; and
it has been finely remarked, that the same ignorance which renders barbarians incapable of
conceiving, and of embracing, the useful
restraints of law, exposes then aked and unarm'd
to the blind terrors of superstition. The German priests, improving this favourable temper
of their countrymen, even in temporal con-
cerns, which the magistrate could not venture
to exercise; and the defects of civil policy,
were, sometimes, supplied by the interposition
of ecclesiastical authority.

We find, too, that ancient Germany, like
ancient Briton, had her bards, whose genius,
character, and office, were extremely alike in
one country and in the other. It is not easily
to be conceived, says one of Rome's best historians, how this singular order of men, (speaking of the German bards) contrived to kindle
the enthusiasm of arms and glory in the breasts

of their audience. It was in the hour of battle, or in the feaſt of victory, that they celebrated the glory of heroes of ancient days, the anceſtors of thoſe warlike chieftainswho liſtened with tranſport to the animated ſtrains. The view of arms, of victory, and of danger, heightened the effect of the military ſong, and the paſſions which it tended to excite, the de‐ ſire of fame, and the contempt of death, were the habitual ſentiments of a German mind.

We may eaſily ſuppoſe, that with the help of a glowing imagination, which was not wanting, the audience imputed to the bards of Germany all the power which poeſy herſelf has, in ſome of her nobleſt flights, attributed to the bards of Wales.—

> " Cadwallo's tongue
> That huſh'd the ſtormy main,
> Modred, whoſe magic ſong
> Made huge Plinlimmon bow his cloud capt head."

Nor have the Princes of Germany degenerated from their anceſtry, none of whom have higher claims on the love of the people, or the eulogy of the modern bards, than the amiable and youthful monarch, who now fills the imperial throne. Of his warlike atchievements, during the preſent campaign, the trump of fame has

ſufficiently

sufficiently informed you, but there is a trait of his *heart* in private and domestic life, which I receive from the most unquestionable authority, and which will endear him to you more than a thousand victories.

Joseph the second, who was an œconomist, left to (Leopold who did not live long enough, after he became Emperor, to diffipate them) an unincumber'd diadem and immense treasures. These all concenter'd in the present Emperor, to whom was bequeathed the difposal of them so unconditionally, that the dowager emprefs his mother was, in a manner, rather a dependent on his bounty, than poffefs'd of powers in herfelf to claim as widow, wife, and mother. No fooner did the youth find himfelf thus dangeroufly placed, than he refolved to put it out of his *own* power to act unbecoming the fon of an Emprefs and Queen. Convening, therefore, his court and council, he appropriated an early day for his coronation, or rather nomination to the emperorfhip,—the regular ceremony being performed long after at Frankfort,—and he intreated the honour that the Queen Dowager would affift at it. The affembly was brilliant, the young monarch rofe in the midft of it, and holding in his hand a fcroll, thus addrefled

himfelf

himfelf to his minifters, in the prefence of thoufands of his fubjects.—" I perceive a paffage of great importance is omitted in the will of my royal father. No fuitable, independent pro-vifion has been made for my beloved and im-perial mother. The long tried virtues of that noble lady, the tender confidence and domeftic love, in which fhe lived with my father, con-vinces me, that it never could have been in-tended, that fo good a wife, fo kind a parent, and fo excellent a woman, could be left in a ftate of dependence on her fon. Much more likely is it that the fon fhould have been be-queathed to the commands, indulgence, and management of his mother. Or if *it was* in-tended that the fon fhould *receive* the whole revenues of the empire, it could only be in confidence that he would act as her agent, and fee that her private, her natural, and proper rights were paid into her coffers with the leaft care and inconvenience to herfelf.

" In the latter cafe, I hope I fhould be found, throughout my reign, a faithful fteward of my dear parent and of the people ; and, fuppofing, for a moment, this cafe a poffible one, I cannot be infenfible to the exalted affection and efteem the late Emperor and King muft have for me,

that

that he could, after his death, confide the
fortunes of such a wife to the trust of his son.
But human nature is so frail, and the trust is so
aweful, that I tremble while I possess it; and
cannot, indeed, be easy, till I have disburthened
myself of the weight it imposes. To this
end, my loving friends, ministers and subjects,
I have herein bound myself, (shewing the scroll)
by an instrument of the last solemnity, to become responsible in a yearly sum suited to her
rank although inferior to her deservings. And
I have, as nearly as may be, made this dispo-
sition from my private funds, and from sources
the least likely to infringe on, or to affect, the
treasures of the state, which I hold in trust
also,—for the honour of my empire, and the
prosperity of Austria; yet I consider myself as
called upon by my subjects to explain, account
for, and justify every expenditure, before I
make an arrangement in favor of any part of
my own family: But I feel at the same time,
that it is an act of duty and justice on my part,
which will be crowned by the sanction of all
my people.

" Here then, madam, continued the royal
youth, dropping on his knee as he descended
from his throne, and presenting the scroll—here
                                                    is

is the deed by which I relieve myfelf from an infupportable burthen,—the idea of your majefty's becoming the victim of a fon's weaknefs, indifcretion, or ingratitude : and you will find that I have, by the fame act, taken the liberty to appoint you the guardian of my youth, in all that can properly be called (if any thing can) my *private fortunes*: I retain in my hand the *public treafures*, becaufe the weight of them would, from the multiplicity of demands, be attended with fatigue to you ; but I fhall not fail, from time to time, as exigences may arife, to derive benefit, in their application, from your known wifdom, goodnefs of heart and judgement, and your love of the empire."

With regard to the public, one might very reafonably expect from fuch an outfet, what has happened in the progrefs of the reign of this monarch ;—we were prepared for his having almoft emptied the coffers of his private property, and almoft ftript his palace of his furniture, many of its neceffaries, and all its luxuries before he invited the affiftance of his people to carry on this unparalleled war, for their fake, for his own, and for that of human kind ! It is a literal fact that he fent all his gold and filver fervices of plate to the mint;

now

now he contents himself with common porce-
lain. Should the *invasion of the rights of men*
continue, he will, probably, be reduced to
earthen ware, and to shew that his spirit in the
field is equal to his generous sacrifices at home,
he left a beloved wife, in the most affecting
crisis of a woman's life, to be the first in danger as in honour. He is now only in the twen-
ty-fourth year of his age,—surely nothing but
a Carmagnol could wish to shorten the life of
such a monarch, or of such a man! but the
name of King includes tyranny it *seems*; and
every head "that wears a crown," according to the new system, deserves to lose it!
The rule does not admit of an exception.
Notwithstanding which, I shall hazard the
treason to wish that the present Emperor of
Germany, the present King of Great-Britain,
and of every other Prince *like unto them*, may
survive, not only the malicious plots of their
enemies, whether secret, or avowed, but the
enemies themselves! and, I trust, I should have
firmness and loyalty enough to breathe this
wish! this prayer! though it should bring me
to the edge of that instrument, which, for a
similar offence, has immolated such hecatombs
of victims.

Yet

Yet there are, amongst the fubjects even of this beloved Sovereign, many thoufands of perfons who would aid and abet thefe extirpations of royalty, in planting a dagger in his heart!—The Brabançons, the people of Liege, and many large bodies of the *higher*, as well as *lower* parts of the empire, conceal their treafon in applaufe, and their difcontent in flattery, but lie in wait for an occafion, like the folded ferpent in the grafs, to fting the bofom that nourifhes, and arreft the arm which defends them. This is fo true, that in Germany, as in other parts of the world, the foe *within our gates*, and even our familiar friends, who can fmile upon their mafter and be villains, are more to be dreaded than the external enemy. Againft the open violence of the latter we can guard, and force may be oppofed to force; but, from the infidious machinations of the firft, the hour of confidence may be that of treachery, and the moment of apparent endearment may mingle poifons, wounds, and death with embraces.

Amidft fo much unnatural conduct in different parts of the world, it is as *refrefhing* as rare to meet with an inftance of loyalty, in *any* part of it. Such was the fplendid and fpirited

offer of the little town or rather village of
Broek in North Holland, whofe beauties and
fingularities I gave in a former Gleaning. The
inhabitants of this place fent word to the Stadtholder and the States General, that if either the
armies, or the treafuries of the provinces,
wanted affiftance, the patriot gift of twenty
or thirty tons of filver, and five or ten of gold,
fhould not be wanting!—but, alas!—on the
per contra fide of this folitary fact, what a long
lift of murmurs, rebellions, maffacres, and of
treafons, might not be fet down, even in the
fpan of earth and water that appertains to the
Dutch!—to go no farther. And though the
laft revolution threw *them* fifty years behind
hand in wealth, and credit, and an hundred in
felicity, and coft them thirty-two millions of
florins befides, they are, *burfting ripe for another
revolution!*—adieu.

LETTER LXIX.

TO THE SAME.

COLOGNE.

WE have now given a general Gleaning of Weſtphalia, as well as of Holland and
Guelderland,

" Tried what the open, what the coverts yield."

From Cleves, Wezel, Emeric, or any of the
port towns, right to left, you may bend your
way to Spa, Chaud Fontaine, Aix la Chapelle,
or any other place which faſhion, the arts of
men, and the ſtreams of nature have made
popular; but of which the deſcription, the
virtues, &c. are as familiar as the ſprings of
Iſlington. From hence, alſo, your path lies
eaſy and direct by water or by land, to all the
other parts of Germany, including its dependent circles. From this town of Cologne, the
world is all before you. To this ancient and
imperial place you may come even from Rotterdam, (by boats of buſineſs or of pleaſure,)
along two of the nobleſt rivers in Europe, the
Meuſe and the Rhine; the delicious courſe of

s 2

which

which I should certainly describe more particularly, and indeed have Gleaning materials
to this end, but that, since I collected them, a
work has fallen into my hands which I recommend to yours, because it is written with elegance and truth; and because it may now be
perused with pleasure by *all* my readers, as I
am informed a good translation of it has just
made its appearance in England. It has for
title, in the original " *voyage* sur le Rhin,
depuis Mayence jusqu'à Dusseldorf,"—a voyage or journey by the banks of the Rhine, from
Mayence to Dusseldorf.

But although this ample tract of land and
water lies, as I said, before you, it is not *now*
either an easy or an eligible path; for " storms
and desolations rest upon it." At the time I
paid it my earliest visit, you could not take a
direction, amidst a thousand routes, that did not
present even *more*, than the ingenious work just
mentioned has spoken to, of every *agrément*
a traveller can desire, but now—in short, my
loved friend, the charm is dissolved,—I have
strayed with you amongst fragrance and fer-
tility, and pursued the devious walk till we
have literally

" wander'd into a sea of *blood*"!

Forgive

Forgive me. I own it was a ftratagem, but done in kindnefs. I wifhed, as long as poffible, to make you forget and to keep you from thefe confines of " fin and death", to which we were approaching:

. " Veil'd in a fhower of fhadowing rofes".*

You have, hitherto, fcarcely perceived that all along I have been conducting you to the very fcenes of action, where even at this moment, " the battle bleeds in every vein".

" Hark ! heard ye not yon giant tread ?
" Heard ye not yon footfteps dread ?
" Tis War.+

I need not inform you dear friend, who have ever a clue to my wanderings, that foon after your receipt of my laft, I in a manner efcaped to England, and during my very fhort ftay there, fent you an ‡ hiftory of my fenfations ; but no fooner, as you know, had I refrefhed my fpirit at the fight of fo much peace and plenty, gratified my heart by the tranfient view of fome who were dear to me at home, and heard of fome important fucceffes abroad, I followed once more the bent of my " truant difpofition",

* Thomfon.   + Mafon.
‡ The hiftory here alluded to, is that which appears in the introduction, what the Author has cal'd Gleanings at home.

and revifited the fcenes from which I had been driven : It was as you recollect in the midft of a month that would foon have ripened all the fruits of the earth, and made " the heart of the hufbandman fing for joy", had not his hopes been deftroyed, torn up by the. roots and trampled under the foot of the mercilefs enemy. I repaffed all my ancient paths, and to a certain diftance found fome traces of the lovely fcenery I had left, and which I have already Gleaned for you.   I advanced a little, and foon came to the *extreme edge of peace*. Words, were they written by Shakfpeare's pen, could, not duly defcribe the change which had taken place in the fpace of an hundred yards farther, meafuring from the fpot from *whence* peace, plenty, and nature, feemed to have taken flight, as if, like other terrified emigrants, they had fought protection in our Queen of Ifles.

A fmall arm of the Rhine feparated me from a territory that had, fome few weeks before, been the fcene of an action, which, though fhort, had been bloody. I paffed over,—and the reft of the river for many a league, blufhed to fancy like the Rubicon.   The earth for feveral miles gave note of what had been doing in abfence of the Gleaner. An harveft, alas,

of the fword inftead of the fcythe had been
made, and whole ranks of human creatures, as
well as the grafs and the corn, had been mown
down,—an iron harveft !—Flocks and herds had
been fo effectually driven away, or deftroyed,
that although it was celebrated as a country for
the choiceft cattle, and I had fo often *seen* them
cover the banks, neither the lowe of an * heifer,

S 4					nor

* By way of fhewing you how thefe worthy gentlemen who
are faid to be fighting for the liberties of mankind, *then* conducted themfelves, when they *took poffiffion of other people's property.* I have gleaned for you a correct copy of one of their
edicts, iffued on the day after their entering Pruffian Guelderland, even when they came as friends, on a vifit of *confraternity.*

Au nom de la Republique Françoife !

Il eft *ordonné* aux adminiftrateurs, treforiers, et receveurs
quelconques, des droits, et impofitions dans le Gueldre Pruffi-
enne, &c. de ne verfer leurs recettes, qu'entre les mains des
perfonnes commifes par leur differentes communautés ; à l'effet
de faire le levée des contributions impofées au nom de la Republique Françoife, jusqu' à parfait et entier payement.

Il eft auffi expreffement defendu de faire fortir des dites provinces aucune beftiaux, vivres, ou fourrages avant d'avoir fatis-
fait aux engagemeuts qu'elles ont contractées vis à vis de la
Republique Françoife, fous peine d'encourir fa difgrace, et
d'être traité comme fes ennemis.

Le General commandant l'avant garde de l'armée du Nord,

(Signé)					LE MARLIERE.

Au Quartier General à Ruremonde, le 23me. Decémbre, 1792,
l'année première de la Republique.

TRAN-

nor the bleat of a lamb was to be heard. A few fad birds, in melancholy notes chanted a funeral dirge over their ruined bowers and thickets, moft of which had heen " hewn down and caft into the fire." In one of thefe groves, being at a walking diftance from the neigh-

TRANSLATION.

In the name of the French Republic!

This is to give notice, that all adminiftrators, treafurers, ftewards, agents, &c. whatfoever, in Pruffian Guelderland, fhall not give any receipts or pay any money, except into the hands of the commiffions appointed and authorifed on the part of the French Republic, until the whole contribution be paid, as ordered by General La Maliere.

And it is by virtue of the faid authority, ftrictly forbidden to let any manner of provifions, beafts, or forage, go out of the faid provinces until the faid engagements with the Republic of France are fulfilled, upon pain of incurring its difgrace, and of being treated as its enemy!

So much for French brotherhood.

In the very little village of Swoegen, confifting of half a dozen poor farms and a few cottages, was a levy, (befides their quota of the provifions) of 1500 florins.
In that of Mierlo, not much larger, 2000 florins.
In other parts of Pruffian Guelderland, 200,000 florins.
Forage, 100,000 florins.
Befides eating, drinking, during the poffeffion of the country.

N. B. Moft of the beautiful trees, walks, fhrubberies, &c. deftroyed by way of frolic, as thefe honeft patriots amufed themfelves during the *leifure of victory*.

bouring

bouring town where I made one of my gleaning pauses, I had in a former visit been at some pains to form a seat of fresh sods, to discipline the foliage on either side, and canopy the branches above, chiefly because it was in the neighbourhood of two or three nightingales, who sang their sorrows to each other, and because a stockdove had built in the back ground. And it had the farther *agrément* of a brook, that after an hundred fantastic mazes, amongst the meadows and fields adjacent, took its course along the underwood, through which I could see it stream as I sat, and I could besides hear it dispute and struggle with the impediments it found in its way. Of these it complained so gently, as very well to associate with the notes of my dove and nightingales. Although I had thrown the arching of my alcove, as far forward, cave like, as I could, with a design to exclude too obtrusive a visit of the sun, and of the world, I could observe at the openings of the oak branches part of a fine field of springing corn, and catch a glimpse of some steeples on the one hand, and several farm-houses and cottages on the other : So that the *tout-ensemble*, you will conceive, afforded to a man of poesy and peace all that his heart could desire. In this retreat I had passed many a sunsetting, and

not

not seldom a sun-rising hour. I returned to lament the change. All that side of the grove which screened and furnished branches for my alcove, was cut away by a sanguine banditti, who came, *sword in hand*, into these environs. The hand of wantonness had hacked off with the sabre whole nurseries of firs and poplars. Most of the houses had been burnt down, and the wretched inhabitants plundered of all their little stores. Some were dead of wounds, some of grief, the rest wandered about the world in search of the very few, who, with the dispo-sition, had the power of benevolence.

The fields which I left so full of vernal pro-mise were despoiled; not an handful of grain remained for a *Gleaner*, who was now literally left to pick his scanty subsistence amidst thorns and briars; and though the steeples of some churches were yet to be seen, they could be viewed only as the monuments of that dread-ful sacrilege which had been committed within. I entered one of these, and found it had, in real and dreadful truth, been turned into a den of thieves. The altars were broken down, and the fragments stained with the blood of its mi-nisters; the ruthless soldiery had converted the most holy places into the most obscene; inde-

cent

cent allufions, and impious mottos were pen-
cilled on the windows, doors, and even on the
fainted reliques; and the images of the Redeemer were demolifhed, with every mark of
mockery and fcorn*. Several tombs were torn
open,

* In that fheaf of our Gleaning, gathered in and fent you
from Wales, I forgot to mention, and, indeed, it will come in
better at this place, that when I was at Bangor, the Warder of
the cathedral of that epifcopal city told me, that one of its
ancient bifhops was ftruck blind by a thunderbolt from heaven,
for the facrilegious act of felling the bells. The confternation
of the Warder, on recounting this as we ftood difcourfing under
the bellfry, could fcarce have been exceeded, had the thunderbolt fallen on his own head. What would this honeft fon of
fimplicity have concluded, had I been then able to inform
him, that the French were cutting off the heads, and mangling
the limbs, of *their* bifhops, not for felling the revenues of the
church, but for daring to affift at, and adminifter divine
worfhip, for attachment to their king, for believing in a Saviour
of the world, and for not turning apoftate to their God: nay,
furthermore, that they condemned the holy men, moft eminent
for talents and piety, to the ftake, the cannon, the mufquet, or
the guillotine; and, laftly, that fo far from fparing the bells
on account of their fanctity, that they convert them into inftruments of murder—the murder of the beft priefts, the beft citizens, and the beft men! And, by way of clofing the climax of
facrilege, were I to obferve that a number of thefe citizens
finding themfelves ficken from the vapours of the charcoal, and
the putrid ftench of the dead bodies, which they were turning
ut of the coffins, that the lead thereof might be made into
bullets,

open, and the " canonifed bones," which had been depofited for centuries, were hung round the pulpit, and the ruins of the altar-piece!

The habitations were in the fame difmantled ftate; all the valuables that were portable had been carried off in waggons, tumbled into the heap of promifcuous plunder, and nothing remained but the *wreck* of the fixtures, and the miferable proprietors who had efcaped the pillagers, mourning, or famifhing over them. One fweetly-ruftic abode, that I had, the preceding year, *diftinguifhed* as the deareft refidence of a numerous, humble, yet not indigent family; the proofs of whofe induftry and content I had feen fhine in every plate, glafs, table, chair, and cup-board, and where I had been accuftomed to fee a groupe of healthy and happy faces, was become a general ruin. The father was marked down, by fome of his bafe townfmen, as an avowed lover of his country, and had; on a late exigence, join'd fome of his neighbours to make head againft a party of

bullets, and balls—would not the poor man, with a better reafon than fuperftition has to offer, conclude that the poifonous naufea thus feizing them, was a fignal mark of divine judgement. Before the æra of liberty, Frenchmen would have confidered it in that light likewife.

foragers,

foragers, who would have driven off the herds and flocks. This was fo foul a crime in the eyes of the French, that they cut off the head of the tree, and mangled feveral of the branches. The very boards and bricks of the rooms were torn up. I ran over the houfe with horror. I paffed through three of the apartments, without meeting one confolatory object. I began to fear every veftige of humanity had been deftroyed by thefe its *fworn exterminators*, when, coming to the broken ftair-cafe, I heard a voice which had *often welcomed* me. I afcended, and faw the wretched remnants of this once-joyful family crouded into the only chamber that remained habitable—two half-grown boys, an old woman, and the young daughter who had fpoken to me. On comparing their prefent with their paft ftate, the latter opened on my mind *new ideas of human viciffitude*. I inftantly called to my remembrance that the laft time I had feen thefe very perfons, the two firft objects were fporting on the green before their door, in all the glee of body and of foul. The old woman and her hufband were fitting on a bench, environed with honey-fuckles that twifted, felf-bent, into a natural canopy, and the daughter was " leaning, half-raifed," on the flowery ground, at the feet of her parents,

and

and laughing at the anticks of her two brothers.

Why should I paint to you the dire reverse!
Alas! the reverse goes almost out of the reach
even of *imagination*. It is not easy to suppose
the ravagers *could*, in so short a space of time,
change *every happy circumstance to its bitterest
opposite*; that they could turn, for instance,
plenty into famine, health to disease, and a
contented mind to an agonized, broken spirit!
Yet all this had been done *by the sons of liberty*,
who too truly put their threat in execution, of
carrying misery and death into every place they
visited.

As to my poor nightingales and stockdove,
though they had more cause than ever to lament
that terror, which, in conventional language,
is *the order of the day*, had sent them to mourn
prematurely in other lands:

" —————————— The very spot,
" Where many a time they carol'd, was forgot."

for the little thicket, which had been their
leafy sanctuary was burnt up by these glorious
free-booters—because, forsooth, the proprietor
was wicked enough to attempt saving himself
and

and family by flight, when he heard that a party of *patriots* were likely to invade his village, and the guilty wretch was another *traitor*, who had unfortunately diftinguifhed himfelf, on a former occafion, as a lover of his country. Nothing, in fhort, remained of the various innocent and interefting objects my heart had appreciated, but a fragment of the brook, part of which had been deftroyed in the fury of extirpating the thicket; and from the broken gaps the water had worked its way into an oppofite current to the left, where, in forming a junction of founds, it feemed to lament the general ruin. But, God knows, the furrounding calamities required no aids from fancy. On the contrary, in this poor fuffering little town, and its environs, there *actually* happened fuch horrors as Fancy, when *moft* difpofed to excite terror, her ftrongeft attribute, never formed. Dreadful *beyond* imagination was a fact which thefe inhuman republicans perpetrated on the fucking infant of the haplefs fugitive laft mentioned. He had information that the enemy would be at Kreutznach in a few hours, and being told that he would certainly be amongft the *profcribed*, on account of the active part he had taken, when a party of peafants bravely defended their all againft a former horde, he

followed

followed the impulfe of a panic-ftruck moment, and filled his two carts, the one with his family, the other with his moveable effects, in order to fend them away to a brother farmer's, where they could find a promifed protection. He followed his little houfehold with an aching, yet comforted heart, but hearing the found of the enemy's guns in the road they were to take, and fuppofing the route had been changed, he returned to his cottage, and had hope that the plunderers would purfue another plan. Alas, this was a flattering expectation. The patriots had heard that a detachment of Pruffians were ftill in Kreutznach, but learning foon after, from a fcout, that they had marched out of the village the preceding evening, the patriots filently made their way into the heart of the town before it was fufpected they were in the neighbourhood ; for it was late in the night, or rather early in the morning, and the peaceful, harmlefs inhabitants were in their beds. You will better judge of the confufion than I can defcribe it. The peafant facrificed the dead to fave the living, and taking his wife in one hand, and his children, linked arm in arm, in the other, the fuckling lying on its mother's breaft, he left his dwelling with a hope of ftill gaining the asylum.

afylum. A patriot *countryman* and neighbour, however, with whom he had often difputed on the fubject of his principles, noticed his departure, and conducted the fanguine enemy into the path he had taken. They lingered about till the dawn, which, alas, broke too foon for the fugitives; who, on hearing the voice of their menacing purfuers, had plunged into a wood to the left; but the crying of their own child betrayed them. The barbarians rufhed into the wood, where, fpreading themfelves, they overtook the female part of the wanderers; whom the poor peafant had quitted for the moment, to explore a track that he conceived might lead them to a fmall hamlet on the left; and which, confifting only of a few fcattered huts that ftood on the fkirts of the foreft, might ftill preferve his family. Meantime, they were feated, as he thought, in fo fecure a recefs, that the " dogs of war," though in full cry, could not harm them during his abfence. He was miftaken. The blood-hounds difcovered their haunt, and, feizing the trembling mother, they tore the babe from her breaft and ftriking off its head, threw the bloody gift into her lap, as a *prefent to her husband*, dreadfully fwearing, at the fame time, that if fhe did not perfuade him to return, and folicit

pardon for his paſt offenſes againſt the *French Republic*, that her own head, and that of every
other child, ſhould anſwer it! They left her
for other miſchief. Cruel as it is, my friend,
you are impatient for the ſequel of this bloody
adventure, which I received, nearly as I relate
it, from the mouth of the deſolate wife.

On the return of her huſband, gueſs, if you
can, his ſenſations—the bleeding head of his
youngeſt infant, the lifeleſs trunk of its little
body, the agonized mother, the no leſs ſhocking proſpect of the remainder of them, all
before him! Let your beating heart have reſt,
however, as to the remainder of this poor
family. After the Carmagnols had paſt ſome
hours in the ravage of Kreutznach, and, in
raiſing ſuch exactions as left famine to finiſh
what the ſword had begun, the approach oɪ
the Pruſſians compelled the enemy to evacuate
the town, and the peaſants returned—they re-.
turned indeed to an heap of ruins: where

    " Once the garden ſmil'd,"

and where I had ſo lately *ſeen*, with delighted
eyes, all that the ſweeteſt poetry has ever fancied or deſcribed,

        " Thoſe

" Thofe calm defires that afk but little room,
" Thofe healthful fports that grac'd the peaceful fcene,
" Liv'd in each look, and brighten'd all the green."

I generally walk with a fmall edition of the author of thefe verfes, an author who was one of the earlieft friends of my youth, and whom my youthful mufe fincerely lamented, in my pocket. *His* exquifite poems, and the Seafons of Thomfon are amongft the deareft of my travelling equipage. On my word of honour, I feel a gratitude, a refpect, an affection, nay, a *paffion of the heart* for every leaf; for with how many charming ideas have they filled it, when my own thoughts were comfortlefs and fad? and, during the fummer months, though I know almoft every paffage by rote, I have one or the other of thefe *Glories of our ingenious ifle*, in my hand, and

" In all my wand'rings round this world of care,"

they appear to be partakers of my pilgrimage. I thus feem to be in the company of two of my moft illuftrious countrymen, and when I perufe their pages, I feem but to repeat their converfation.

But never did I think I fhould be a dweller upon earth, when almoft every beauty and

innocence

innocence of nature that each has so sweetly sung, should be cut down for so many leagues together, and left by the cruel spoilers to clot and wither in human gore! Still less did I suppose I should so often have occasion to *apply* or to *contrast* so many of their passages. Had the author of the " Deserted Village" lived in these times, and gleaned, like me, the places which the enemy of mankind have over-run, all the distress of that poem, which bewailed, in some measure, an imaginary, or, at least, a partial evil, would quit its objects, to lament others, a thousand fold more to be deplored. To see

> " The rural virtues leave the land,"

as an effect of that luxury, which

> " Indignant spurns the cottage from the green."

And while

> " Trade's unfeeling train
> " Usurp the land and dispossess the swain."

And still further to observe

> " Contented toil, and hospitable care,
> " And kind connubial tenderness,————
> " And piety, with wishes plac'd above,
> " And steady loyalty, and faithful love,
> " Pass from the shore, and darken all the strand,"

is a melancholy sight, and worthy to be
mourned

mourned by the mufe of Goldfmith. But, while the poor exiles took with them many of their deareft confolations,

> " The good old fire that firft prepar'd to go,
> " The lovely daughter, lovelier in her tears."

And while the fond mother could

> " —Kifs her thoughtlefs babes with many a tear,
> " And clafp them clofe in forrow doubly dear."

their paffage to

> " New found worlds, beyond the weftern main,"

and all their deftiny is blifs, compared with the execrable deeds which have been heaped on the head of the inhabitants of the countries, that border on, or rather comprehend, the theatre of the prefent war.

And, in fine, when I left one defolated place, in the hope of gaining more repofe; and feeing lefs forrow in another, it was, generally fpeaking, but going from bad to worfe! An irregular and ftill, difappointed tour which included moft of the towns and villages in the neighbourhood of the Saar, the Sambre, the Mozelle, the Zorn, the Meufe, and the Lower Rhine, (in thofe branches which ftretch along the frontiers, in different directions;) com-

 prehending,

prehending, one way, an excursion from Coblentz to the Duchy of Deux Ponts—from Louvain to Givet another, from Binche to Bouchain a third, and so on, (till I returned, like an hunted hare, to the place from whence I set out) presented me with nothing but

" A bitter change, severer for severe! *"

I have followed the *victorious* in their burning pursuit of the flying enemy, even when my way has been sometimes impeded by the bleeding bodies, and mangled limbs of the *vanquished!* Unable from wounded feelings to proceed, I have returned to the spots where the action began, and there seen the horror, desolation, and famine by which even *conquest* has been gained. Even on the day when such conquest has filled the dismantled, and half depopulated streets of the rescued town with the shout of victors—when solemn *Te Deums* have been appointed to be sung in all places of public worship, I have beheld that mass of private misery which is frequently no less the companion of victory than the attendant of defeat—the shriek of the widow, the orphan, and the childless parent were still nearly the same,

Had

* Young.

Had my poor friend Goldsmith survived to witness them, how much more reason would he have had to exclaim, while on *one day* he heard or saw in *several* villages, not inferior to his Auburn:

" The swain responsive as the milk maid sung,
" The sober herd that low'd to meet their young,
" The noisy geese that gabbled o'er the pool,
" The playful children just let loose from school,
" The watch-dog's voice that bay'd the whispering wind,
" And the loud laugh that spoke the vacant mind."

What additions I say, my dear friend, would have been given to his reasons of complaint, were he to have been an auditor and spectator of these objects on one day, and, on perhaps, the very next, to find the swain ruined or murdered, the milk-maid violated, the head driven into the enemy's camp, the children deprived of a father, and the whole country destroyed! Had the subject of his pen been only the sanguinary annals of a *few hours* depredation, in the village of Dudelange *, a small place in the disastrous

---

* Or of Chimay, a sweet little village upon the beauteous river Blanch, between the picturesque forests of Thierach and Fagne, in the fine county of Hainault. But, for many ages, the demon of war has ravaged the charms of Chimay.—Wholly however to extirpate them, to turn the town and the environs into the tomb of their harmless inhabitants, of the proprietors, and their property, was reserved for the French Republicans!

T 4

province

province of Luxembourg, where decrepid old
men, sick persons, women labouring with child,
babes at the breast, or in the cradle, became
the indiscriminate victims of these monsters,
had he seen the lives of those miserable
beings taken away, by absolutely *innovations in
cruelty*, and attested the wanton iniquity of
tearing up the young and tender crops which
their industry had sown, he would *indeed* have
had reason to exclaim

  " Sweet smiling village, loveliest of the lawn,
  " Thy sports are fled and all thy charms withdrawn;
  " Amidst thy bowers the tyrant's hand is seen,
  " And desolation saddens all thy green
  " And trembling, shrinking from the spoiler's hand
  " Far, far away thy children leave the land!

But it is far beyond the reach even of * Goldsmith's poetry to offer an adequate description of
                atrocities,

* Enthusiast as I am to the energy of his muse, and dearly
as I love the memory of the man, with whom I have past so many
happy hours, when life and poetry were young to me, and con-
sequently when both were more full of charms, I must acknowledge that even when I have, in the course of this last journey
amongst the ruins of humanity, applied the choicest language
from the muse of my deceased friend to deplore that I saw so
many proofs of a tyrant's power, I have felt that language too
feeble for the occasion.

And when in surveying the wreck of some spot that once
realised the flights of his happiest fancy, I have exclaimed:

                  " Here

atrocities, of plunder, fword and fire, which throw into fhadow the utmoft barbarity of the Goths and Vandals.

And

“ Here as I take my folitary rounds,
“ Amidft the tangling walks, and ruin'd grounds,
“ And *not a year elapfed*, return to view
“ Where once the cottage ftood, the hawthorn grew,
“ Here as with doubtful, penfive fteps I range,
“ Trace every fcene and wonder at the change,
“ Remembrance wakes with all her bufy train,
“ Swells at my breaft, and turns the paft to pain.”

Even this have I found a faint though beautiful picture of tha facts.—I do not recommend any man to make the fame experiment, but if the fober headed or cold hearted reafoner who has read the effufions of a warm imagination, and given to human calamities a ftronger pathos, and a deeper colour than the critic in his elbow chair fuppofes *can* belong thereto, a journey to thefe fcenes of private grief and public mifery would foon convince him, that we live in a world in fome parts of which there are daily, perhaps, hourly, happening diftreffes far too poignant for the pen or the pencil, though Rubens were to hold the one, and Shakfpeare the other; and, indeed, that much of what has been condemned as romance, is but an underwritten or underpainted hiftory of circumftances in real life. But, after all, it is wrong in me to fet down fuch condemnation to a cold heart or head.—Thefe will never be amongft the defects imputed to the Gleaner, and yet had he not been an eyewitnefs to the different calamities defcribed in thefe volumes, he muft have attributed fome of thefe calamities, had they been reprefented by any other perfon, to the work of fiction,

And the evil is ftill growing, ftill extending its horrors. Though I have at length turned from them, the memory of the paft is never to be erafed; the prefent is full of apprehenfion; and the miferies of the future cannot be calculated. Remote as is now this peaceful place from the immediate fcenes of action, it fhields me not from a thoufand dreadful fights of the wounded and the defolate. Two waggons loaded with the former this morning pafs'd my window, and an equal number are expected tomorrow. If you afk me why I threw myfelf fo much in the way of fcenes like thefe, fo foreign, fo repugnant to every feeling of my foul? why I remained in their view fo long? I can only anfwer that, in the firft inftance, I went to revifit places and people which had once given me pleafure, and I defired to fhare their pain, in a reverfe of fortune; fecondly, when once involved, it was not eafy to difentangle my fteps; and laftly, I loft myfelf in the bloody mazes!

LETTER LXX.

TO THE SAME.

Valenciennes.

HOW often, in surveying these hor-rible wrecks of human affairs, have I reiterated that apostrophe, which you did me the honour so much to approve on the first publication of a work, whose chief design was to paint the miseries of war in general, and of civil war in particular. You will accept one passage, which came to my mind many times in the course of these military Gleanings amongst surrounding scenes of death, of ruin and of havock.

" * Ah earth thou common parent—thou whose nourishing bosom furnishes to all the children of content that will cultivate thy kindness; how art thou made the object of sanguinary ambition! Into what ridiculous portions of ideal property art thou cut out, quarrelled and contended for! How often does the bounteous sun that shines upon thy surface to expand the grain and to cherish thy various productions, leave thy verdant mantle dipt in gore?

" O peace,

* Emma Corbett.

" O peace, thou image of divinity itself—
defcend upon that earth from whence the
miftakes of altercating relations have fo long
affrighted thee. Subdue gentle power the
fierce foul of rebellion. I call upon thee in
the names of nature, reafon, humanity and
juftice.—I call upon thee in the name of
nature's God!"

But left, my loved friend, you fhould deem
this in fome meafure the rhapfody of a poetical
mind, ftrongly moved by the fad fcenery that
environs it at this moment, when I am in the
midft of the horrors that have been produced
by conflagration, famine, forrow, defolation,
defpair, and all the evils of war, fuffer me to
call in the fupport of one, who, though he was
writing in a well fecured city, in times of profound peace and public profperity, at leaft when
the rumours of war could reach him, but by a
medium long after the mifchief apprehended,
and who, tho' he reafoned as a politician and
philofopher, felt as a man. " War," fays he,
" is the laft of all remedies, *cuncta prius tentanda:*
all lawful expedients muft be ufed to avoid it.
'Tis wonderful with what coolnefs and indifference the greater part of mankind fee war com-
menced. Thofe that hear of it at a diftance, or
read of it in books, but have never prefented

its

its evils to their minds (much more thofe, let me add, that write as I do now on the polluted fpots where thofe evils have juft happened) confider it as little more than a fplendid game, a proclamation, an army, a battle, and a triumph. Some, indeed, they allow muft perifh, perhaps, fome of their deareft friends, in the moft fuccefsful field, but then they died upon the bed of honour, refign their lives amidft the joys of conqueft, and filled with glory, fmile in death.

" But war has means of deftruction more formidable than the cannon and the fword. Of the thoufands and tens of thoufands that have perifhed in the late contefts a very fmall part ever felt the ftroke of the enemy; the reft languifhed in tents and towns, or places of refuge amidft damps and putrefaction: pale, torpid, fpiritlefs, and helplefs; gafping and groaning; unpitied amongft men, made obdurate by the continuance of hopelefs mifery, and many of which muft, at laft, die without notice and without remembrance. Of that number are multitudes now lingering or agonizing in the hofpitals which I have vifited with a very akeing heart. If he that fhared the danger enjoyed the profit, and after bleeding in the battle grew rich by

the

the victory, he might shew even his gains with‑
out envy; but at the conclusion of a ten years
war how are we recompensed for the death of
multitudes, and the expence of millions, but by
contemplating the sudden glories of paymasters
and agents, contractors, and commissaries,
whose equipages shine like meteors, and
whose palaces rise like exhalations."

All this is unquestionably true of war in
general, and no less certainly founded in fact
is the exception which has been made; that
as there are diseases in animal nature which
nothing but amputation can remove, so there is,
by the depravation of human passions, some‑
times a gangrene in human societies for which
fire and sword are the necessary remedies. That
the force collected against France is of this
sort, I think there are few, even of those who
wished a reform, and silently approved the
primary measures taken towards it, but must
acknowledge; at the same time that they must
applaud the caution that withheld the British
empire from joining in the dreadful operations
while there was yet room for gentler methods.
Never, perhaps, in the annals of history was
there a crisis at which Bolingbroke's remark
could be so apposite, as that at which we have

now

now arrived; " If ever fays he, a teft for the trial of fpirits can be neceffary, it is *now:* if ever thofe of real liberty and clamorous faction ought to be diftinguifhed from each other, it is *now*; if ever it is incumbent on nations to know what truth is, and to follow it, it is *now*. If we do not take advantage of the ftanding water of faction, the tide will foon turn one way or the other, and carry *all before it.*"

" A people, fays his lordfhip, who will maintain their liberties, far from jogging on filently and tamely like the afs between two burthens, muft preferve fome of the fiercenefs of the lion and even make their roar to be heard like his, whenever they are injured, or fo much as threatened;" but to fhew that he does not in this obfervation mean to recommend that difloyal feditious fpirit which creates a perpetual fcene of tumult and diforder, and expofes the ftate to dangerous and often fatal convulfions, he confeffes that a fpirit of faction may deftroy a free conftitution, though founded on

" The nobleft bafis
" Our rights, our natural inheritance."

But that a fpirit of real liberty never can, and left we fhould imagine that fuch a fpirit is inconfiftent with the loyalty we owe our

7   fovereign,

fovereign, or chief ruler, by what ever name
his fupremacy is diftinguifhed, he remarks,
" that in every kind of government fome powers
muft be lodged in particular men, for the good
order and prefervation of the whole community. Nothing can be more clear than that
the lines which circumfcribe the powers, are
the bounds of feparation between· the prerogatives of the Prince, or other magiftrate, and the
privileges of the people. We hence infer that
every ftep which the prince or magiftrate
makes beyond thefe bounds is an encroach-
ment on liberty, and every attempt towards
making fuch a ftep is a danger on liberty;
but if it is righteous to draw the fword againft
tyrants. who endanger this liberty, it is not lefs
fo to unfheath it againft traitors who cover the
crimes of rebellion and regicide under the
mafk of patriotifm."

Notwithftanding which we muft deeply regret the dire neceffity of man thus preying
upon man, and fhudder to reflect there are really
thofe amongft us meriting the cenfure which
an excellent writer has paft on them—Wretches
who without virtue, labour, or hazard, while in-
commodious encampments, and unwholfome
ftations, where courage is ufelefs, and enterprize

is

is impracticable, are filently difpeopling fleets and fluggifhly melting away armies, are growing rich as their country is impoverifhed; who rejoice when obftinacy or ambition adds another year to flaughter and devaftation; who laugh from their defks at bravery and fcience, while they are adding figure to figure, and cypher to cypher, hoping for a new contract for a new armament, andcomputing the profits of a fiege or a tempeft.

The fighting fanatics are not much more praife worthy, either as to their precepts or practice; nor the blind mob who follow their doctrine, and who talk of liberty becaufe it is a better name for idlenefs. I never hear this clamour for freedom without calling to mind thofe lines of Milton, which fo juftly characterife the prefent innovators and their adherents. See how they apply:

" A barbarous noife environs me,
" Of owls and cuckoos, afles, apes, and dogs,
" They bawl for freedom in their fenfelefs mood,
" And ftill revolt when truth would fet them free,
" Licence they mean when they cry liberty;
" For who loves that muft firft be wife and good:
" But from that mark how far they are we fee,
" *For all this wafte of wealth and lofs of blood!*"

LETTER LXXI.

TO THE SAME.

LIBERTY, fays my Lord Bolinbroke, is a tender plant which will not flourifh unlefs the genius of the foil be proper for it. Notwithftanding it has been watered with human blood, and manured by human bodies, great muft be the reform of the prefent fyftem, ere I can be perfuaded, my friend, that France is that genial foil. The ftate of and the late tranfactions in that miferable country, cannot be thought of, without leffening the * dignity of the human fpecies; for comparing what once was that kingdom, with what it is, one cannot help affociating with the godlike attributes of man, a capacity of exhibiting and triumphing in qualities † fo Satanic that the arch foe of mankind might blufh to avow them as parts of his nature.

Yet a day is to come when the hiftorian muft detail the particulars of the French Revolution.

The

---

* At the all-devouring moment in which this letter was written.

† The Gleaner fpeaks here of the reign of Roberfpierre, *now* abhorred alike by the Englifh and French nations.

The fugitive accounts of the temporary, or diurnal writers,—thofe " *brief* chroniclers of the times", muft be collected by fome great and impartial pen for the information of pofterity. What a foul-affrighting mafs of mate-rials. If to his literary endowments, the biographer of thefe horrible facts fhould pof-fefs the milder and more compaffionate feelings of the heart, what agonizing martyrs muft thofe feelings be to the truth! How muft his page be ftained with the blood of innocents! In every leaf the crimes of an age committed in a day are to be recorded! Where fhall be found the man whofe foul, whatever be his talents, is firm enough to detail them. And after all, he can fcarce hope Pofterity fhould give him credit. The clofer he advances to the truth, the lefs is the probability of his being believed. We are at the prefent day fo accuf-tomed, fo familiarifed to the hiftory of hor-rors,—to the maffacre of infants in the firft, and children in the fecond ftate of human be-ings, then onward to the affaffination of bed-rid age, and to the violation of all places which ufed once to be moftholy,—mothers, off-fpring, and fwaddled babes,—fanctuaries, churches, and facred altars,—that the tales, which, in the beginning of their atrocities, *literally*

> " Did harrow up the foul, froze the young blood,
> " Made the two eyes like stars start from their spheres,
> " The knotty and combined locks to part,
> " And each particular hair to stand on end,
> " Like quills upon the fretful porcupine:"

make now a weaker impreſſion even on the breaſt where pity has a throne.

I heard one of the moſt tender-herted of men declare, that the ſight of mangled human bodies in the field of battle was diſregarded after a month's cuſtom ; and we know, that the appearance of an open grave, or of a deceaſed perſon carried to it, are almoſt imperceptible, at leaſt unheeded, objects in a populous city, where funerals are amongſt the ordinary occur-rences of the day ; whereas, in a ſmall village, a coffin, and a tomb, retain their power of intereſting and of affecting the mind, even of the gay and diſſolute.

Thus it is in the ſtory of France, polluted as it is with abominations : but when more than a century of interval from theſe ſhall arrive, (and ſuch a period muſt come) the moſt candid reader will impute ſome part of the narrative to prejudice, to paſſion, or to fancy.

                          Indeed,

Indeed, how can the hiftorian himfelf expect or wifh fucceeding generations fhould fuppofe there had ever entered into the heads, or hearts of their anceftors, thofe *innovations* in cruelty, as I have before called them,—thofe *original fins* in the *old age* of a wicked world, that, even *now*, we could not believe but that we *know* them to be facts.

It will, neverthelefs, be the melancholy, though faithful, office of the biographer of the French Republic, to ftate, that, whatever is moft repugnant to reafon and nature,—moft offenfive to the laws of man and of God, were the means to bring about the beft end in the French nation,—a nation long celebrated for its manly gentlenefs and polifhed urbanity, and which was fo univerfally allowed to merit the character given of it by one of its beft poets,

"Where men adore their wives, and woman's power
" Draws reverence from a polifh'd people's foftnefs,
"Their hufbands equals, and their lovers queens."

He muft reverfe this picture, and fhew this very people embrueing themfelves in the life-blood of the fex they idolized,—extending their ferocity towards it beyond the practices of the common murderer. He muft inftruct children yet unborn, that their parents were capable of

U 3

violating

violating that * religion, the very hem of whofe garment had been facred. For proof of which tremendous affertion, he muft enumerate thofe plundered churches, demolifhed altars, and fainted images, which for fo many ages were deem'd hallowed, even by the moft reprobate of tyrants, and moft abandoned of the people. To which enormities muft be added, the pillage of coffins, and turning out of them the very bones of their forefathers, to convert the materials, with which filial piety had guarded them, into the inftruments of a bloody war *upon each other*. To thefe muft fucceed the fhuddering annals of prifons forced, and their contents, amounting to thoufands and tens of thoufands of human beings, murdered with more than Druidical barbarity, for refufing to become apoftates to their King, their Country, and their God.

In fine, the tiffue which fuch an hiftorian muft weave for his readers, would confift of all

* You probably remember the prophane fpirit of that Letter which Chaumet, one of the members of the convention, read, after his long fpeech on the liberty of religious worfhip : If fo, you will particularly bear in mind that paffage which mentions, that at Nanci every kind of religious worfhip was abolifhed, and that every object that could recall religion to the *imagination* was deftroyed ! This letter was diftinguifhed by the *loudeft applaufes* of the people !

that

that is vile and incredible,—of flaughters, continued many days and nights without re-miffion of a moment; till one * of the magif-trates avowed, that though the number of butchers amounted to an † hundred, daily contracted for, in the fingle city of Paris, they declared themfelves fo fatigued, that in pity to themfelves, though with acknow-ledged regret, they were obliged to give their exhaufted arms *a little reft* ; after which, they returned to their bloody bufinefs with reno-

* Pethion.

† It is well known that thefe day labourers in murder were hired by the National Convention, at fo much a day, or fo much per head or per hundred ; and that there was frequently an horrid emulation amongft the affaffins with refpect to the number of victims immolated.: many wagers were laid by thefe competitors for the bloody wreathe as to the quantum of blood fhed in the fame given fpace of time : each became jealous of the other's prowefs, deeming a murder more than he or fhe had committed as a draw back on glory. But one of the long fummer days, that the republicans commemorate by an annual feftival, and which humanity, and nature, and nature's God, join to expunge from the hiftory of time, was diftinguifhed by a victor, who put in his claim to the fanguinary palm, on the merit of having beheaded with his fingle arm two hundred of his fellow citizens !

> Quis talia fando
> Mirmidonum Dolopumve aut duri miles Uliffei
> Temperet à lachrymis ?

vated vigour, till one of the moft populous capitals in the world was inundated with the blood of its beft and braveft inhabitants.

He who fhall " thefe unhappy deeds relate", muft defcribe monfters whofe appetite for murder every hour " increafed by what it fed on", and which,

> " Rav'ning firft the lamb,
> " Seized then the garbage".

Wretches, who exhaufted all the *modes* of cruelty that a wanton and wicked imagination could fuggeft :—of victims ftuck on fpits, which pierced through the fcull and entered the brain,—or hewn limb from limb, were toffed into the air, or dragged along the earth, yet quivering with life, or pounded to atoms, and then hurl'd into the water, or the flames :— Of holy men, like poor Jofeph de Villette, torn from their retreats where they had

> " pafs'd a life of piety and praife"

as ignorant of the revolutions as of the vices of the world, and of the world itfelf: of fhamelefs women, mad with the infection of enthufiafm, who forgetting their fex, forgetting their nature, feated themfelves upon the dead bodies of their victims, and with more than favage ferocity

ferocity throwing the mangled members in horrid paftime from murdcrefs to murderefs, or compreffing the blood from the yet palpitating heart—drink it in execration of the murdered !—or devoting their *own* off-fpring to death, with a mockery of Roman barbarity, for deeds that the *worft* of the Roman matrons would have deemed worthy of a triumph, even in times of pagan obfcurity ; or turning the coftly furniture of the royal palaces, and the facred offerings of gold and filver of their altars, with the altars themfelves, into a *feu de joie*,—(a bonfire,)—fing and dance around the flames;—of mothers initiating their own children in the myfteries of blood,—the blood of babes !—and, more mercilefs than Herod, of men, who not contented with the maffacre of five little ones—in the fight of *her who bore them*, who hack'd off the maternal arms, even while holding to her bofom, and kiffing the bleeding head of the * fuckling at her breaft !

* The fentiment of Lady Macbeth has been thought by many humane perfons to exceed the bounds of poffibility. But do not the above facts prove the profound knowledge of the Poet, in the vices as well as virtues of the heart:

" I have given fuck, and know
How tender 'tis to love the babe that milks me,—
I could, while it was fmiling in my face,

Have

breaſt! and, for ſome time after, refuſing
the compaſſion, implor'd upon her knees, of
diſpatching the parent :—of devoting a noble *
lady and her blooming daughters to the
conſuming fire, but firſt anointing their naked
bodies with oil that they might ſuffer a more
excruciating death,†—but the tender-hearted

reader

Have pluckt my nipple from his boneleſs gums
And daſh'd the brains out."

* The Counteſs of Chevres.

† The murder of Madame de Perignac was attended by the
following terrible circumſtance: her eldeſt daughter who ſuffer'd
with her, unable to endure the torture of deliberate death, ſup-
plicated the executioner appointed to nurſe and feed the flames,
and enforc'd her requeſt on her knees then half-conſumed, to
ſhorten her miſery by the ſword, by a fiercer fire, or any other
means of ſpeedier diſſolution.—The murderer either from fear,
or cruelty, refuſed; when a youth who had been a ſpectator, and
had ſtruggled with his diſtreſs, (being indeed the young lady's
lover,) ran to the place where the beloved of his ſoul was burning, and diſpatched her with a piſtol, which he had indeed
reſerved for himſelf; at this the ſurrounding mob were ſo exaſ-
perated that they made a circle round the blaze to prevent the
young man's eſcape, and exclaim'd that it was a pity to part
lovers! Amongſt the perſons moſt offended at this action, (I
mean of the youth) were four young *women!*

In truth, the female ſex when they have once paſſed a certain bound of cruelty, are cruel indeed, and ſuch as caught the
ſpirit of French patriotiſm, ſeem to have adopted the whole
ſhuddering doctrine of the evil genius, which Lady Macbeth
invoked;

Come

reader muft not be left to fuppofe the tyrants
were guilty of the *mercy* of a *rapid* deftruction,
like that of quick lime ; no !—he is to be told
that thefe innocent facrifices were to be con-

> Come all ye fpirits
> That tend on mortal thoughts, unfex me here;
> And fill me from the crown to the toe, top-full
> Of direft cruelty : make thick my blood,
> Stop up th' accefs and paffage to remorfe,
> That no compunctuous viiitings of nature
> Shake my fell purpofe !——
> Come to my woman's breafts ye *murdering* minifters,
> Whereever in your fightlefs fubftances
> Ye wait on nature's mifchief.
> Come thick night
> And pall me in the dunneft fmoke of hell !

How fublimely terrible!—Would I could add,—what long I
thought, —how *finely imagined!* But could a fpirit lefs fell
that this make females ftab thofe who were but fufpected of
loyalty to their king, and honour of their god, tear off the
flefh with their teeth, and faftened with pins to their drefs, wear
it as a mafk of *Revolutionary virtue !*

Shall not the Gleaner, fhall not even every lover of liberty,
execrate means like thefe to attain a reform of abufes, however
great and manifold ? Reader, of whatever party thou art,
confult thy bofom counfellor, and if there be as much of compaffion, as would beftow a figh on human fuffrance, it would
induce thee to reprobate fuch meafures, even though they led
thee to perfect freedom.

fumed

fumed *à petit feu,* by a flow fire, and lafcivious fongs, and impious hymns, were to chorus the piercing groans of the victims. Lives there, in the round of a very cruel world,—roams there a favage along the famifhing fands of Africa; lies there in the dungeons a criminal, expecting and *deferving* death, fo loft to the innocence that attended him in his cradled hours, as to fuppofe any act of an hellifh nature could be added to the horror of this unqueftionable fact? And yet the hiftorian is to be told, that fix unhappy priefts who were next to be thruft into the flames, were conftrained to eat of the flefh of thefe martyr'd *women,* as it dropped blacken'd and peace-meal from their bones! Alas! the climax is not yet wound up!—a blamelefs man in his extremeft age, was the firft facrificed of the fix Ecclefiaftics abovementioned, no fooner was he roafted by thefe furely more than demoniacs, than the five others were commanded to inform the *French Republic* whether the body of a Parfon or of a Countefs was the moft to their tafte!

Well might the banifhed brothers of the infulted, dethroned, imprifoned, and fince beheaded Louis the fixteenth, in their pathetic and juftificatory addrefs to commiferatg

Europe,

Europe, exclaim " who is there that would not
" be affected to fee that once flourifhing king-
" dom, to which nature has been lavifh in the
" means of making it fuch,—fo rich in popu-
" lation, fo fruitful in its productions, and
" which once abounded in money; fo opulent
" from its refources and commerce, from the
" induftryof its inhabitants, and the advantages
" of its colonies,—that kingdom provided with
" fo many ufeful inftitutions, and whofe happy
" abodes have been fo univerfally courted,—
" prefenting at this moment nothing but the
" appearance of a barbarous country; given
" up to rapine; ftained with bloody ruins;
" and deferted by its principal inhabitants; an
" unorganized empire, torn with inteftine dif-
" traction, ftripp'd of all its riches, threatened
" with every fpecies of fcarcity, enervated
" from four years of internal diforder; and on
" the brink of diffolution, from peftilence and
" famine, from battle and murder, and from
" fudden death !"—Mad wickednefs my friend
has fwept all away! Was there ever feen, ever
recorded, fuch inquifitorial examinations, fo
many oppreffive fhackles, fo many violations of
the moft facred places, fo many maffacres of
citizens?—No—France is itfelf alone!

LETTER

LETTER LXXII.

TO THE SAME.

THOUGH the enormities committed by these would-be-Republicans upon the species in general, absorb any acts of cruelty exercised on individuals, it is, I feel, impossible to pass over the fate of Madame de Lamballe, one of their most illustrious victims, without a particular mark of my attention,—the rather as she was even before the miserable revolution one of those sacrifices which the ribbald pamphleteers of France mangled without any just cause.

Besides a personal acquaintance with her myself, from which I am able to assure you of her claim to your respect, on the basis of many very generous actions; I am, also, in friendship with many who were in the habits of intimacy with her both before and since her unfortunate visit to the court of France: and although I cannot say with the Thane of Cawdor, that,

> " She has bought
> " *Golden* opinions from all sorts of people".

I can

I can very truly affert that by many of the wife
and good in her own country, and in England,
during her refidence there, her graceful manners,
her general charity, in France, and in many
other virtues which are held in reverence by
the common confent of mankind, will make
her death bewailed and her memory refpected.
Of the private failings which fome have been
fo fedulous to impute to her, fince her alliance
with her royal and unhappy friend, I cannot
pretend to fpeak; but it may at leaft be as
fair to fet all this down to the fcore of envy,
malice, or uncharitablenefs, as to that of
rruth. She has often been denied the virtues,
of which fhe was known to be in poffeffion by
all thofe who knew herfelf; and it is reafonable to fufpect fuch vices may have been attributed, (by thofe who knew her not,) the dark
fhadows of which never paffed her fancy or
her mind. To be the favourite lady of a Court
and of a Queen, of whofe favor fo many cour-
tiers were jealous; to be pre-eminent for beauty, grace and talents, are in themfelves frequent
objects of malice and ill-report, and not lefs
productive of hatred and envy, than of love
and admiration; nor lefs dangerous to the pof-
feffor, than to be the favourite minifter of a
king,—a title to whofe kindnefs, though made

out by high and meritorious qualities, with refpect to the fovereign who diftinguifhes and
rewards them, muft always become the fubject
of fecret malignancy, or open detraction, with
refpect to that part of the public, whofe vanity
fuggefts to them, at leaft an equal fhare of the
fame qualities, and who therefore make pre-
tenfions to at leaft equal recompenfe; and being
difappointed, become flanderers of courfe;
and flanderers not only of the faid favourites,
but of the faid kings and queens: for it is a
rule in defamation not only to abufe thofe
whofe merit is better rewarded, than the de-
famer's, but to involve the perfons reward-
ing it in the like cenfure. And I have often
wondered that you, my friend, who have fo many
attractions, and fo many friends ready to acknowledge it, fhould have had fo few enemies,
covert or avowed, to difpute your claims. I
muft confefs I am amongft the number of
thofe who regard perfons whom "*every body is
faid to fpeak well of,*" as fufpicious characters;
and I have, on nearer approaches, generally
found them over-rated, efpecially for the virtues moft lavifhly *bepraifed:* And by the fame
principle I always believe, and have as frequently found thofe people, who have a contrary report from this very officious Mr.

Everybody,

Everybody, who paints his angels and monsters larger than the life have few vices but
what have been given to them, and that the
particular vice most insisted on, is the very
one from which the party accused is most ex-
empt. Perhaps the truth of a character is
between that partial one given by a friend, that
inveterate one imputed by a foe, and that in-
sipid neutral one furnished by an indifferent
person, that has no interest to abuse, nor any
passion or affection to praise you. It floats on
my memory that I am repeating an observation
sent you in a former Letter ; if so, accept this
renewal of the remark, as an evidence of its
being a truism. But then where, you will say,
shall we look for, where find such a dispassion-
ate reporter, neither influenced by fondness,
enmity nor languor? And if we could find
him, would his portraits be agreeable?—even
if they were strong likenesses, they would be
without the essentials to render them touching.
We had better I believe yield up the pencil,
and ourselves, to friends and enemies,—if the
latter give the shades too dark, the former can
throw in lights to relieve them,—and if the
deadly colouring of the one is too violent and
too sombrous, the lovely tinting of the other,
and even the flattering touches, which fondness

works into the features, will soften away whatever appears too harsh and too heavy.

Applying this to the unhappy lady, who drew forth the remark, I am persuaded she deserves what has been said of her virtues, by her friends, as much as she *could* do what has been asserted of her by her enemies; while both must surely join in lamenting her fate; the particulars of which, blended with some account of her character, are as follow.

Her maiden name was Maria Teresa Louisa of Savoy Carignan; she married Louis Alexander Joseph Stanislaus, of Bourbon, Prince of Lamballe, President of the Council, and a Prince of the Blood. The Princess, who had formed her attachment to the Queen of France in the day of royal prosperity, resolved not to forsake her in the day of distress. A series of invitations from some of the first families in England, who laid a regular siege for her company, yet at last obtained it almost by storm, took her from her friend for a short time. Her reception in London, in the best circles, and at court, reached her affections, and won her gratitude, and pointed out a safe protection from the tempest that began to roll over the

house

houfe of Bourbon : but none of thefe had power to hold her from taking her fhare of peril anddiftrefs at Paris; to which city fhe returned, where a flight fummer friendfhip would have trembled to approach. She found the unhappy Antoinette, as fhe expected to find her, furrounded by many infults, many dangers, and hourly in expectation of more. And that fuch previous knowledge of her auguft friend's fituation was the fuperior magnet that drew her from the admiration of St. James's, cannot be doubted ; fince to be partaker of fuch dangers and infults, fhe quitted fuch admiration. In a word, fhe returned to Paris, while every body elfe of character, or of no character, were flying from it by ftratagem, and by every means poffible. The friendfhip of courts has been a fruitful, and a favourite theme of poets, who echo the afperfions of ignorance from one to another. Let that of the Princefs de Lamballe for the Queen of France ftand on record as a proof that fuch cenfures, even if they were admitted to be generally true, have their happy and honourable exceptions. And furely no vicious feeling could have, at fuch a moment, drawn the one Princefs to the other; fince there is in guilt that fort of daftardy which induces us to leave and efcape from its

 accomplice

accomplice in the searching hour of calamity, rather than hasten to receive our share; and, were any wanting, I should add this circumstance as a weighty one, in evidence of the purity of the principles which united Madame de Lamballe to the Queen.

But even in her prison-house she not only performed the gentle offices of a friend to the Queen;—the general duties of a friend to the indigent were not forgotten. Poverty and sorrow were never sent empty or weeping from this amiable Princess: and her benevolence was, even more than her beauty, the subject of admiration: the people of Paris, in a more especial manner, were the objects of it; and it was by the hands of that very people, in that very city, this illustrious visitor was to die; in a manner that would have been thought by justice itself, too cruel, too shocking, for the vilest criminal that ever disgraced human life, or the laws that protect it.

On the third of that September (1792) which will ever be enrolled in the history of the world, amongst the days that have most disgraced and stained it, this unfortunate and exalted woman, who had long been imprisoned in the Hotel de

la

la Force, was difturbed by the ruffians of the Republic while fhe was yet on her bed of ftraw, to leave that dreadful place for another. On her telling them fhe had no fault to find with her prefent place of confinement, they rudely anfwered fhe muft be transferred to the prifon of the Abbey, and that fhe muft go without delay; adding that her life depended on her obedience. She then begged of the leader of thefe ruffians, who was one of the national guard, to ftep afide with his myrmidons, while fhe dreffed, and that fhe would attend him. In a few minutes fhe recalled the officer, who conducted her through the dungeon to the light, the leaft rays of which that dreadful place excluded. They reached the prifon-doors, the other fide of which they had fcarce gained, when the unhappy Princefs found reafon for preferring the darknefs of her fub-terraneous cell to long-loft day light, which prefented her with nothing but an

" Affembly
" All made up of villains,"

whofe faces, hands, and garments were embrued in blood. The murderers were purfuing their defolations under her 'eyes. In fhort, it was in the middle of that tremendous day on which

x 3

affaffination

aſſaſſination was the moſt rapacious. Some of the fierceſt of theſe executioners pauſed from blood to interrogate her, to abuſe and menace. " Alas (replied the Princeſs) I have nothing " to ſay: whether I die a few days ſooner or " later, Sirs, is a matter of indifference to me, " ſince I perceive that I am devoted; and I " am prepared for death." She was then hurried to the tribunal, where the preſident, being told ſhe refuſed to anſwer queſtions, exclaimed, " Away with her to the Abbey." This was a ſignal for all that was to follow, and her executioners did not ſuffer it to eſcape. Scarce had ſhe paſſed the firſt ſtreet ere they ſtruck their auguſt victim ſeveral times on the back part of the head, with a ſabre, which was covered with blood—the blood of ſo many kings and heroes. Two wretches then took her arms, and obliged her to walk over the dead bodies. She fainted at almoſt every ſtep. In this ſituation they ſtripped her, inſulted her, forced her to ſtoop down, embrace, and kiſs the carcaſſes of the murdered citizens. Shocking to ſay, they then mangled her beautiful boſom, and, refuſing to ſhew her the indulgence of a ſpeedy releaſe, ſtabbed her firſt in every part they knew not to be vital. Unable to bear up any longer, ſhe ſunk on the earth,

when

when the wanton villainy of the rabble proceeded to the worst and basest extremities.
After which, being asked whether she would
yet save herself by cursing the French Queen
and family, she struggled even with death to
exclaim with energy, " No, never!—bless them
" now and ever !" After which, turning to
her persecutors, she said, " Behold I am ready."
Then, dropping on her knees, she cried, " O
" God all puissant preserve my friends, and
" receive my soul." It was in this pious moment the butchers cut off her head, from which
hung those most beautiful tresses, to receive
the blood. It was then stuck upon a pike, and
carried by one of the wretches, while another
followed with her lovely hands, and generous
heart, a third bearing her bowels folded round
his brutal arms, in a wreath of triumph, while
a fourth fastened her other members to a
hurdle, and drew them after him. It was in
this manner they paraded the streets of Paris,
pausing at every place, which contained those
who were known most to love and honour this
unhappy Princess. They first stopped under
the windows of the Duke of Penthievre, whom
they compelled to survey the mutilated limbs
of his daughter-in-law; and then proceeding
to the temple, they forced the royal prisoners

to gaze upon their friend and favourite, defiled with blood, and difhonoured in the duft,
and when the Queen fainted at the fight, the
heartlefs monfters mocked at her anguifh, and
aggravated it by every infult, which the facred
reliques of her friend could receive.   As the
horrible proceffion returned, they obliged the
paffengers, whether on foot or in carriages, to
kifs the head of the Princefs, and one of the
abandoned creatures, with a loud voice exclaimed, that he had feafted like an emperor,
having dined on the heart of a beautiful
Princefs.

But all thefe terrors were alas in the infancy
of their crimes, or, to ufe the language of
patriotifm, in the dawn of that *indivifible and
immaculate* Republic, which has fince reached
the fummit of its virtues, in the extirpation
of the King, Queen, Princeffes, and nobles
of the land.

In the melancholy annals of the world, there
certainly have been periods of time fufficiently
on the memory to leave an afflicting impref-
fion.   That of the Goths and Vandals, when
they came to take vengeance on the Roman
empire, or roving from their foreft homes,
when

when they sallied, like trooping wolves, in
quest of plunder, or of new settlements, was a
dreadful æra. The cruelty of Maximin, when
by a single act of authority, the whole mass
of wealth, we are told, was at once confis-
cated for the use of the Imperial treasury, and
the soldiers, hardened as they were in acts of
violence, blushed as the sacrilegious plunder
was distributed amongst them—this was another crisis, when, according to the historians,
a general cry of indignation was heard, im-
ploring vengeance on the common enemy of
humankind. Ancient tradition but too well
authenticated, multiplies the examples by hundreds, and were we to carry the survey to modern times, they would extend to thousands;
amongst the latter must ever be enumerated the
disaffection and dismemberment of the blooming States of America! But neither these, nor
any other in the crimson registers of tremendous occurrences, equal the enormities
which have been long practised by the French
UPON EACH OTHER: and taking history * from
the

* " What history never related, cried Robespierre, what romance never dared to imagine, we have done".

That is very true indeed Mr. Robespierre: You and your
indefatigable coadjutors have out-heroded Herod with a vengeance;

the beginning of the world to the prefent hour, the aggregate of offences, perpetrated againft God and man would juftify our pronouncing that the *moft* calamitous condition of the human race is to be dated from the æra of the *French Republic, during the abfolute monarchy of the tyrant Robefpierre!*

When we reflect that thefe are the times *before us,* that we *live in them,* that frefh reports, and experience of frefh horrors, reach our eyes, ears and hearts every day,—that the now * *fworn* enemy of the affrighted globe, is every hour either multiplying mifchiefs abroad, or at home, and that he does all that in him lies to deal deftruction through the land; threatening to involve all nations, to overturn all governments, laws, liberties, and religions,

geance: And to prove further that your famous expreffion, (in your famous manifefto of murder! your folem *proclamation of blood* delivered to your fellow citizens, November the feventeenth, one thoufand feven hundred and ninety three, by way of *Sunday* difcourfe,)—" we have heaped up ages within the limits of one fingle year"—to prove—great *leader of the unfaithful!* that this is alfo a truifm, you have contrived to turn one of the moft extenfive nations of the inhabited earth into a butchery!

* Liberty, reafon, and humanity, all France, all nations, and all nature triumph that he is now no more.

and

and in fine, that the growing evil fcarce gives more affurance of tranquillity to *you* that are remote, than to thofe who are nearer even than I am now to the immediate fcenes of action, what hope have we but in *Him* whom the moralift beautifully defcribes, as " holding " the reins of the whole creation in his hand, " and who moderates them in fuch a manner, " that it is impoffible *for one to break lofe upon* " *another* without his knowledge and per- " miffion".

Thrice happy he, who, in a general difafter like that which now defolates fo large a por- tion of the globe, and from the fpreading mifery of which no fecurity can be derived from riches, honours, poverty or innocence, happy is he who can fay with the man who exempli- fied at his death the precepts of his life.—" In " fuch cafes, I know but one way of fortifying " the foul; and that is, by fecuring to ourfelves " the friendfhip and protection of that Being, " who difpofes of events and governs futurity. " He fees at one view the whole thread of my " exiftence, not only that part of it which I " have already paft, but that which runs forward " into all the depths of eternity. When I lay " me down to fleep I recommend myfelf to his
.." care;

" care: when I awake I give myfelf up to his
" devotion. Amidft all the evils that threaten me
" I will look up to him for help, and queftion
" not but that he will either avert them or turn
" them to my advantage. Though I know nei-
" ther the time nor the manner of the death I
" am to die, I am not at all follicitous about it;
" becaufe I am fure that He knows them both,
" and that He will not fail to comfort and fup-
" port me under them."

May fentiments like thefe foothe every mif-
fortune that my friends, my readers, and my
countrymen may be called upon to bear !—
And may peace revifit the world!—a peace
founded on real liberty, but not upon frantic
licentioufnefs.

Such has all along been the private prayer,
fuch fhall now be the public wifh of your ever
affectionate friend and fervant,

THE GLEANER.

P. S.—How far the Divine Power, in the
wifdom of his fublime and inexplicable dif-
penfations, may fuffer thefe inftruments of
vengeance to proceed, it is not for mortals to
determine: In the mean time one cannot but
notice the apparent connexion betwixt the

late

late events and certain prophetic parts of the facred writings.*

Voluminous

* In a book called *Liber Mirabilis*, written by the Bifhop of Arles, who died in 543, there are a number of things foretold which feem to warrant our confidering the Author, not only as a divine but a prophet. Amongft other. fingular predictions refpecting his devoted country are the following.

" The nobles fhall be ftripped of their dignities and of their riches.

" The proper defenders and protectors of the kingdom fhall be conftrained to leave it.

" There fhall be as great an effufion of blood as in the time of the Gentiles.

" The church univerfal, and the univerfe itfelf, fhall bewail the deftruction and the pillage of one of the moft celebrated cities of the earth.

" The holy men fhall be driven from their fanctuaries.

" The virgins fhall be polluted, and fly from their monafteries.

" The church fhall be defpoiled of its temporals.

" The very heads of the nation and the holy temples fhall be defiled. The miftrefs of France fhall be left defolate.

" But the black eagle fhall appear, and the lion fhall come roaring from a far country.

" Woe unto thee once opulent city ! Thou that enjoyeft all things in proud abundance, thy fated hour will come ! Woe

unto

Voluminous have been the reflections made in the rise and progress of these horrible, these unparalleled events. The most obvious, yet the most perplexing to all reasoning and all order, is the consideration that such events happened under the eyes of those who created to themselves new laws, new authorities, and a new Constitution :—That, at the time when these massacres began, the self-erected Republican governors were in the full origin of their power; and that, to have put an end to such disorders, in the first instance, it would have been a very trifling exertion of such power to have prevented, if not, the bloody effusions of the tenth of August, at least those of the

unto thee city of philosophy! Thou wilt see thyself brought low!"

The above is given as a literal translation. I have not seen the original, and offer it you, by a German medium. How far the prophecy is fulfilled, the above faithful accounts, and others which must have reached you will testify: And well-knowing the gentle virtues of your heart, I may exclaim

" Tant d'horreur vous surprend! mais de leur barbarie
" Je ne vous conte que le moindre partie!
" Tout unite Paris; la mort sans resistance
" Couvrit en un moment la face de la France".

If this was true, in the days of blood which the Henriade has sung, it is more eminently so at this sanguinary period.

second,

fecond, third, fourth, and fifth of September, in the tremendous year of one thoufand feven hundred and ninety two; for, in each of the places where the lives of the citizens were taken away, the executioners,—or if they better like the term—the patriots—butchers— did not, I am inftructed from the beft authorities, exceed more than between thirty and forty, and thefe

" Made up of wretches
" That look'd as if all hell had drawn them into league:"

mercenary robbers, condemn'd highwaymen, hir'd affaffins, fellows efcaped from the gallies, girls of the town, and fifh women. Such were the original active difturbers of the public peace, who might have been brought to order with a flight effort of any one of the protectors of the new-rais'd republic : And to the blufh of all thofe who affumed a fhare in the infant commonwealth, glorious in its defign, but villainoufly mangled in its cradle, it is to be remembered, as an eternal monument of their difgrace, that there exifted at that crifis, even on thofe bloody days, an Executive Power, a minifter of juftice, a minifter of the interior, a mayor, a municipality, a department, a legiflative affembly, a national guard, a commander

mander in chief of that guard—in short, the forty-eight sections. There does not seem the shadow of an excuse to be made, either as men or magistrates for any one of them. If the carnage had been perpetrated in an hour, they might have said, we wanted time, for we could not under an hour have put our authorities in force. But that carnage continued three days, and three nights successively! Had the assassins been composed of an army formidable by their numbers, the legislative bodies might have said, we wanted strength to repel such a force of insurgents; but those assassins consisted of an handful of men and women: and during the whole time of their assassinations, the forty-eight sections were assembled and constantly sitting. The National Assembly had power to save two of their own members, M. M. Jancourt and Jonneau; why did they not extend their generosity or their justice to the rest? These their friends were rescued amidst the outrages of the populace who had proscribed them.

With respect to Revolutions in general it may be a curious speculation to trace their merits and their progress.

A

A reform in governments may be abfolutely
neceffary, and a revolution has fometimes fet
out well, * as unqueftionably did that of France,
under

* There is an inftance, which is at the fame time an example, and a very rare one, of a revolution *continuing* under thofe
principles : and if ever there was one act of dire oppreffion
more infamous than another, it.is to be found in the *Syftem of
Tyranny*, under which that injured country has long, and is ftill,
labouring.   We talk loudly of Afiatic flavery, of the hard fate
of the fable race, and pitying Europe, no lefs than the Gleaner,
feems to take the alarm on *their* affecting fubject; but againft
the property, liberty and lives of thefe poor people, (who certainly *have* undeniable and everlafting rights to their own country, and the fruits of their own induftry and inheritance, while
they trefpafs not on the inheritance and induftry of other
nations,) againft thefe often, and ftill mark'd victims of *defpotifm* there is form'd a cruel combination, headed by two of the
moft powerful *defpots*, both of whom by the bye are amongft
the loudeft declaimers againft the *French* Revolution, and by
way of fupporting this *illuftrious inconfiftency*, one of thefe powers
has one grand army in Brabant to affift in deftroying *tyrants,*
and another grand army elfewhere to exterminate a free and
generous people ! And his IMPERIOUS colleague in this celebrated *bucchanneering*, orders, and joins in, public prayers, fafts
and feftivals to beg of the God of equity to turn the hearts of
the French ; and then, at the tag end of this mockery, hitches
in, endways, another prayer for the fuccefs of her.arms againft
thefe Unfortunates.   The firft prayer is hypocritical, and the
laft is fincere ; but the fincerity has, if poffible, lefs " relifh of
falvation" in it than the hypocrify, in the degree that it is a
greater turpitude to be earneft in a vile caufe than fimply to
affect compaffion in a good one.   In this matter, however, the
affectation is intended to give a colour to the earneftnefs. When

under the fanctions of reafon, honour, public
good, and the caufe of religion.   But, nine
times

a plunderer wants an apology, (in a cafe of felf-intereft,) pity,
(I mean a piteous prayer, which is extremely cheap) about the
intereft of others—Pity, has a mighty convenient mantle to
throw over the fhoulders, and accordingly the plunderer always
makes a fpoil of it (amongft the reft of the pillage) to cover
himfelf, and his real defigns.   Unluckily, however, in the prefent bufinefs, the mantle is too thin : The noble perfonage in
queftion has, in the courfe of a long life and reign, had fo many
occafions to put it on and throw it off, juft as it became commodious or troublefome, that it is thread-bare in fome places,
and torn in others ; and though the fublime wearer is drefs'd
in it at this very moment, all the world can *fee through it*.

I have been at fome pains to *glean* the great perfonage above
mentioned, and have picked up fome curious anecdotes.   And
not a few on this very fubject, an *hypocrify in benevolence* ; the
public and private inftances of which will amufe you when we
meet ; and the whole of which delectable Gleaning is calculated
to prove that " *all which gliflers is not gold* ;" and that when a
foreign trumpeter (whofe breath belongs to the power who paid
for the trumpet, or commanded it to be blown) founds a vol-
ley—I can by no means call it a *voluntary*—about magnificent
prefents, jewel boxes, picture in brilliants, &c. each of immenfe
value, it ought to be told at the fame time, that in certain parts
of the world there are mines of fparkling trumpery which the
flave digs, and the *tyrant* gives away, juft as any would-be-
thought generous perfon in our own country might beftow
Briftol ftones and pafs them off for diamonds ! In doing which
there feems to be no great danger, as the receiver, conceiving
the gift a mark of honour, muft ftarve rather than difpofe of it.
But fome men there are who do not choofe to carry the point of
honour

times out of ten, it degenerates into a mere
perfonal quarrel, in which public good, and
every

honour quite fo far; and who maintain that the laws of felf-
prefervation are ftronger and more binding than thofe of delicacy. On this right of nature, it has come to the ears of the
Gleaner, that certain perfons have, in the laft extremity, *parted*
with their fuperb keep-fakes and love-tokens received from the
gracioufly imperial hands in queftion, and found like the juggler's trick :

> " Shake but the bag, and all feems fair,
> " The fingers fpread—and *nothing's there.*"

We know that in fome hands both abroad and at home, this
juggling art has

> " Rais'd both fortune and renown."

And that VICE perfonified in a *female* character was the beft juggler after all. In a ftory that I know, of a fword fet, or *faid*
to be fet, with brilliants of the firft water, according to court-
arithmetic worth 5000 florins, the ever honoured receiver
wanting bread, could, with difficulty, get enough to purchafe
ve and twenty loaves! and a fplendid ring from the fame ever-
honoured giver, eftimated at 2600 l. fterling, was pronounced
by a famous jeweller to have coft about 200l. In fhort, the
Gleaner has, with very few variations, had occafion to apply
every inftance of Slight in the fable, and thinks that the illuftrious juggler above-mentioned might exclaim with better preten-
fions than Gay's trickfter :

> " Who dares with me difpute the prize,
> " *In juggling I fubmit to none!*"

Y 2

But

every other generous motive is, forgotten, to
make way for the gratification of private ambition, avarice, and hatred. The original caufe
in the abforbing ferment of party is fpeedily
fwallowed up: what was principle becomes
paffion. Or what at the commencement was a
brave and daring conteft betwixt the governors,
for prerogative and the governed for privilege,
—a determined affertion of real or fuppofed
rights on the one hand, and of natural claims
on the other at length fettles into a mere party
madnefs.   And the infanity is contagious.
Every body catches it.   Men, women, and
children rave about it. The time of reafoning is paft, confequently the time of entering
its caufes.   It is then the bufinefs of the individual whatever be his party to follow where
that leads, to defeat or victory, to life or death.
In the feverifh paroxifm of indignation, each
perfon eafily perfuades himfelf his quarrel is
juft; every angry man imagines he has a good

reafon

But then this perfonage has the reafon to give which triumphant
vice herfelf made ufe of, and every fubordinate trickfter, crown'd
or uncrown'd, might obferve

> " How practice has improv'd her hand,
> " But now and then *we* cheat the throng!
> " *She* every day, and all day long."

But it is a tempting theme, and I am breaking into my Corps de
Referve.

reafon to be fo; and the more we are wandering from the right, the more violently and inveterately we infift that the objects of our difpleafure and enmity are in the wrong: and in public as well as private contention the tranfition from generous ftrife to illiberal rancour is almoft immediate, the flighteft wound foon turns into a gangrene. Each perfon becomes odious to one party and honoured by the other, as he gives proof of fteadinefs to his own caufe. The maffacre is called patriotifm on the one hand, and loyalty on the other, and very frequently the object firft in contention, like the fquabble betwixt the two dogs and the fhadow, is not worth having: but, meantime, it is fought for as fiercely as if it was the one thing neceffary to our comfort in this world, and our falvation in the next. In the end, the point is given up, and when accounts are cool enough to be reduced to rules of arithmetic, it ufually turns out, that, in point of damages, each party has fuffered in blood and money from thoufands up to millions, and on the credit fide we have nothing to fhew for them but units and cyphers.

On fair calculation, therefore, my friend, whatever advantage may be derived to pofterity,

Y 3

little

little is to be gained by the prefent generation:
Since, after every ten years war, (I mean a civil
war of courfe) fo much havock has been done
to property in general, and the paffions of
hatred have fo rankled in the heart, privately
fpeaking, againft friends, neighbours, and families (even in the miferable feptennial fquabble
about elections, this is manifeft) that I queftion
much whether there is a being on the face of
the earth, (except the ftock-jobbers, foreftallers,
agents, and other vultures in fociety, who
thrive in time of public calamity,) can expect
to be the better for it. The ravages ufually
drain the beft blood, fortunes, and feelings of
the country, for, at leaft, half a century: and
fuppofing there is then a regeneration, with
fome few benefits that were not before enjoyed, we fhall probably have loft many
that were better before the reform began.
Befides the melancholy confideration that
our pofterity will look upon the party and
perfonal love and hate, that has defcended
to them, as part of their inheritance, our immediate offspring will have been educated in
all the prejudices of our own particular party,
and the next age will lofe little or nothing of
hereditary attachment to one fide, and ill-will

to another, while remoter generations will trace the hiftory of their forefathers, and make what the politics or fafhion of the day fet down as rights and wrongs, the caufe of new murmurs, new exactions, new rebellions, new patriotifms, and, in fine, the fparks that will be found in ftirring up the embers and afhes of the old world, fhall ferve as a match to burn down the new. And, knowing, my friend, what we know of the difcontented, repining, fpirit of man, (knowing that even if God him-felf does not difpenfe his funfhine and his fhowers, exactly in proportion to our fancied good, we rebel) have we not the experience of feveral thoufand years that thefe fires will be kindled up in human fociety till the coming of that conflagration which

    " Lightnings with the meteor's blaze confpire,
    " And darted downward fet the globe on fire."

Far, however, am I from wifhing to " check the genial current of the foul" that afpires to liberty. 'Tis the true ftate of nature, the genuine fpirit of life, the health, beauty and fupport of fociety. We cannot even extend our ideas beyond the fphere of this world, and raife them to another without fuppofing that *perfect freedom* is the bafis of immortal felicity.

        A

A defpotic heaven is a contradiction in terms; indeed the generous ftruggles of human beings for liberty, when wanton cruelty no longer debafes her caufe, are but affertions of the divine part of our nature. Thofe jarring atoms which fhake a nation and which are, perhaps, infeparable from revolutions, give way to wife, wholefome, and humane arrangements; and when order is called out of that political chaos, though humanity muft ever fhudder at the dire effect of thofe convulfions which have preceded fuch arrangements, as tyrants feldom long furvive their victims, we muft venerate the " end while we never ceafe to deplore fome of the means by which it has been brought about."

In fine, applying thefe general obfervations to the particular inftance before us of the French people:

"— When the dread thirft of blood is o'er,
" And RUTHLESS RAGE SHALL STAIN THEIR CAUSE NO
 MORE;
" With honeft joy ALL nations fhall embrace,
" Their Gallic foes and own them of a kindred race."

——————

" FIRM AND IMMOVEABLE ON NATURE'S BASE,
" STANDS THE GRAND CHARTER OF THE HUMAN RACE,
. " AND HE WHO GAVE US LIFE, BADE LIFE BE FREE!"

a facred

a facred truth, and which, not only in the * work from whence thefe lines are copied, but in every other work of his hand, and movement of his heart, has and will ever influence the thoughts, converfation, or compofition, however imperfect in other refpects, of one who is equally a foe to tyranny and cruelty, whether in monarchs or multitudes, and a friend to liberty. Farewell.

* Humanity,

HUMANITY,

HUMANITY,

OR,

THE RIGHTS OF NATURE,

A

POEM;

IN TWO BOOKS.

A NEW EDITION:

CORRECTED BY THE AUTHOR.

WHAT I ventured abroad many years since under the title of SYMPATHY,—a poem, which, on account of the interests created in the heart, by the subject itself, was received by the public with so much generous warmth—was INTENDED to serve as a preliminary to what I had farther to observe on SOCIETY, or a prospect of the HUMAN RACE, under the combined influences of CLIME and GOVERNMENT, RELIGIONS, LAWS, and LIBERTIES—From these, the transition to TYRANNY was natural and strongly in connexion; and from TYRANNY, I felt myself called upon by all the awakened emotions of HUMANITY, to consider SLAVERY; but not only that species of it which consists in buying and selling our *Fellow-Creatures* in

Africa

Africa—BUT EVERY OTHER KIND, in EVERY OTHER PLACE. Views, therefore, of FREEDOM and BONDAGE, throughout the different parts of the globe, have been taken, as well from experience, as the beft hiftorical evidence.

How far the *entire Abolition*, fo warmly contended for by the fupporters of this meafure, may be confiftent with human policy, it is not my purpofe particularly to enquire. It is not the *name* of Slave in *itfelf*, which produces the great mifchief. An hired fervant in Europe may be as little at his own command, and deftined to as hard labour as a purchafed Negro in Africa; but the effential difference confifts in the one being guarded by the laws of the land, which fpread before his perfon and his property a fhield that defends him from every *abufe of power*; and the other is left naked and defencelefs to the " infolence of office."

HUMANITY requires that the RIGHTS OF NATURE fhould be enjoyed by every *Human Being.*

Being.   It is therefore againſt the ſhocking barbarity,* the unqueſtionable cruelty, and the too well atteſted horror, growing out of theſe, that I ſtill contend.—An abolition of *theſe enormities* is abſolutely neceſſary.   For the reſt, whether the commerce flouriſhes or falls, is a matter of no moment to the Philanthropiſt: without engaging in the heats of political controverſy; without attending to the pleas of intereſt on the one ſide, or the ſallies of enthuſiaſtic zeal (though generous in its exceſſes) on the other, it is ſufficient to Him that the happineſs of the *ſpecies* in *general,* is

made

---

* I am glad, however, to have it in my power to obſerve, that we have not ſuffered the HUMANITY of the French and other nations to ſurpaſs our own, at leaſt in *one* of our iſlands, as the following authentic extract from the Jamaica Councils will atteſt, dated *November* 29th, 1787.

" This day the Hoaſe of Aſſembly went into a Committee on the Conſolidated Slave Bill, and continued ſitting upwards of three hours ; we underſtand, that by this Bill the whole ſyſtem of the law reſpecting Negroes, is entirely changed, a Council of Protection is eſtabliſhed in each pariſh, and many humane proviſions are introduced for rendering their condition eaſy and happy; it is alſo made felony, without benefit of clergy, to murder a Slave; a clauſe, which, to the great honour of the Houſe, paſſed without a ſingle diſſenting voice."

made independent on the tyranny of *particular individuals*,—that the laws of *subordination*, in the different classes of SOCIETY, should not violate the laws of *humanity*,—and that so much of *liberty* should be allowed to every man, as to feel a consciousness of his being a link in the great chain of the community; and that till by some act of his own it is necessary for the *good of the whole* that he should be considered as an outcast of society, he is, by the Rights of nature and of Reason, entitled to protection from insult, misery and death.—So far as the *wealth* can be reconciled to the *happiness* of nations, and the Establishments of Civil *Society* to the Rights of Nature, every lover of his country must subscribe: at the same time, as the *wealth of worlds* cannot justify the least wanton infraction of the *laws of Humanity*, whoever vainly attempts to support an argument for the one, at the expence of the other, erects a building which hath its foundation in the sands, and which must tumble into ruins at the slightest touch of Reason and of Truth.

HUMANITY

HUMANITY.

BOOK I.

FROM vernal blooms and many a fragrant bow'r,
The red'ning bloffom and unfolding flower,
From breezy mountains and the covert vale,
The gliding water and the whifpering gale,
From gayer fcenes where carelefs Fancy-ftray'd,
Bafk'd in the fun, or frolick'd in the fhade,
Ambitious grown, and touch'd by generous praife,
Now turns the MUSE to more advent'rous lays ;
No more fhe paints the tints of blufhing morn,
Nor hangs the dew-drop on the trembling thorn ;
No more the brook runs murmuring in her line,
No more fair Spring, her florid verfe is thine;
Farewell, a long farewell, to founts and flow'rs,
Far loftier themes demand her thoughtful powers.

Sublime Society! where'er expands,
By art or nature form'd, thy potent bands,
Thro' realms of heat, where faints th' expiring
          breeze,
Or piercing climes, where the sun seems to
          freeze;
In darksome caverns, on tremendous steeps,
In bowery forests, or in billowy deeps;
Where roars the gulph, or where the streamlets
          flow,
Or dazzling mountains rise of endless snow,
Soon shall she dare to wing the vast domain,
Thy awful power the subject of her strain.

But, ah! first kneeling at Compassion's shrine,
Her opening lay, HUMANITY, be thine!
Thee she invokes, oh! soother of distress,
Who with our kindness wove our happiness;
For as thy circling virtues round us move,
From our best *deeds* thy brightest *joys* we prove;
Oft as our neighbour sinks in sudden grief,
Thou wak'st as sudden to afford relief.

Oft as the stranger's bosom heaves with sighs,
The soft responses in our bosoms rise :

The

'The cries of terror and the throes of care,
The groan of misery, and distraction's glare,
Sickness that droops, disease that gasps for breath,
The howl of madness, and the shrieks of death,
Deep sounds of agony that most affright,
Dread views of horror that most blast the sight,
Dire as they are, like wond'rous magnets draw,
And own, HUMANITY, thy sacred law.

And oh ! 'tis THINE, when vital breath seems
    fled,
To seek the awful confines of the dead ;
Beneath the billow, tho' the victim lies,
Thy dauntless zeal the roaring main defies ;
Inspir'd by HIM, whose hallow'd touch restor'd
The darling son the widow's soul deplor'd,
Her matron bosom eas'd of dire alarms,
And gave the youth to her despairing arms,
'Tis THINE to plunge into the bloating flood,
Clasp the swol'n frame and thaw the frozen blood ;
Breathe in the lips reanimating fire,
Till warm'd to SECOND LIFE, the DROWN'D
    respire.

                Hark !

Hark! as those lips once more begin to move,
What founds ascend of gratitude and love!
Now with the GREAT REDEEMER'S praise they
    glow,
Then bless the * agents of his power below;
New sprung to life, the renovated band,
Joyful before their second Saviours stand;
And oh far sweeter than the breathing spring,
Fairer than Paradise, the wreaths they bring!
The blissful homage rescu'd friends impart;
Th' enraptur'd incense of a parent's heart,
Oe'r-aw'd, and wond'ring at themselves, they see
The magic power of soft HUMANITY!

When sovereign Reason from her throne is
    hurl'd,
And with her all the subject senses whirl'd,
From sweet HUMANITY, the nurse of grief,
Even *thy* deep woes, O PHRENZY! find relief;
For tho' the tresses loose and bosom bare,
And maniac glance thy hapless state declare,

                            With

* Promoters of that glorious Institution the HUMANE
SOCIETY.

With gentle hand *she* still supports thy head,
Beguiles thy wand'ring wit, and smoothes thy
  bed;
Assists thy roving fancy in its flight,
To crown thy airy sallies with delight;
An healing balm to thy warp'd sense she brings,
Till from her sympathy some comfort springs,
And joys which reason with a frown denies,
Her tender pity with a smile supplies;
In thy lone prison-house she bids thee draw
From the rush sceptre, and the crown of straw,
The mimic truncheon, and the love-knot true,
Full many a transport Reason never knew;
Ev'n at thy grated cell she oft appears,
She culls thee flowers, and bathes them with
  her tears;
The perfum'd violet or the blooming rose,
On thy hurt mind a transient bliss bestows; -
Into a thousand shapes the garlands change,
As fairy fancy takes its antic range;
Then while thy brows the fragrant wreaths
  adorn,
The roses seem to bloom without a thorn.

z 3

Yet

Yet not to woes confin'd, fair PLEASURE's song,
The reckless frolics of the village throng;
Ev'n as we pass them by in distant lands,
Thou mak'st our own, and oft we join the bands;
The sudden sounds of happiness we hail,
And swell the chorus echoing in the gale;
Gladly we pause, then blythe pursue our way,
While brighter sunshine seems to gild the day;
Slow from the jovial groupe as we depart,
Thy richer sunshine beams upon the heart;
Thus bliss is doubled, and thus pain can warm,
From thee, HUMANITY, both boast a charm;
We chear, are chear'd, now grant and now re-
    ceive,
And need, in turn, the comfort which we give.
Thus thy fair streams spread plenty where they
    run,
Yet bless the fountains whence those streams
    begun;
Although a thousand channels they supply,
Like the rich NILE their source shall never dry.

But Thou from whom these bosom'd comforts
    flow,
Thou equal Friend of happiness and woe,

Hast

Haſt ſtill ordain'd grief ſhall to crimes belong,
And keen affliction wait on ev'ry wrong;
Pride, hate, revenge, and tyranny, and ſtrife,
As they mix poiſons in the bowl of life,
Daſh their *own* cup, and impotently try
To break, *unpuniſh'd*, nature's *ſocial tie:*
Good is of good productive, ill, of ill,
Conſcience o'er both exerts her empire ſtill,
And this great truth ſhall ev'ry tyrant know,
THE WOE HE GIVES, SHALL BE REPAID BY WOE.

Is there a land where echoing Fame extends,
From her proud cliff to earth's remoteſt ends,
Where gently ſlop'd the teeming vales are ſeen,
Adorn'd like Eden's with eternal green,
Where ev'ry village glows with every wealth,
The ſhowers are riches, and the breezes health;
Where ſun ſerene beſtows the genial ray
But never ſcourges with exceſſive day;
Where female beauty ſheds her faireſt blooms,
And lovelieſt feature, lovelieſt grace aſſumes;
Darts ſtrongeſt magic from the potent eye,
Adorns the bluſh, and arms the conqu'ring ſigh;

Z 4

Where

Where ev'ry scene is prodigal of charms,
True courage kindles, and true glory warms,
Where rear'd to Virtue, Christian temples tow'r,
And melting Charity chastifes pow'r,
Conducts the naked stranger to her dome,
And grants the houseless wanderer an home,
Where equal laws their social mildness shew,
Till mercy beams upon the captive foe?

O native Britons! here assert your claim,
Boast of your ISLE and justify her fame!
Tell, how her youth by sacred science led,
To all the soft'ning charities are bred;
How second childhood, like the first, receives,
From *her* the cradle which compassion gives!
Tell, how her palaces of mercy rife,
Large tho' the wants still larger the supplies;
How, her kind *GILBERT frames protective laws,
A faithful champion in the poor man's cause;
How, even now, intent on god-like deeds,
Thy wants and woes, O! POVERTY, he pleads:

Earnest

* Vide his Bill for the Relief of the Poor.

Earneſt thy oft-invaded rights to ſpare,

From the hard hand that would thy pittance tear,

E'en from thy lip, nor heed thy tear-dimm'd eye,

Thy ſpectre form, and pity-moving cry :

Tell how her * BIRCH, whoſe heart is form'd to

   blefs,

The ſad to ſuccour, and the wrong'd redrefs;

The raviſh'd morſel of the poor to ſave,

The work to crown her warm aſſiſtance gave.

Tell how her † POTTER aids the generous plan,

As bard her pride, her nobler boaſt as man :

Tell, how her HOWARD's ſympathizing foul,

The Saviour-arm outſtretch'd from pole to pole

Crutch to the lame, and viſion to the blind,

Tell, how ſhe ſooths the ills that ſcourge man-

   kind :

All this proclaim, till nations blefs the zone,

And happy Britons mark it for their own !

The

---

* This Lady is Author of a Benevolent Project on the ſame Subject ! and of innumerable other good works.

† Prebendary of Norwich, who took an active Part in inſtitu-
ting and regulating an Houſe of Induſtry in his own County.

The boaft is juft! yet why to *home* confin'd
Are the foft mercies of Britannia's mind?
Why, at her bidding, rolls the crimfon flood,
To deluge other lands in kindred blood?
Why are fires torn from children and from
      wife,
Dragg'd at the Car of Trade, and chain'd for life;
And why do human hecatombs expire,
Smote by her mangling whip and murderous fire?
Thofe ftripes, and killing fhrieks that rend the
      air,
Ill fated Africa, thy wrongs declare?

O! that my Mufe could mount on Nature's
      wing,
Soar like her "darling," her lov'd Shakfpeare,
      fing!
Then ev'ry word fhould "harrow up the foul"
And Afric's wrongs refound from pole to pole!
Thrice humble Howard, ah! do *thou* infpire
And breathe thy Godlike fpirit in my lyre,
For, all accuftom'd as thou art, to fee
Heart-rending fcenes of human mifery,

Ne'er

Ne'er did thy eyes fuch marks of horror trace,
As hourly agonize the *Negro race !*
Prove then the prifoner and the mourner's friend,
And once again thy virtuous influence lend ;
" So raptur'd notes, as if by Angels giv'n,
" Once more fhall peal the harmonies of Hea-
      ven".*

Unfeeling INT'REST ! dark, infidious power,
Whofe fanction'd arts wafte nations in an hour ;
Whofe mining frauds, more fatal ftill, deftroy
Hope's tender bloffom, and the fruits of joy ;
Thou, to whom all the coward flights belong,
Thy heart too cruel for each generous wrong,
For fierce Revenge, that fever of the foul,
Hate that defies, and Love that fpurns controul,
Or mad'ning Jealoufy when Reafon bends,
Or Zeal, extravagant to liberal ends,
Thou, who, for noble faults like thefe, too cold,
Whofe vices ne'er afpire, but ftoop to gold,
That groveling paffion of the fordid breaft,
Like Aaron's ferpent fwallowing up the reft ;
                              Theft,

* Triumph of Benevolence.

Theft, rapine, plunder, fraud, and murder, ftend,
Fell minifters! to wait thy dire command.
Yes thou, the founder of this impious trade,
Mad'ft *him* a flave, that nature never made,
Tore the poor Indian from his native foil,
-And chain'd him down to never-ending toil.

Say, Muse, from whence th' unnatural mart
　　　began,
This fordid merchandife, this fale of man?
From Egypt firft the Ethiop traffic came,
But mild its dawn, then flavery was not fhame;
While nature yet preferv'd fome generous right,
The yoke was eafy and the burden light;
Soon o'er th' Ægean waves the trade was
　　　brought,
And Greece receiv'd, and Rome th' infection
　　　caught;
Yet temperate ftill, no tyranny arofe,
Till baneful Luxury marfhall'd all her woes;
Conquerors, their captives, with a fmile receiv'd,
And whom the brave embrac'd they ne'er deceiv'd;

The

The battle o'er, they bade contention ceafe,
And foes in war were humble friends in peace,
The pledge was folemn, and the vow fincere,
The union facred and the compact dear.

But oh ! fair ATHENS, when the commerce drew
To thy lov'd fhore, the bonds yet gentler grew,
In rofy fetters were thy pris'ners bound,
And e'en the captive was with freedom crown'd;
Wifdom in peace, or valour in the war,
The faithful counfel, or the glorious fcar,
Attachment prov'd, or fervitude fuftain'd
With manly zeal, his liberty regain'd:
With his own hand the mafter loos'd the yoke,
And fcarce perceiv'd the flave his bonds were
　　　　broke :
Captive no more, he ftill purfu'd his toil,
And grateful vow'd allegiance to the foil.
Yes, claffic ATHENS, nurfe of generous arts,
Thine was the throb HUMANITY imparts;
While fhamelefs 'SPARTA butchering half HER
　　　　flaves,
Convulfive fhook, and dug untimely graves :

To

To all a tyrant's guilt and fears a prey,
Despis'd, abhor'd, and dreaded was her sway.
Thou too,. loft ROME, how galling was thy chain
In the dire times, when mercy fu'd in vain;
When cut to atoms was the debtor's heart,
That each hard creditor might claim his part!
And thou ! degraded GREECE, how fall'n thy state,
Once like thy splendid rival wife and great;
How dimm'd thy orb, when *Sages* could ordain,
The fanguine whip, and vindicate the chain :
When thy grave PLUTARCH, wife, difcreet, and
       brave,
In ftern philofophy could ftab his flave ;
And thy DEMOSTHENES, in thunders urge,
The fovereign virtues of the mangling fcourge ;
O blind to think, where fmiles and kindnefs fail
That frowns and ftripes, and cruelties prevail !

Hail * tender ADRIAN, firft on Rome's record,
Who drew diftinct the line 'twixt flave and lord;
                                   Who

---

* It muft be confefs'd there were ftrong fhades as well as lights
in the character of Adrian ; his Hiftorians all agreeing that he
wanted ftrength of mind to preferve his general rectitude without
violation; he feems neverthelefs intitled to the epithet (*tender*)
here given him, on the teftimony of thofe very Hiftorians, who
                                              pronounced

Who with sweet mercy temper'd awful power,
While pity's angel hail'd th' auspicious hour!—
Thou too, * just CONSTANTINE, with gentle
    sway,
Bade all be free and all that God obey;
The fire from Heav'n a general lustre shed,
And the foul mists of superstition fled;
Fair Truth was crown'd, Dissimulation fail'd,
Sunk was the crosier and the cross prevail'd.

But ah! once more to stain the bloody shrine
And fell mankind, O PORTUGAL, was thine;
To thee ill-fated Afric owes her pain,
The scourge fresh-pointed, and the new-forg'd
    chain;

                    Thine

pronounced him affable to friends, and gentle to persons of
meaner stations; relieving them in their wants, and visiting them
in their sickness; in short, an Emperor, according to his own
constant maxim, not for his own good, but for the benefit of
mankind.

* The Justice of Constantine may be impeached, in some
strong instances, for his character was certainly composed of a
mixture of great vices and virtues; but the Page of History has
declared that after a public avowal of the Christian Faith, he
was just and indulgent to all Christians; and although he pursued
a scheme of Politicks that destroyed the Empire, he established
a Religion that continues to be the blessing of mankind.

Thine the bafe arts the fons of gold applaud,
The fmile deceptive, and the fnare of fraud,
Th' extended hand that chafes fear away,
Th' embrace that wins affection to betray,
The league of peace, in policy devis'd,
The compact broken, and the oath defpis'd,
To lure the heart all fmooth feductions try'd,
And the heart gain'd, difguife is thrown afide:
The plot avow'd, the promife boldly broke,
By the harfh driver and the galling yoke.

    Accurs'd Gonzales taught thee firft the art,
To fix this ftigma on his country's heart;
The dire example fpread with barbarous rage,
Thrift was the vice, and fpar'd nor fex nor age;
At length the traffic into *fyftem* came,
Th' infection fpread, till Britain caught the
      flame;
Detefted Hawkins arm'd his pirate hoft,
And wolfe-like prowl'd on Guinea's fated coaft;
Force, fraud, and flattery, were by turns employ'd,
O fhame! till twice ten millions were deftroy'd.
Chriftians taught favages new modes of ftrife,
And burft afunder all the ties of life;

Chriſtians taught ſavages to worſhip gold,

Till, for their idol, ſons and ſires were ſold :

Till ſleeping tribes at midnight's hour were
    caught,

And ſeiz'd as prey, to *public market* brought ;

Till from the breaſt the babe was ſnatch'd away,

And children kidnapp'd in the face of day.

Next tawny SPAIN the ſhameful trade purſu'd,

Theft grew familiar, tyranny enſued ;

Commerce, like this, might well command *thy*
    zeal,

O patron of the agonizing WHEEL!

Engine abhorr'd ! from where with deafning
    ſound

The fatal Biſcay throws its foam around,

Ev'n to the ſteeps where Pyrenees aſcend,

And like a rocky chain their links extend,

The nations ſhudder'd as it ſprang to birth,

And throes unwonted ſhook the lab'ring Earth.

Curs'd Torquemada! who couldſt calmly bear

To hear the notes of anguiſh and deſpair :

With horrid joy, behold the flame devour

The hapleſs victims of thy torturing power ;

Deck them for facrifice in rich attire,
Then dance like Satan round thy feaft of fire.
Behold where fated FLORIDA extends,
His blood-track'd courfe the fell VELASQUEZ
  bends,
See, as he gains the chain-devoted land,
The fable natives hurry to the ftrand,
His failing caftle on the waves they view,
And gaz'd with wonder as it nearer drew;
But on the deck when *human* forms appear'd,
And peaceful fignals fmil'd, their hearts were
  chear'd;
Twas MEN they trufted, MEN who feem'd fo
  fair,
Cajol'd their faith, and lur'd them to the fnare!
For now as guefts they land, as guefts are led,
Thro' palmy groves to every Indian fhed;
The Spaniards there their glitt'ring ftores unfold.
The fhining mirrour, and the toy of gold;
Each gaudy bauble, cheats the Indian's eyes,
And tricks his paffions into fond furprize,
Suggefts, alas, a want before unknown,
'Till Europe's vanity becomes his own;

The

The ufelefs ornaments his fenfes fire,
And each frefh gewgaw kindles frefh defire.

To purchafe thefe what impious frauds were
    taught!
With their own blood was every trinket bought.
For, in their turn, as guefts the Indian bands
Fated, alas! to quit their native lands

No fraud fufpecting, mount the treacherous fhip,
Where, as in ambufh, lie the chains and whip,
Like nefted fnakes whofe poifons are enroll'd
Mid'ft wreaths of flowers, in many a fhining
    fold;
The faithlefs Spaniard leaves the plunder'd fhore,
The fraud fucceeds, and freedom is no more.
Then o'er th' affrighted waves is heard the yell
Of mingled thoufands in their wat'ry Hell,
In the dark caverns of the bark they lie,
Live to frefh horrors, or by piece-meal die;
Thus fhut from light, unknowing yet their doom,
The veffel proves a dungeon and a tomb:
While the bafe tyrant glorying in his fnare,
Mocks at the loud rebuke and dumb defpair.

Soon

Soon as the veffel bears the tribes away,
What horrors feize upon the trembling prey !
Ah ! hear the fhrieks of kindred left behind,
Roll to the wave and gather in the wind !
Matrons with orphans, fons with fires appear,
But vain the orphans fhriek, the parents tear:
The Spanifh robber ploughs the wat'ry plains,
And plants his cannon at the thin remains;
The flaming balls the wailing natives reach,
And added flaughter ftains the crimfon beach;
All, all is loft, yet ftill with generous pride,
Slaves fpurn at life, when freedom is deny'd:
" Free, ftill be free, loud echoes to the fky,
Dare not to live in bonds, but dare to die !"

Then oh ! ye Chriftian favages, declare
On what unknown prerogative *ye* dare ?
Peaceful and bleft, where rich Bananas grew,
And nature frefhen'd as the fea-breeze blew,
Where harvefts fmil'd without the aid of toil,
And verdure gladden'd the exuberant foil,
Where fummer held fo bountiful a fway,
Scarce claim'd their year the culture of a day,

The

The plants at twilight trufted to the earth,

The following morn fprang blooming into birth:

Grac'd with the bow, the Indians harmlefs ran,

And undifturb'd enjoy'd the rights of man :

The rights of man by nature ftill are due,

To men of ev'ry clime and every hue ;

Their arrows fought the monfters of the wood,

The chafe at once their paftime and their food,

Bower'd by th' umbrageous vine, they thought no
    wrong,

Now wreath'd the dance and caroll'd now the
    fong.

And oft fome fable miftrefs of the foul,

Prepar'd the banquet, and partook the bowl :

Love's captive only wore fair beauty's chain,

And pleas'd fubmitted to the blifsful pain.

If giant Power confers this wanton fway,

Subdues the ftrong, and makes the weak obey,

Does power give Right? beware that dangerous
    plea,

Perchance, fuch power may fpread its right to
    thee.

The flave once ftronger than thyfelf, fhall ftand,
And feize the fceptre of ufurp'd command;
Arm'd with thy iron fcourge fhall bid thee toil,
Scar thy white fkin, and chain thee to the foil:
Thy fpirit fainting in the glare of day,
Shall bid thee naked brave the Syrian ray,
Thy fcorn retort, retaliate all thy rage,
Wear out thy youth, and murder thee in age;
Tear from thy fetter'd arms thy child and wife,
And blaft the budding promifes of life;
Repay, in turn, each ftroke thy bafenefs gave,
And make THEE feel what 'tis to be a Slave.

Ah! falfe as fatal! to the Weak and Strong,
Th' inherent rights of nature ftill belong:
No partial principles the juft impel
To thinking wifely, or to acting well;
And liberty, of all mankind the caufe,
Becomes a forfeit *only* to the laws,
Thofe facred compacts which like links fuftain,
Connecting parts of the great focial chain:
And while, with thefe, no member is at ftrife,
As full the right to liberty as life:

Avaunt

Avaunt affertors of *fuperior* right,
And vain diftinctions betwixt *black* and *white*.
Firm and immovable on nature's bafe,
Stands the grand charter of the human race;
And HE who gave the bleffing gave it free:
Life were a curfe if robb'd of Liberty!

 Whence then this wond'rous difference in our
  race?
Come crefted Pride, and thy diftinction trace:
Lo, from th' Equator to the northern pole,
Tho' colours change, unchangeable the foul!
If juftly bought the man of *deepeft* die,
By equal laws the *next in fhade* we buy;
So, foft'ning on, till fcarce a tint between
The haughty lord and humble flave is feen;
Springs the vain boaft from thy fuperior WHITE,
Vain prepoffeffion of thy partial fight?
Beware, fallacious reas'ner, left the North
His *whiter* rival fends indignant forth!
Ah! rather, blufhing *hide* thy fnowy fkin,
For know thy flave paints white the fire of *fin*;
But darker than *himfelf* he draws the Pow'r,
The fovereign *good* his fable race adore;

A A 4

Thy

Thy cruelty has taught him to defpife,
Like hell, *thy* hue, his *own*, like heav'n to prize.

NATURE and HABIT, human kind controul,
The needle one, and one th' attractive pole;
And what, in Europe, we a grace may call,
Is found in Africa no grace at all;
And what abhorr'd deformity we name,
In many a climate dignifies with fame.

Survey the various globe from fhore to fhore,
Weigh MANNERS, CUSTOMS, and be proud no
    more;
Obferve how all to fix'd opinion bow,
Or fond caprices, which no ftandards know;
Thou, who would'ft fix her to thy pallid face,
Behold her beauty fhift the ever changeful grace:
Here BEAUTY proudly boafts the length'ning
    head,
There on the fhoulders bids it broadly fpread:
Here fmalleft gems muft grace the fair one's ear,
And there the pendents large as logs appear;

Here

Here fee her afk the locks of fnowy white,
Yet beg the charm of teeth more dark than night,
Here muft the broaden'd eye-brow fhade the face,
There foftly curv'd the crefcent arch muft grace:
While here again, that crefcent arch muft part,
Ev'n from the root and yield to brows of art:
Here, BEAUTY loves the cheek fupremely fair,
There boafts the gafh and cherifhes the fcar.
In Britain, rofe and lilly muft unite,
While Damian's Ifthmus, claims the milky white:
The beard muft here e'en to the girdle flow,
There not a briftle muft prefume to grow;
Here the fwoll'n body; there the flender waift,
This wrap'd in filk, and that in dog-fkin grac'd:
Here BEAUTY triumphs in her wooly hair,
But waves in wreaths her auburn treffes there:
To grace the dames of Europe, fair they flow,
Long and profufe upon a neck of fnow,
In ev'ry curl a Cupid feems to lie,
To aid the conquefts of the fparkling eye.
The thickeft lip here beauty makes her care,
More foftly fwell'd, like dewy rofe-buds there;
The dazzling white is in this clime admir'd,
The gloffy black in that is more defir'd.

Feel

Feel humbly then, nor deem all grace thy own,
Nor think that *Nature* charms in thee alone;
The poorest native of the poorest coast,
Hath still his beauty, still his good to boast;
From earth's beginning to its utmost ends,
Proportion'd charm, proportion'd blifs she sends,
Exact division, but adapted still,
To what in different climes her children feel,
To what, when undebauch'd by man's desires,
Or fancied wants, neceffity requires;
Nor sparing, nor yet prodigal her plan,
With pois'd equality she bleffes man:
On the worst soil some heartfelt joy beftows,
Which the glad son, she there has station'd knows,
And what from us extorts the taunting sneer,
May to his fenfe an happinefs appear,
And the fond gifts which we indulgent deem,
To him an aggravated curfe may seem.

Thus kind is nature in her zone ferene,
But not more kind than in her torrid fcene;
Not lefs a parent where the frozen Power
Refides for centuries in his icy tower,

Where

Where the hoar monarch in his veft of fnow,
Afcends the hills where funs refufe to glow.
Vain all difpute of colour, form or fize,
* In pride, in pride alone the difference lies;
Whence, then, prefumptuous man, deriv'd thy
    right,
And by what law does olive yield to white?
Their nature, origin, and end, the fame,
Why has not brown, black, copper, equal claim?
Tho' fhifting colours like their parent earth,
Alike their fpecies and alike their birth.

If not in *colour* then, perchance in *fenfe*,
In the *foul's* power, may lie the proud pretence,
Ah no! from Nature's hand all equal came,
Thro' ev'ry clime an helplefs babe's the fame,
The fame frail emblem of our ftate appears,
A weak and helplefs being born in tears!
If cultur'd climes refine on nature's plan,
They change the mode, but never change the
    man.

The

* "In pride, in reas'ning pride, our error lies."
                        POPE.

The human paffions ftrongly are imprefs'd,
In the untutor'd, as the polifh'd breaft ;
In the fwarth African that's bought and fold,
As the fair plunderer that fteals his gold,
Heav'n form'd his eyes to love his native hue,
And pointed all his appetites as true,
Thofe fable tints, at which with fear we ftart,
Are the lov'd colours that attract his heart :
Our polifh'd arts, refinement may beftow,
But oft enfeeble nature's genuine glow.

In polifh'd arts unnumber'd virtues lie,
But ah ! unnumber'd vices they fupply ;
Here, if they bloom with ev'ry gentler good,
There are they fteep'd with more than favage
        blood ;
Here, with Refinement, if fweet Pity ftands,
There, Luxury round them mufters all her bands ;
'Tis not enough that daily flaughter feeds,
That the fifh leaves its ftream, the lamb its
        meads,
That the reluctant ox is dragg'd along,
And the bird ravifh'd from its tender fong,

That

That in reward of all her mufic giv'n,

The lark is murder'd as fhe foars to Heaven:

'Tis not enough, our appetites require

That on their altars hecatombs expire;

But cruel man, with more than beaftial power,

Muft heap frefh horrors on life's parting hour:

Full many a being that beftows its breath,

Muft prove the pang that waits a *ling'ring* death,

Here, clofe pent up, muft gorge unwholefome
    food,

There, render drop by drop the fmoaking blood;

The quiv'ring flefh improves as flow it dies,

And Lux'ry fees th' augmented whitenefs rife;

Some gafh'd and mangled feel the torturer's art,

Writhe in their wounds, tho' fav'd each vital part,

Afk you the caufe? the *food more tender grows,*

And callous Lux'ry triumphs in the blows:

For this, are fome to raging flames confign'd

While yet alive, to footh our tafte refin'd!

    O power of mercy, that fufpends the rod!

O fhame to man, impiety to God!

Thou polifh'd Chriftian, in th' untutor'd fee,

The facred rights of fweet HUMANITY.

Thine

Thine is the World, thy crimson spoils enjoy,
But let no *wanton* arts thy soul employ,
Live, tho' thou do'st on blood, ah! still refrain,
To load thy victims with *superfluous* pain;
Ev'n the gaunt tyger, tho' no life he saves,
In generous *haste* devours what famine craves;
The bestial paw may check thy human hands,
And teach *dispatch* to what thy want demands,
Abridge thy sacrifice, and bid thy knife,
FOR HUNGER KILL, BUT NEVER SPORT WITH LIFE.

Relief appears as the Muse shifts her place,
To where pure manners bless the gentlest race;
Lo, where the BRAMINS pass their blameless life,
Free from proud culture, free from polish'd strife
To man, brute, insect, nature's constant friends,
The heart embraces and the hand extends:
See the meek tribe refuse the worm to kill,
No murder feeds them, and no blood they spill;
But crop the living herbage as it grows,
And quaff the living water as it flows,
From the full herds, the milky banquet bear,
And the kind herds repay with pastures fair;

From

From fanguine man, they drive the game away,
From fanguine man they fave the finny prey,
The copious grain they fcatter o'er the mead,
The bird to nourifh and the beaft to feed,
The flowers their couch, their roof the arching
    trees,
And peaceful nights fucceed to days of eafe.

O! thou proud Chriftian, aid fair nature's
    grace,
And catch compaffion from the Bramin race:
Their kind extremes, and vegetable fare,
Their tender maxims, all that breathe to fpare,
Suit not thy cultur'd ftate, but *thou* fhouldft know,
Like them to fave unneceffary woe;
Like them to give each generous feeling birth,
And prove the *friend* not *tyrant* of the earth.

O fweet HUMANITY! might pity fway,
All, all like Bramins would thy voice obey;
All need, alas! thy tender help below,
To heighten rapture and to folace woe.
One leans on all, for aid, not all on one,
What worm fo feeble as proud man alone?

The

The veriest giant, by himself is found,
Frail as the reed that every breeze can wound,
But even the pigmy with associates join'd,
Strong as the oak, can brave the rudest wind;
The Social Passion opens with our breath,
Pursues thro' life, and follows us to death.

See, as yon infant lull'd in slumber lies,
How the fond mother to its cradle flies,
Soft on her faithful breast reclines its head,
Her faithful breast its banquet and its bed:
Tho' many a suffering for its sake she bore,
They all but serve to make her love it more,
For soon a *kindred* passion *equal* burns,
The parent's tenderness the child returns,
Runs by her side, or struggles to her knee,
And owns the touch of fair HUMANITY:
The child arrived at man, the parent lies,
Sick'ning at life, in haste her offspring flies,
And when, at length, the mother yields to fate,
Stretch'd round her breathless form the affections
        wait;
In mute distress, and with uplifted hands,
The child she cradled, at her coffin stands,

6   Ivokes

Invokes her fpirit to affuage the woe,

And teach him patience to endure the blow;

Bleffes the holy fhade which gave him birth,

Moves to the grave, and views the opening earth;

A filial fhudder thro' his frame he proves,

As the duft falls upon the duft he loves:

Then, as the time fteals on with thief-like power,

And brings to *him* the all-fubduing hour,

Himfelf, ere this a parent, foon fhall prove

The foft'ning offices of *filial* love,

Soon thofe who owe *him* life fhall weeping bend,

And his attracting couch as fondly tend,

Watch his dim'd eye, obferve his changing cheek,

And drink his dying breath to hear him fpeak,

As fainted founds of oracles divine,

His lateft accents in their hearts enfhrine;

Thus fhall he *feel* the tendernefs he *gave*,

And equal tears fall faft upon his grave.

Tyrants o'er brutes with eafe extend the plan,

And rife in cruelty from beaft to man;

Their fordid policy each crime allows,

The flefh that quivers and the blood that flows,

The furious ſtripes that murder in a day,
Or torturing arts that kill by dire delay:
The fainting ſpirit, and the burſting vein,
All, all are reconcil'd to Chriſtian gain.

In cold barbarian apathy behold,
Sits the ſlave-agent bending o'er his gold;
That baſe contractor for the chain and rod,
Who buys and ſells the image of his God.
Callous to ev'ry touch that nature lends,
The bond that ties him to his kind he rends,
Robber at once and butcher of his ſlaves,
Nor grief, nor ſickneſs, age, nor ſex he ſaves,
But plung'd in traffic, coldly can debate,
The parent's deſtiny, the infant's fate;
The teeming mother of her hope deſpoil,
And poiſe the gains of child-birth or of toil;
The ſighs and groans which ſpring from both he
　　　ſpurns,
For life or death 'tis gold the balance turns.

* O! Pride and Avarice of deluded fools,
Deſpotic maxims taught in foreign ſchools!
　　　　　　　　　　　　　　Where

* Although in conformity to the change in the *time*, the
　　　　　　　　　　　　　　　　　　Author

Where late the fcience of a flave was taught,
To check the growth of every generous thought;
Where one proud mortal own'd the fubject;
        breath,
Whifpers were treafon, and a word was death,
Tenets like thefe to polifh'd † France belong,
For all fhe licens'd was the dance and fong !
The hands were fetter'd tho' the feet were free,
And clos'd the lips in dread of tyranny :
The poor, proud fubject, ftill was idly gay,
Skipp'd off his thoughts, and humm'd his cares
        away;
As the cag'd bird tho' pris'ner till it die,
Will fometimes fing altho' it may not fly.
Thy tree, O LIBERTY! forbade to tafte,
A Frenchman's richeft genius ran to wafte :

B B 2

Oft

Author has chang'd the *tenfe* in this Apoftrophe, he trufts he fhall
not be underftood as intimating that the late good and unhappy
Louis XVI. was a tyrant. The tyranny was then in the Conftitution, and fatally for him the public Indignation broke out during
his mild, and perhaps too merciful reign.

† See the Note inferted at the clofe of this, and the next
apoftrophe.

Oft were the feeds of freedom in his foul,
But none could fpring amid fuch hard controul :
In life's frefh morn if chance they dar'd to fhoot,
The bud fcarce peep'd ere Power deftroy'd the
      root.
Ah what can profper in a flavifh foil,
Save ftinted fhrubs unworthy of the toil,
Like pallid fweets of ineffectual May,
That faintly bloom and wither in a day.
Not fo the plants which LIBERTY beftows,
That in our Albion's favor'd garden grows;
There lifts the oak its top into the fkies,
While with glad heart the Briton fees it rife,
Uninjur'd there, for ages fhall it ftand,
Nor ever quit it but to guard the land : .
Then on the deep in gallant pomp it moves,
To ferve that freedom which its country loves.

    Oh! ever fail, fair Bark, upon thy waves,
Still guard thy England, from a realm of flaves :
Oh ! ever flow, fair Sea, to guide our coaft,
Still to divide us from yon abject hoft ;
                And

And fwell ye Cliffs that canopy our ftrand,
To frown indignant on that fervile land;
That land of mutes, of one proud Lord the prey,
A clime where to be dumb is to obey,
Unheard, unfeen, where wretches meet their
    dooms,
For whom no tear muft dare to bathe their
    tombs,
Conceal'd the parent's pang, the lover's fighs,
Baftiles for ever frown before their eyes;
Like thofe they mourn, down precipices thrown
Are all that venture nature's laws to own;
Buried alive, from youth to age they lie,
And ev'n, at laft, in agonies they die. *

Oh! hail'd by men and angels, be the hour,
Which clipp'd my Country's wing when ftretch'd
    for power!

B B 3

Which

---

* Such was the Character of France in the *old*, and though it
is not applicable to the *new*, EXCESS, either extreme, the Author
confiders as *equally fatal* to that Rational Liberty he wifhes to
fee eftablifhed amongft Human Beings.

Which taught the monarch where his rights
　　should end,
And to what point the subjects should extend;
Bade the encroacher know his proper sphere,
Or for each wrong the monarch subject fear.
Once Kings controul'd the law, in infant times,
Plunder'd at will, nor answer'd for their crimes,
Freedom's fair system snaps the tyrant's chains,
Corrects his nature, and his rage restrains.

As the small acorn to a forest grows,
By gradual steps Britannia's glory rose,
Mark by what stern varieties of fate,
Terrors of war, and anarchies of state,
What direful griefs by foreign fury bred,
Rivers of blood, and mountains of the dead,
She past, advent'rous, ere her wrongs were o'er,
Complete her triumphs, and confirm'd her pow'r.

Behold the painted natives of our isle,
Rough as the coast, uncultur'd as the soil;
Half-naked and half-cover'd see them go,
For sport or war accouter'd with the bow,

3

The

The plumy helmet nodding on the head,
And the loose skin across the shoulders spread,
A rude Society without a plan,
Above the brute, yet scarce arriv'd at man;
But then, e'en then was felt the patriot flame,
And from these sparks our noon-tide radiance
    came;
To guard the huts that stretch along the strand,
Arm'd with the scythe and wicker shield they
    stand,
The chariot mount, or leap upon the ground,
And shout victorious to the trumpet's sound.
The hardy Chiefs e'en Romes proud Host defy,
For Britain conquer, or for Britain die.

Thus, in the earliest hour of England's morn,
A Briton's hate of tyranny was born!
Abhorrence sacred, to repel the hand,
That dar'd to wrong the charter of the land.
Hence rose our liberties, and hence our laws,
The Good was common, common was the Cause
Yet, conflicts, murders, massacres ensu'd,
And many a Saxon, Danish sword embrued

In

In Englifh blood, and many a monarch's life,
And many a Monk's, fubmitted to the ftrife,
Ere Laws were fix'd, as *now* fublime they ftand,
The fhield, the fpear, and buckler of the land :

  At length bloom'd forth, diffufing all their
    charms,
The arts of peace more ftrong than thofe of
    arms ;
Like mifts difperfing at the dawn of day,
Barbaric Ignorance refin'd away.
The fword was fheath'd, the trumpet heard no
    more,
And the Lyre tried its humanizing power,
Religion came the Idol to explode,
And rear'd her Altar to the Living God.
In place of Deities with frowns pourtray'd,
Cherubs appear'd with heaven-born fmiles array'd.
Hence wife, and potent, aweful, and humane,
The Chriftian Syftem holds the guideing rein ;
Prop of HUMANITY, and feen from far,
Bright as the luftre of the morning ftar.

Thrice

Thrice hail! thou * hero of the Saxon line,
Britannia's LAWS, Britannia's FREEDOM's thine!
Enrich'd by Nature, and adorn'd by art,
Thine were the varied powers of head and heart,
Thine, by a kind felicity of fate,
The reconcil'd extremes of *Good* and *Great,*
Conduct with Courage, thought with action
   join'd,
And all the Virtues temper'd and combin'd;
Ardent in war, in gentle peace ferene,
Wife in the public, as the private fcene;
Coolnefs to plan, and vigour to purfue,
And born to mould a rugged ftate anew,
Whate'er Philofophy has drawn fublime,
Or poets fung, in all the pride of rhime;
Whatever hiftory of good has giv'n,
The Boaft of nature and the fmile of Heav'n,
Adorn'd thy youth, and to complete the plan,
And give the perfect model of a man,
Nature beftow'd each fafcinating grace,
The princely ftature and attracting face,
Then, in the nobleft light her work to bring,
In times of trial, ftamp'd thee for a King!

Scarce

* Alfred.

Scarce shone the crown upon thy princely head,
Ere rapine paus'd, and foul disorder fled;
And when compell'd to quit the regal seat,
Still, like thyself, was sought the soft retreat;
Veil'd by the shepherd cot and clown's attire,
Still glow'd within thee all the patriot's fire:
Dismiss'd the regal pomp, its train resign'd,
No fate could sink the *monarch in thy mind*;
The kingly glories *there* their state maintain'd,
There, unsubdu'd, majestic Virtue reign'd;
Expiring LIBERTY engag'd thy care,
For her to heav'n still breath'd thy fervent prayer:
Beneath the humblest shed she fill'd thy breast,
The humblest shed, ennobled by the guest,
There, while th' unconscious neat-herd toil'd and
　　sung,
The dart was pointed and the bow was strung;
Then, while thy country's foes repos'd supine,
Again in arms the Foe beheld thee shine,
Th' Invaders soon a Conqueror allow'd,
And every haughty Lord to ALFRED bow'd!
To Arts as Arms thy Genius led the way,
And the glad Olive mingled with the bay;

Of

Of focial Life, too, thine the faultlefs plan
Foes warm'd to friends, and man acknowledg'd
    man,
Fair Times ! 'when monarchy was happinefs,
When Rule was Freedom, and when Power
    could blefs !

'Twas thine to call where'er the atoms lay
The Rights of honeft Nature into day;
'Twas thine, O royal architect! at length,
To give her Charter, beauty, foftnefs, ftrength;
'Till on a firm foundation Freedom ftood,
And Reafon faw that all was fair and good.

END OF THE FIRST BOOK.

HUMANITY.

B O O K II.

PROUD of the contraſt, with indignant lay,
Once more O Muſe, to Gallia bend thy way;
Explore yon Cavern, frowning on the fight,
Where one faint lamp ſends forth a ſickly light!
Through folds of darkneſs where yon wicket
  glooms,
Perfidious POWER has ſcoop'd the living tombs,
Along the filth that oozes from the walls
The ſlimy ſnail, with track aborrent crawls,
And oft, augmenting poiſons, from the top,
With ſullen ſound, falls ſlow the withering drop.
The peſtilential toad that ſquats below
Gathers freſh venom as thoſe poiſons flow;
* Here,

* Here, many a fathom down, defpotic rage
Hung human victims in the dreadful cage;
Here the poor Captive, torn from child and wife,
From youth to age, groan'd out detefted life:
Nor nature's fun, nor arts fupplying blaze,
E'er ftole one beam of comfort on his days,
Nor human form, nor human hand was nigh,
To footh the grief that gather'd in his eye,
Save one brief glance of man, as thro' the hole,
His daily bread, the filent goaler ftole,
No human voice beguil'd the endlefs night
That cruel fhut him from creation's light!
To footh a miftrefs wanton Louis gave,
To one who dar'd be juft, this lingering grave,
To one who dar'd a proftitute pourtray,
And bring his honeft Satire into day;
How finks the heart to pace this gloomy round,
How pants the Mufe to leave this tyrant ground!

But ere fhe turn, to Afric, let her fly,
Where flav'ry groans beneath the faireft fky;

To

---

* How does HUMANITY triumph in the annihilation of this impious manfion of defpotifm! on the firft fuggeftion of thefe thoughts, how little did the Author imagine the Triumph was fo near!

To defolated Asia, once the bleft
In every charm of lavifh nature drefs'd,
The holy fpot by many a prophet trod,
Seat of the faints, and fojourn of the God,
Where Faith her Chriftian temples rear'd
    around,
And blood of Martyrs fanctified the ground,
Where ev'n Redemption like a Cherub came,
And Revelation, fpread th' enlight'ning flame.

But oh! thou Land, of Heav'n itfelf belov'd,
What dire events, what changes haft thou prov'd?
How has time alter'd ev'ry charm of youth,
Since firft thou heard'ft the oracles of truth!
Difgrac'd the truths, which all th' Apoftles gave,
Thy Prince a tyrant, and Thyfelf a flave!
Forgot the Heavenly claims that once were thine,
Forgot the precepts breath'd from lips divine:
Vain all the fathers, all a Saviour taught,
And God expell'd for what th' Impoftor brought,

Ah! what avails thy medicinal floods,
Thy citron breezes, and thy palmy woods,
                     What

What tho' the Caffia breathes along thy fhore,
And trickling manna adds its effenc'd ftore;
Tho' gums balfamic in thy vallies grow,
And both the Indias in thy region glow,
Thine, tho' Olympus, dear from claffic fame,
And honour'd Hermon, a more holy name:
Tho' the tall Cedar decks thy fragrant fhrine,
And lofty Lebanon himfelf be thine,
From fair Euphrates ev'n to Jordan's wave,
Tho' thy rich Coaft the hallow'd waters lave,
And tho' thy fruits, voluptuoufly difpenfe
A keener relifh to th' invited fenfe,
'Tho' on thy flowers a bolder bloom prevail
Which fends more piercing odours to the gale,
And tho' thy fkies, yet falient and ferene,
Call fair Hygea to the tempting fcene,
All, all thefe bleffings a ftrong balance find
In one broad curfe that feizes on thy kind;

Nor this the Peft that oft has thinn'd thy plains,
O'er thy devoted land a TYRANT reigns.

More fell, more fatal, than thy torrid fun,
Fierce thro' the Eaft fee DESPOTISM run,

4   Frantic

Frantic before him move a fanguine band,
The ruthlefs agents of his murd'rous hand ;
Crouching behind, in dumb allegiance wait,
Nurs'd up in blood, his various tools of fate,
In varied fhapes of cruelty they rife,
To torture life, or hideous deaths devife :
Dey, Sultan, Signior, Emperor and King,
Chief, Vifier, Cailif, each inferior Thing.
Some, do his bidding in the noon of day,
And fome, at midnight, feize upon his prey ;
Submiffion, terror, chaftifement, combine,
To fink the abject vaffal to the fwine,
Below degraded inftinct Reafon falls,
And Man is bound like herds within the ftalls,
His fpirit dies fubdued by hard controul,
The ufelefs body moves without a foul ;
No fpark of heav'nly fire the mafs can warm,
Nor public virtue touch, nor private charm,
But general cowardice, by horror bred
Courage unftrung, and manly honour dead :
For oh! the dart, the gibbet, and the wheel
Are the leaft terrors that a flave can feel,
Of thefe the anguifh fcarce can rage its hour
Ere Death appears in foft relief of power,

Death, a kind refuge in the laft defpair,
But long a LIFE OF SLAVERY who can bear?

' Lo PERSIA's tyrant, with unnatural ftrife,
To pleafe a minion robs a child of life,
With favage rage can blind the firft-born fon,
And partial lift a fecond to the throne;
When the proud Sopha has confign'd to death,
Tis treafon but to beg a parent's breath,
The fentence paft, the *look* that aims to fave,
Condemns to equal fate the pitying flave;
Senfual religion aids the tyrant's will,
And blood for ever reeks along the fteel;
In dire fufpence, like Damocles's fword,
By a flight thread hangs life—a TYRANT's word,
Impofts and Edict vex the groaning land,
And ev'n the fountain flows but at command.

Oh haplefs Afia, while fuch horror reigns
What Britifh Mufe will reft upon thy plains.
Yet fhould fhe fteer again to AFRIC's fand,
There too, fhe fees Oppreffion lift his hand,

Within

Within the tropics fiercer than the blaze,

That fires the earth, with iron rod he sways,

Ev'n from the fertile Nile to Niger's waves,

'Tis but a change of tyrants and of slaves.

O pride enormous! impudence of man!

But let not Britons imitate the plan,

Frame no false systems and then call them wise,

Or make distinctions where no difference lies;

Alas! full oft the European face

Masks a mind darker than the darkest race ;

The Negro's heart may be a purer shrine,

For thoughts devout O! haughty White, than
          thine,

Acceptance find more gracious from its God,

Than the proud master who uplifts the rod,

His prayer to holy KANNO more prevail

To the great SPIRIT whispering in the gale,

His pious vows to QUOJA 'midst the trees

Or high BASSEFO walking in the breeze,

These may more virtues and more truth impart,

Than Christian incense from a savage heart,

                          And

And the wild Tambour beat to idol shouts,
To heav'n ascend before the organ's notes;
Say, what the pomps of science or of prayer,
If the poor Indian's *fervor* glows not there?
In different forms tho' men the God adore,
Shap'd as the brute or painted as the flow'r,
As marble here, and there as feathers seen,
There the birds bone, and here the fishes fin,
Each, as it marks *sincerity*, shall rise,
And welcome find in the recording skies;
Shall more be cherish'd by the powers of Heav'n
Than less true worship where more aids are giv'n,
Than the mock homage of th' enlighten'd train,
For whom a Saviour liv'd, and died in vain.

A doctrine this too harsh for human pride;
Resort to facts and be the doctrine try'd,
With faithful hand, cull'd from th' historic page,
Proofs throng to proofs might vanquish Christian
        rage;
Oh! tyrant WHITE, forget awhile thy gold,
And every virtue in thy BLACK behold,
All that is honour'd, lov'd, or priz'd by thee,
In thy scourg'd Negro, blushing, shalt thou see.

Lo

Lo, as the Mufe to Anticofta fteers,
Mid'ft the wild waves HUMANITY appears!
Efcap'd the wreck, although their barks were loft,
Whole crews were dafh'd upon a favage coaft;
The coaft, tho' favage, there the Chriftians find,
Each God-like feeling in an Indian mind,
For touch'd by cries that pierc'd the piny wood,
The natives fought the margin of the flood,
Then as th' expiring Chriftians caught their view,
To human grief the generous Indians flew,
The focial paffion glowing in his face,
Thus fpoke a Chieftain of the fable race:
" Hafte children hafte, behold where brothers
        lie,—
" Rife ftrangers rife, the hand of help is nigh:
" Men, like ourfelves, throughout the globe,
        command,
" The fhelt'ring bofom, and the aiding hand,
" All, all are kinfmen of a different hue,
" Our faces vary, but our hearts are true;
" Ye poor white wanderers on our bounty
        thrown,
" Your griefs are facred and your wants our own."

c c 3

This

This faid, he gently to his Cottage led,
Smil'd on his guefts and yielded up his bed;
Then watch'd till morn, a guardian at the door
Blefs'd and was bleffed—*could a Chriftian more?*

To trace each VIRTUE thro' the fultry Sands,
Next Negro HONOUR all thy praife demands;
In CUJOE's generous foul it meets the view,
And darts a glory thro' his tawny hue.
A band of Chriftian pirates fought the fhore,
And many an Indian from their forefts bore,
To CUJOE's cot a Foe was feen to fly,
Pierc'd by a dart, and begg'd, in peace, to die;
But foon the Tribes purfue, demand their prey,
" Scalp, fcalp that wretch, they cry, in open day!
" CUJOE conceals the Man whofe blood is ours,
" 'Tis not our rage, 'tis juftice that devours."
Mean time th' exhaufted Chriftian gafp'd for
　　　　breath,
As Cujoe rofe, and ftopp'd th' impending death:
" My Friends forbear, the guilty feek and flay,
" Purfue the race that ftole our tribes away,
" May Ocean whelm them in the deepeft wave,
" The guilty punifh, but the blamelefs fave!
　　　　　　　　　　" Lo,

" Lo, this fick Chriftian on my faith relies,
" Of Gueft and friend, ah! reverence the ties !
" Here, in the rights of Friendfhip fhall he reft,
" This arm his buckler, and his fhield this breaft,
" This Cot his Citadel, and ere *he* die
" Here muft your hatchets fall, your arrows fly!"
Honour prevail'd, their vengeance dy'd away,
And fafe in CUJOE's hut the Chriftian lay.

Next, let us fpeed to yonder fainted plains,
By mountains fcreen'd, and crown'd with dulcet
          canes,
Where the mad Ouragan in phrenzy roars,
Affrights the Ifle, and defolates the fhores,
While many a rill and flow'ry vale between,
Smile in the ftorm and reconcile the fcene :
There fee a Hero of the Negro line,
Boafts an high FEELING, Briton, proud as thine.

The faithful QUA-SHI with his mafter bred
The fame their manfion and the fame their bed,
Together us'd in infant times to play,
Their friendfhip ftrengthen'd in life's riper day ;

                          The

The flave was trufty and the lord was kind,
To Qua-shi's care the property affign'd,
His labours clos'd, he took the tranfient reft,
Then chid the Sun yet loit'ring in the Eaft ;
Ere peep'd the dawn his daily toils he fought,
And daily wealth to his lov'd lord he brought.

Envy, at length, a poifon'd arrow drew,
Which wing'd with mifchief to the mafter flew,
Of dire neglect the accufation came,
And lo, the fentence paft for Qua-shi's fhame;
A public punifhment was now decreed,
And the next Morn was Qua-shi doom'd to
        bleed !
The injur'd Slave with fhudd'ring terror heard,
And at deep midnight fought his barbarous Lord,
Then wrought to agony, thefe words addrefs'd,
The poignard trembling at his Mafter's breaft.
" O Thou, whom no rememberance can move,
" Nor cradled tendernefs, nor manly love,
" Dare not to think that Qua-shi's foul will bear
" The public Infults which thy hands prepare,
                              " Think

" Think not the bloody Morn thefe eyes fhall
       view,
" Nor think for pardon that thefe lips fhall fue,
" No Monfter, no, my foul's above my fate,
" Scorns thy proud mercy as it braves thy hate;
" Thus Tyrant, thus, thy fury I defy,
" Live Thou to Shame, while I in honour die."
He fpoke—the Poignard fluic'd the crimfon
       flood,
And bath'd the Mafter in the Servant's blood.

If thou would'ft Negro TENDERNESS behold,
Seek with the Mufe the coaft where broods the
       gold;
A * Briton there—immortal be his name,
By pity's Angel mark'd with endlefs fame !
A Briton there, an Indian Infant found,
For favage rites by fuperftition bound,
The Negro King amidft the croud he fought,
And at the Sacrifice the victim bought,
Then to the Ship his trembling Charge convey'd,
While all the fable train with awe furvey'd ;

But

* Snelgrave.

But scarce the Babe was plac'd upon the deck,
Than loud was heard a female's piercing shriek,
" 'Tis he! 'tis he! it is the babe I bore,
" Whom savage Acqua from this bosom tore,
" Ah! come my own—resume thy couch of rest,
" And cling once more to this maternal breast,
" Blest be the hand, by Echo form'd to save,
" Thrice blefs the Hand that led me here a slave,
" Blest be the Author of these transports wild,
" And blest the power which has restor'd my
        Child!"
She could no more, but still the speaking eye,
Own'd the rich gift of sweet HUMANITY!

But when she heard her infant had been bought,
Ev'n as the flame its tender limbs had caught,
" O Indian God, Oh! God-like White, she said,
While o'er her sable cheek the crimson spread,
" All that a parent, all a slave can give,
" O God-like White, O Indian God receive!"
Kneeling she wept, then kifs'd her refcu'd Child,
While in her jetty arms the Infant smil'd;
Dances and Songs of Praise now struck the waves,
And one strong charm like magic touch'd the
        slaves,
'Thro'

'Thro' the long voyage obedient they remain,
Nor founding whip is heard, nor clanking chain.

Touch'd is thy heart, O Merchant of thy kind,
Does human Softnefs fteal into thy mind?
Rous'd is the fpark, too long reprefs'd by Gold?
Then bend thy heart to what we next unfold:
Now, while perchance the human paffions move,
O view the force of friendfhip and of Love,

In Negro bofoms fee thofe powers at ftrife,
Which form the blifs and agony of life.

ZEBRON and ZABOR of the jetty race,
Were firft in feature and proportion'd grace,
Bright as the Antelope their radiant eyes,
As the proud Palm-tree tow'r'd their equal fize,
Both wore alike the Tyger's fpeckled fpoil,
Brothers in drefs, in paftime and in toil;
Slaves tho' they were, ev'n Slav'ry had its charms
For ZEBRON's comfort was in ZABOR's arms,
And ZABOR fainting on the arid fand,
Was rear'd to Joy by gentle ZEBRON's hand,
By blifs united much, by forrow more,
A Negro's Fate they foften'd while they bore;

But

But Love, at laft, a keener pang imparts,
For fable ZELIA triumph'd o'er their hearts;
Her fkin of Ebony beftow'd a grace,
That far outfhone an alabafter face,
So thought the youths, with equal truth infpir'd,
With all their paffion, all their climate fir'd;
Each fcorn'd to ravifh, each refus'd to yield,
And Love and Friendfhip both maintain'd the
          field;
Devouring torments fpread the mutual flame,
But ftill their friendfhip, ftill their love the fame;
When beauteous ZELIA in their view appears,
ZEBRON and ZABOR melt in mutual tears,
Oft, both embracing, to renounce her fwear,
And Friendfhip feems to link them in defpair;
At length their conflicts, big with every grief,
And ev'ry paffion, fought a dire relief.
At clofe of day as ZELIA trac'd the wood,
The Lovers follow'd and before her ftood,
The wand'ring Maid too fatal in her charms,
Now fnatch'd to ZEBRON'S now to ZABOR'S arms;
The fondeft vows that ever Lovers fwore,
The deepeft groans that ever heav'd they pour,

Then

Then, with clos'd eyes, and heads declin'd, they
     dart,
The mutual daggers in her bounding heart;
Speechlefs fhe fell, her fobs their fhrieks confound,
They clafp the victim, and they kifs the wound,
Then raife the poignards ftreaming in her blood,
And with their own augment the crimfon flood.

Thus Negro Virtues, Negro Frailties fhine,
Say, *fairer* Savage, do they yield to thine!
Their ardent virtues emulate thy own,
Their errors are the errors of their zone;
And art thou ftill Supreme of human race,
Still boafts thy Nature the imperial grace?
Ah no! without the aid of borrow'd arts,
Worth, greatnefs, goodnefs, elevate *their* hearts,
The tow'ring fpirits in their bofoms move,
They hate with vigour, as with force they love,
Together leagu'd, till death they faithful toil,
And fmooth the wrong that chains them to the
     foil;
Still hand in hand their direful loads they bear,
Divide each joy and mitigate defpair:
Vivid

3

Vivid as Thine the fenfe of joy and pain,
Thrills in each pulfe, and vibrates in each vein;
When hope infpires, behold, as bright a ray,
Illumes their eyes and o'er their features play;
When grief affails, the tears as copious flow,
To mark the foft or agonizing woe;
When the lafh fcourges, or the pincers rend,
A fhriek as piercing from the heart they fend;
Ere the brave fpirit of the man is broke,
Ev'n with a Briton's fcorn they fpurn the yoke,
Love of their native Land, that magic charm!
Againft a hoft hath made a handful arm,
They love like Thee the foil that gave them birth;
And treafure up each particle of earth
Fondly embofom'd, ere they leave the fhore,
And kifs the facred relique o'er and o'er.

Muficians, Poets, too, by nature taught,
A fong fpontaneous burfting from a thought,
Swift into meafure fubjects feem to fly,
As tranfient objects tranfient themes fupply,
Each nerve extatic fprings to the rebound,
And every motion feems to paint a found;

The

'The fweet enthufiafm ev'ry grief beguiles,

And the fcourg'd Captive even in anguifh fmiles,

With thrilling paffion ev'ry feature glows,

So ftrong the charm it cheats awhile their woes.

Yet, who the Negro's *fufferings* can relate,

Or mark the varied horrors of their fate;

Where, blufhing Truth! fhall we their griefs
    begin,

Or how commence the catalogue of Sin?

Demons of torture! ye who mock at woe,

And fmile to fee the crimfon blood-track flow,

In horrid triumph rife from central Hell,

Th' inventive pangs of Chriftian growth to tell,

Oh! aid the fhuddering Mufe to paint the grief,

Which calls on death for pity and relief;

Oh! powers of Mercy, loofe that maffy yoke,

Oh! hold that Arm, for murder's in the ftroke!

Behold that axe the quivering limb affails,

Behold that body weltering in its wails!

Ah! hear that Bludgeon fall, that lafh refound,

And fee thofe wretches writhing on the ground!

See yonder mangled mass of Atoms lie,
Behold that Christian's hands the flames apply,
At the bare feet is laid that sulphurous train,
It Climbs the heart and burns into the brain.

Survey the triple horrors of their state,
Doom'd in each change to be the sport of fate;
Torn from their native land at first they come,
And then are thrown into the sailing tomb,
In wat'ry dens like coupled beasts they lie,
And beg the mournful privilege to die;
But Death, more kind than Man, oft brings relief,
Releases one, while one survives to grief;
The living wretch his dead associate sees,
The body clasps and drinks the putrid breeze,
Chain'd to the noxious corpse, till rudely thrown,
In the vex'd sea, then left a slave alone.
Ah! wretch forlorn! *thy* lot the most severe,
Assassination would be mercy here!
Methinks I hear thee cry, " Ah! give me death,
" Give the last blow and stop this hated breath,
" Oh! for a sword to waft me to the shore,
" Where never Christian White may torture more,

" Curse,

" Curfe, curfe me not with Being, inftant throw
" This loathfome body to the waves below!" .
His prayer deny'd, condemn'd 'midft flaves to
    groan,
The cruel Merchant " marks him for his own,"
The fcar by Chriftian cruelty impreft,
Smoaks on his arm, or blackens on his breaft,
The wattled oziers form his rugged bed,
And daily anguifh earns his daily bread;
Short food, and fhorter reft, and endlefs toil,
Above the fcourge, below the burning foil.

Soon with his fable Brothers muft he go,
" Doom'd to a fad variety of woe,"
Like harnefs'd Mules o'er Afric's dreadful fand,
In flow proceffion move the mournful band,
The length'ning files begin their circuit wide,
While on their limbs are galling braces ty'd;
Fraught with coarfe viands, fee the ftraining
    throng,
Drag the oppreffive caravan along,
The maffy iron and the direful log,
Their naked bodies ev'n in flumber clog,

An iron collar o'er each neck is paft,

And iron rivets hold the collar faft;

A tighten'd chain acrofs each fhoulder goes,

While the dark driver takes his own repofe;

At length arriv'd, the miferable band

Like the ftall'd oxen pafs from hand to hand.

Ye friends of Man! whofe fouls with mercy
          glow,

Throb not your breafts with fympathifing woe?

Fires not the focial blood within your veins,

To make the White Man feel the Negro's pains?

Beat not your hearts the mifcreant arms to bind,

Of the proud Chriftian with a favage mind?

Doft thou not pant to fnap the impious chain,

And rufh to fuccour the infulted train?

From fervile bonds, to free the haplefs race,

And fix the haughty tyrants in their place?

Make *them* the weight of Slav'ry to know,

Till their hard natures melt at focial woe,

Nor till they humanize to focial men,

Would ye reftore them to their rights again!

                              Oh!

Oh! FREEDOM, facred Goddefs! who infpires
Th' untutor'd Savage with fublimeft fires,
Oft have the Chiefs o'er lifted troops prevail'd,
And Nature's warriours fped where armies fail'd;
While the bought foldier in his trade of death,
With fordid contract bargains for his breath,
While the brave Indian from his fetters broke
Ev'n Famine braves to feel no more the yoke :

What will not FREEDOM's Heav'n defcended
    fire,
In cultur'd, or untutor'd Souls infpire?
The RIGHTS OF NATURE and of GOD to fave,
Men fcoop the rock and build upon the wave,
Explore the barren fand, the marfhes drear,
And the free Cottage in the defert rear,
Delight in hollow of fome cave to dwell,
Or dig thro' Earth the independent cell.

See where MARINO lifts her craggy brow,
Half hid in clouds, and cover'd half with fnow,
Beyond the Appenines, there Freedom reigns,
And fcorns the thraldom of Italian plains;

D D 2

There

There fee untax'd the proud republic grow,
And fpurn the bondage of the vales below,
Clofe on the liberal Heav'n behold it ftands,
And looking fcorn on tributary lands,
What, tho, thofe tributary lands difplay
The bloomy fragrance of perpetual May,
Like the coy fenfitive each lovely flower,
Still feems to tremble at the touch of power.
Bleft be the good Dalmatian's generous earth,
·Which boafts, Oh ! Rome, than thine a nobler
　　　birth,
Thou, but the refuge of a robber band,
To his devotion rais'd the folded hand,
And many a century his little ftate
Has ftood the ftorms of Fortune and of Fate,
Whilft thy funk cities, once the boaft of Fame,
Are mark'd by Ruins, and an empty name :
What tho' no ftreams here lave the fcant domain
But melting fnows and refervoirs of rain ;
Tho' hillocks fcatter'd round the parent hill,
At once thy pride and penury reveal,
A narrow circuit, and a labour'd foil,
Which yields fubfiftance but to endlefs toil,

Dear

Dear is the grain that decks the Mountain's fide,
Beyond the harveft of Italia's pride.

In this fmall fpot behold one path alone,
Where jealous freedom guides us to the town,
There, entering, arts and arms and trade we
    view,
For ev'ry Citizen's a Soldier too ;
There laws are form'd on patriot Wifdom's plan,
For each enjoys the honeft rights of Man ;
There all for general happinefs combine,
To that great aim, with hands and hearts they
    join.
Oh ! fainted founder of this virtuous land,
Sublimely rais'd, I fee thy ftatue ftand,
Ev'n where the Virgin confecrates the place,
It fills with holy zeal thy generous race,
With free-born men thy Mount is cover'd o'er,
While loft CAMPANIA glooms a defert fhore.

Say, what but FREEDOM chear'd the Savage
    bands,
That once o'erfpread CANADIA's conquer'd lands ?

D D 3

Wild

Wild as their woods behold uncheck'd they go,
For sport or food accouter'd with the bow,
They ask'd no bounty from the sullen soil,
The casual chace their banquet and their toil,
And when at eve the warm pursuit was o'er,
Nor twang'd the bow nor sped the arrow more,
They sprung from light repose ere peep of day,
And thro' the humid desarts took their way;
Active, ferocious, bold, unaw'd they stood,
Troops of the lake and armies of the wood,
Vers'd in no science, lesson'd in no art,
They breath'd the eloquence that reach'd the
        heart;
Unknown the classic pomp of pedant schools,
Above th' ungenial check of colder rules,
It beam'd defiance in the flashing eye,
Storm'd in the shout and melted in the sigh;
In tranquil hours it gave the smile serene,
In public tumults show'd th' indignant mien,
While every vivid tone and glance exprefs'd
All the strong paffions of the warriour's breast.

                                    When

When   the   rude Chief his brave harangue
    began,
The Savage rofe to Hero and to Man,
And when th' invader tore him from the foil,
Dear fcene of all his pride, of all his toil,
No artificial mockeries of woe,
Or taught his cheek to change, his tears to flow;
With pious awe he kneel'd to kifs the ground,
And fondly prefs'd his forrowing friends around,
" Oh! weeping Brothers! this our place of birth,
" Our fathers Afhes confecrate the earth ;
" Should the foe drag us to a foreign fhore,
" Thofe facred afhes we can guard no more,
" Leave, leave not thus our Sires to Chriftian rage,
" But ah! with filial wrath the conflict wage."

Thus thro' the globe in Nature's earlieft dawn,
For FREEDOM only was the arrow drawn,
The plain rough ancient at his threfhold ftood,
And held that freedom dearer than his blood;
Whate'er the foreft or the lakes beftow,
Fruits of his lance, his angle and his bow,

          The

The fur that warms him or the hut that fhields,
The fcanty harveft which his culture yields,
Earn'd by his ftrength, was by his ftrength main-
    tain'd,
And Freedom held what honeft labour gain'd,
Part of himfelf, the Swain his Freedom thought
His reafon fanction'd what his nature taught,
Nor force of bribes nor frauds of gold he knew,
For Life and Liberty to arms he flew.
For thefe, fee fmiling in their realms of froft,
The fons of Labradore's inclement coaft,
Tho' darknefs fheds deep night thro' half the
    year,
And fnow invefts the clime,—that clime is dear,
Where blows the arctic tempefts icy gale,
And famine feizes on the fpermy whale,
The bearded Efquimaux half robb'd of fight,
Roves uncontroul'd content with Freedom's
    light,
To all the ills his Country knows conforms,
Sports in her caverns and enjoys her ftorms;
For the huge Sea-dog tugs the lab'ring oar,
Nor fighs for bleffings of a fofter fhore.

6

Such

Such too, Britannia, were thy favage Sons,
Thro' all thy tribes the dread of Slav'ry runs,
Tho' mild heroic, honeft without laws,
They brav'd each peril in fair Freedom's caufe.
But ah! full many an age in Gothic night,
Was veil'd th' effulgence of their native right;
Tho' like the rocky Barrier of their coaft,
That Freedom now is her fublimeft boaft,
Full many an age diffenfion fhook her Fane,
From Rome's fierce Cæfar to the ftormy Dane.
In whelming tides pour'd in the Saxon clan,
And Normans finifh'd what their rage began;
The favage Briton to his Mountains fled,
Alternate triumph'd and alternate bled;
War upon wars, on conqueft conquefts throng,
Vandal drove Goth, and Goth urg'd Gaul along;
On human flefh the favage Victors eat,
And miftic Druids fhar'd the fanguine treat;
Impoftor-priefts before their Idols ftood,
And talk'd of Heav'n with hands embru'd in blood;
Before their eyes imagin'd fpectres glare,
Spirits were heard, and fancy'd ghofts were there,

Religion,

Religion, Law, and Government their own,
Bloody their Altars, bloody was their Throne ;
Thro' the vex'd Ifle the fanguine edict fpread
'Twas Heav'n demanded mountains of the dead ;
In the dark grove which Superftition trod,
Priefts hid their fpoils, yet commun'd with their
        God,
And muttering rites within the fearful gloom,
Firft ftab a victim then the feaft refume ;
Unfelt as yet the foft'ning ties of life,
Deep in the prifoner's breaft the ruthlefs knife
The defperate Female plung'd—could man do
        more !
Then idly prophefied as flow'd the gore ;
A rage of flaughter then the Sex poffeft,
Now with each grace of Love and Pity bleft.

But foon the favage Tyrant was the Slave,
For fell Invaders pierc'd the Druid cave ;
Forth from the Baltic pour'd the deathful hoft,
And train'd to havock, crimfon'd all the coaft,
The Northern Hive fwarm'd terrible around,
And every altar fmoak'd upon the ground,

4

Promifcuous

Promiscuous carnage, spotted every hand,

Swell'd the gorg'd tomb and deluged all the land.

Different in mind, and manners, as in face,

The Normans came, an innovating race;

Their power, their passions, and their pride, they
      brought,

Fierce, bold, and bloody, and with conquest
      fraught,

From the forc'd mixture of a foreign breed,

Unnatural customs, laws, and wars succeed;

The *Saxon* superstition, weak as dire,

In two extremes of water and of fire,

But these were lenient mercies to the strife,

That *then* with horror hung a cloud on life,

For then, the ties of social Good unbound,

Assassination took its deathful round;

In every grove some lurking stabber lay,

And human bloodshed clotted all the way,

Frequent the mangled corpse obscene, appear'd,

And mutual hate the sanguine standard rear'd;

In slavish homage to a haughty Lord,

Each home-felt joy was broken at the board,

From

From houfe to houfe the Tyrant's edict ran,
And the Feaft ended ere the Mirth began,
At the eighth hour toll'd out by dread command,
The dreary knell that darken'd all the land;
Friendfhip no more her magic could impart,
Nor fhare the glad, nor raife the drooping heart,
The " blazing faggot" chear'd the hearth no
        more,
And all the foft'ning blooms of life were o'er;
To ruin'd Juries the dire fword fucceeds,
And at each pore infulted Juftice bleeds,
The favage beafts, which Nature gave to all,
To glut the rage of fcepter'd pride muft fall;
No more the chace, no more the woods were free,
All, all was Hate,—for all was SLAVERY.
The Lawyer-Clergy too, and *Baron* proud,
Aping their Prince, ftruck terror thro' the croud;
Next, bigot *Priefts*, th' impofing mandate bring,
And yoke the Neck of each fucceeding King;
Fair truth in fetters was with reafon bound,
And dread Anathemas were peal'd around,
Pontiff Hypocrify, parade of prayer,
Pardon, or curfe, indulgence or defpair:

                              The

The heart was tainted, and the head confus'd,
And all the attributes of God abus'd;
Kings, Priefts and People in one chaos hurl'd,
And Virtue left with Liberty the World!

Eventful BRITAIN! fhould the Mufe difplay,
The bloody tracks which mark'd thy homeward
          way,
Or trace the Deluges of Foreign Gore,
That ran in purple torrents thro' thy fhore,
As conqueft oft her crimfon pinion fpread,
And different victors different horrors bred;
Thy hardieft Sons would tremble but to view,
The fearful picture that her pencil drew.

Laft, and what greater proofs can now remain?
Touch we the border of SURINAM'S plain,
Lo, there the purchas'd NEGROES may'ft thou fee,
Burfting their bonds indignant to be free,
From rocks and caves in daring Bands they come,
And wrought to blood like warring Lions roam;

Fire,

Fire, Plague, and Death th' untutor'd Bands
    defy,
Refolv'd on Freedom or refolv'd to die.

Then bleft the * man and worthy to be bleft,
Friend of the Wretched, Guardian of th' op-
    prefs'd,
Bleft be the Man—ye Negroes bow the knee,
And blefs him, Thou, Oh! fweet HUMANITY—
Who, fcorning intereft, thus pourtray'd the plan,
That gave to Men the awful rights of Man;
" Oh! Race difhonour'd, whofe fad forms we tear,
" Nor heed our kindred, heed our Maker there;
" Too long on fordid Altars have ye bled,
" From Chriftian hearts too long has Mercy fled:
" At length return'd, behold fhe brings relief,
" From Heav'n fhe comes to footh the Captive's
    grief;
" My brethren rife, the galling chains unbind,
" And give the generous Model to mankind;
" What Avarice feiz'd let Juftice now reftore,
" Let Negroes ferve, but ferve as Slaves no
    more;
                                " Or

* Penn.

" *Or if the* NAME *of Slave muſt yet remain,*

" *Strive not for words, ſo we remove the pain ;—*

" *Strive not for words, ſo we the rights ſupply,*

" *The raviſh'd rights of ſweet* HUMANITY!"

The good Man ſpake, applauding thouſands
    bow'd,
The Hero triumph'd, and the Chriſtian glow'd,
Unnumber'd Hearts by great example fir'd
Bent to the Law HUMANITY requir'd ;
Unnumber'd Manacles that moment broke,
Unnumber'd Slaves were loofen'd from the yoke,
Unnumber'd Hands were folded up in air,
Unnumber'd Voices breath'd a grateful prayer,
Unnumber'd Eyes late bath'd in tears of woe,
Ah blifsful change ! with tears of joy o'erflow :
From God the ſpark began, to Man it came,
Till all perceiving, all partook the flame ;
Heav'n's fire electric, as one touch'd the ball,
It ſtruck a ſecond till it ſpread to all.

And ſhall not generous England catch the flame,
And add the Wreath of Mercy to her fame,

Shall

Shall not HUMANITY affert her caufe,

And Albions Slave find *Juftice in her Laws* ?

Thofe equal Laws, whofe amicable fway,

The rich and poor, the high and low obey.

Bleft Land ! where *Sovereigns* view their roofs
      afcend,

While Law and Liberty their thrones defend,

Bleft *Subjects* too, whofe guarded manfions ftand,

Too firm for Tyranny's rapacious Hand,

Where the poor *Peafant* knows his Cot fecure,

Humble in fize, but on foundations fure ;

Where boldly fenc'd his little Garden grows,

And not a King Dares rob him of a Rofe.

Thus in the crouded Hive, tho' all agree

To choofe their Monarch, the proud Swarms are
      free

Plebeian Cells, as facred as the Great

And both contribute honey to the State.

   Launch then the Bark, unfurl th' impatient
      Sails,

Swell ye kind Seas, and blow ye foftering Gales,
                   Oh

Oh hafte fome Angel thro' the realms of air
To Afric's Sons Britannia's tidings bear!
Thrice happy he who firft fhall reach the ftrand
To fpread the joys of Freedom thro' the Land,
His the rich blifs to fee " his fellows bleft,"
His the glad welcome of fome Heavenly gueft.

And lo! methinks on Fancy's wing convey'd
The MUSE already gains the palmy fhade,
Herfelf the meffenger, to Afric's plains
Ardent fhe flies to break the tyrant-chains,
Her voice already hails the lift'ning croud,
And thus fhe fpeaks her Embaffy aloud,
" I come, I come to fet the Captive free
" Ye fuffering Heirs of fweet HUMANITY.
" Whofe Minds can reafon, and whofe Hearts
        can move,
" With all the joys and agonies of Love,
" Sublime on Nature's fcale again ye rife
' Equals on Earth, as equals in the fkies.

" Where Freedom bids, now take your blithfome
     way
" Yours the fair morn, and yours the clofing
     day,
" Yours is the jocund eve, its fports command
" Or on the cooling wave or barren fand,
" If in your breafts the Patriot paffions burn
" To your lov'd Country, to your Homes return,
" Free, unconfin'd, where'er your courfe ye
     bend,
" Still, ftill fhall LIBERTY your fteps attend !
" Negroes are Men, and Men are Slaves no
     more,
" Fair Freedom reigns, and Tyranny is o'er !"

And now they trace each fcene of former love
Explore each favour'd haunt, hill, vale, and
     grove,
And foon the well-remember'd huts they find,
Where faithful Friends and Loves were left be—
     hind,
Sudden before her fable lord appears,
Th' enfranchis'd wife adorn'd with faithful tears,
Mothers

Mothers again their kidnapp'd babes behold,
Sons clafp their Sires in flavery grown old,
Here their own Niger rifes to the fight,
And there their Nile's prolific banks invite ;
Far as extend thefe parent floods they range,
Feel all at large and triumph in the change :
And ftill in fond delight their triumphs rife,
And this glad Truth re-echoes to the fkies,
NEGROES ARE MEN, AND MEN ARE SLAVES NO
MORE,
FAIR FREEDOM REIGNS AND TYRANNY IS O'ER.*

* In the firft Quarto Edition of this Work, publifhed in
1788, the Poem contained feveral more pages, but, as thefe
fketch'd the Author's defign, and might, indeed, be confidered
as a poetical profpectus of the intended poem of SOCIETY, the
materials of which are loft, and with them, the probability of
the Author's having leifure, courage, or life, to begin his
labour again, with any well-founded hope of reaching the point
of which he once cherifh'd the ambition—for what cannot Youth
and Poefy make us believe—? he has judg'd it better to end the
prefent performance here; only obferving, that, in this revifion
of it, he has avail'd himfelf of every criticifm which, on reflexion,
he *felt to be juft*, whether fuch criticifm was public or private,
expreffed with mildnefs or with rigour.

DIALOGUE LETTERS;

CONTAINING

NECESSARY FIRST QUESTIONS AND ENQUIRIES

IN

ENGLISH, GERMAN, AND DUTCH,

AS

PROMISED BY THE GLEANER.

TO THE READER.

As well to perform a promise, as from a thorough conviction of their GREAT UTILITY to travellers of all descriptions, these Letters are added; but as there is nothing in them which can be either profitable or amusing *on this side* of the Continent; and as *the other side* is, alas! still forbidden ground, without offering fruits or flowers, or gleanings of any kind for the head or heart, the Gleaner can neither expect or wish his Readers to lose the *present* time in such barren occupation; but when, long-wish'd for and long-wanted Peace shall *renew* the Earth, and *revive* wounded Humanity, he would as a Friend, advise all those who carry their gratulations on that joyful event abroad, to take these Dialogues along with them, even though they should refuse the other parts of the work that honour: not but that he would feel himself proud to be their Fellow Traveller, in a literary sense, *altogether*.   And

*** As it is *impossible* to write down the words exactly as they would sound, when pronounced, to an English ear, the following observations may be of use: A, in the German, and Dutch Languages is pronounced as in the French, excepting when there are two strokes over it, as thus—ä—it is then the same as in English.   The v', in both Dutch and German is always pronounced as an f.

DIALOGUE LETTERS,

IN

ENGLISH, GERMAN, & DUTCH.

LETTER I.

ENGLISH.

HOW late is it landlord? waiter? chambermaid?

GERMAN.

Wie fpät ift es, wirth? aufwärter? kammermädchen?   As fpoken, i. e. as it founds to the ear.   We fpate ift es, wurt? aufwerter? kammermadeyen?

DUTCH.

Hoe laat is het, kaftelyn? oppaffer?   Kamer meid?

Is there a good fire?

GERMAN.

Ift ein gutes feuer da? As f. Ift ein gootes fire da?

DUTCH.

Is 'er een goed vuur?

E E 4   Bring

Bring breakfaft, tea, coffee, both; below, above.

GERMAN.

Bring das frühftuck, thee, caffé, von beyden, unten, oben. As f. Bring das freeftick, téé, caffé, fom byden, oonten, oben.

DUTCH.

Brengt het ontbyt, thee, coffé, byde, boven, beneeden.

Is water and towel in my chamber?

GERMAN.

Ift waffer und ein handtuch in meine kammer? As f. Ift waffer unt eyen handtooch in myne kammer?

DUTCH.

Is 'er water en een handdock in myn kammer?

Go for the hairdreffer, barber, both.

GERMAN.

Hohlt dem frifeur, barbier, beyde. As f. Holt dem frifeur, barbeer, byde.

DUTCH.

Haalt de kapper, (prukmaker) barbier, byde.

GERMAN.

Bring my boots, shoes.

GERMAN.

Bringt meine stiefeln, shue. As f. Brinkt myne steefeln, shue.

DUTCH.

Brengt myne laarsen, schoenen.

Brush my coat, hat.

GERMAN.

Bürste meinen rock, huth. As f. Bürste mynen rok, hoot.

DUTCH.

Borstett myn roek, hoed at.

Are there any things which travellers go to fee in this town, village, country?

GERMAN.

Ist etwas merkwürdiges für reifende in diefer ftadt zu befehen, dorf, gegende? As f. Ist etwas merkwerdéges fear ryfende in deefer ftadt zu befaen, dorf, gegende?

DUTCH.

DUTCH.

Is 'er iets merkwaardigs voor ryzigers te feen, in deefe ftadt, dorp, land?

Get fomebody to attend me to them.

GERMAN.

Shaffe mir jemand um mich darhin zu begleiten. As f. Shaffe meer yamaant um mich darhin zu beglyten.

DUTCH.

Beforgt my iemand om my daarheen te geleyden.

If there is a play, opera, concert to night, conduct me to it, at the proper hour.

GERMAN.

Is diefen abend eine comedie, opera, concert, begleite mir dahin, zur beftemten zeit. As f. Is deefen abend eyene comedie, opera, concert, beglyte meer dahin, zur beftimten zyt.

DUTCH.

Als 'er heeden avond| comedie, opera, concert is, brengt my daarheen ter regten tyd.

What hour do you give the table d'hote— one, two, half paft, or three?

GERMAN.

GERMAN.

Welche ſtunde geben ſie die table d'hote um ein, zwey, halber drey, oder drey uhr? As. ſ. Welche ſtunde geben ſee dee table d'hote um ine, zwy, halber dry eder dry oor?

DUTCH.

Wat uur geeft gy de table d'hote ten een, twee, half drie, of drie uure?

I wiſh to dine in private to day, at one, two, three, four; on fiſh, veal, beef, mutton, pork, lamb, veniſon, ſauſages, ſallad, broth, peas.

GERMAN.

Ich werde heute allein eſſen, um ein, zwey, drey, vier uhr, fiſch, kalbfleiſch, rindfleiſch, ſchafsfleiſch, ſchweinefleiſch, lambfleiſch, wild-prét, würſte, ſallade, ſuppe, erbſen. As ſ. Ich werde hyte alline eſſen, um ine, zwy, dry, fear oor, fiſh, kalbflyſh, rindflyſh, ſhaaflyſh, ſwine-flyſh, laamflyſh, wildpret, werſte, ſallade, ſuppe, erpſen.

DUTCH.

Ik wenſchte heeden voor my zelfs teeeten, ten een, twee, drie, vier uuren, fiſch, kalbsfleeſch, rundfleeſch, ſchapefleeſch, ſpek, lamsfleeſch, hartefleeſch, worſt, ſallaad, ſoup, erten.

I would

I would take an airing this morning, after-noon, evening, to-morrow. Take care to get me a carriage.

GERMAN.

Ich wolte diesen morgen spatzieren fahren, nachmittag, abend, morgen. Sorgen sie für eine kutsche. As f. Ich wolte deefen morgen spatzeeren faaren, naachmittag, aabend, mor-gen. Sorgen fee fear ine kutsche.

DUTCH.

Ik wilde deefe morgen lugt scheppen, namidag, heden avond, morgen. Dezorgt my een hoets.

Let me have a supper ready on my return. eggs, cutlets, sallad, spinage, tarts.

GERMAN.

Laffet ein abend effen by meiner rückkunft fertig feyn. Eyer, carbonade, fallade, fpinat, pafteten. As f. Laas ine abend effen by myner rickkunft fertig fine. Eyer, carbonaade, fallade, fpenaat, pafteten.

DUTCH.

Laat teegen myn terugkomft fouppe gereed fyn. Eyer, en korteletten, fallaad, fpinage, taarten.

I defire

I defire my fheets may be thoroughly dry, and hung by my own fire, till I order them on the bed, and I wifh to have my bed warmed. I burn a light. Let there be a good fire made up.

GERMAN,

Ich verlange meine betlaaken durch und durch trocken, und bey meinen eigenen feuer zu hangen bis dafs ich felbige aufs, bette haben will, ich verlange mein bette gewärmet, ich brenne ein licht; lafs ein gutes feur gemacht werden. As f. Ich verlaange myne betlaaken durg und durg trocken, und by minen eigenen fire zu haangen bis dafs ich felbege aufs, bette haaben will, ich ferlaange mine bette gewermet, ich brenne ine licht; laffe ine gootes fire gemaacht werden.

DUTCH.

Myn bedlaakens moeten door en door droog fyn, en by myn eigen vuur hangen, tot dat ik defelve opt bed ordonneere, ik wenfch myn bed géwarmt to hebben, ik brand een ligt; laat een goed vuur aanleggen.

Let me fee your printed lift of wines and their prices. Let me have a bottle of wine —half a bottle.

GERMAN.

Laffet mir eure gedrückte lifte von weinen
fehen, und deren preifen, gebt mir eine bouteille
vom — wein, eine halbe bouteille.   As f.
Laaffet meer ire gedrickte lifte fon winen fehen,
unt déren prifen, gabet meer ine boüteille fon
— wine — ine haalbe bouteille.

DUTCH.

Laat my een gedruckte leyfte van wynen fien
ende preifen, geeft my een flees—wyn—een
halfe flees.

I fhall not want a fire in the morning; or
let me have a fire in my chamber early. I fhall
go after breakfaft.   I fhall go before breakfaft.
To-morrow; the day after; in three days; four,
five—in a week.   Call me at four, five, fix,
feven, eight, nine o'clock.

GERMAN.

Ich werde des morgens kein feuer nottig
haben; *or* lafs ein feuer in meinen zimmer
früh anlegen; Ich reife nach fruhftück ab.
Ich werde vor fruhftuck] abreifen. Morgen,
den folgenden tag, innerhalb drei tagen, vier
Funf, in einer woche. Rufe mir um 4, 5, fechs,
fieben, Acht, neun uhr.   As f.   Ich werde des
morgens

morgens kine fire natig haaben; *or* laas ine
fire in minen zimmer free anlegen. Ich rife
nach freeftick aap. Ich werde fore freeftick
aaprifen. Morgen, den folgenden tag, innerhalb dry tagen, fear finf, fex, feehen, acht,
nine oor.

DUTCH.

Ik zals' fmorgens geenvuur nodig hebben; *or*
laat my froeg een vuur in myn kamer hebben.
Ik fal fertrekken voor't ontbeit. Ik fal
fertrekken naar't ontbeit. Morgen, de folgende
dag, in drie, dagen, vier, fife, in een week;
wekt my om vier, fife, fes, feven, agt, neegen
uur.

Take me a place, two, three places, in the
poft waggon, for to night, to morrow, Monday,
Tuefday, Wednefday, Thurfday, Friday, Saturday, Sunday; *or* befpeak me a private carriage;
faddle and bring out my horfe; he wants fhoe-
ing; he is lame; this bridle, girth, ftrap is
broke, let it be mended; bring my bill.

GERMAN.

Nehmet mir einen platz, zwey, drey plátze
auf dem poft-wagen für die nacht, für Morgen,
Montag, Dienftag, Mittwochen, Donnerftag,
Freytag.

Freytag, Sonhabend, Sontag. Oder, bestellt mir extra post; sattelt, und bringt mir mein pferd; er mus beschlagen werden; er ist lahm, dieser zaum, gürtel, riem, ist gebrochen; last es wieder zurechte machen. Bringt meine rechnung. As s. Namet meer eynen plaatz, zwey, dry pletze ouf dem post-waagen, fear dee nacht, fear morgen, moantag, dinstag, mittwochen, donnerstag, frytag, sonnaobend, Sontag, oder bestellt meer extra post; saattelt, unt brinkt meer mine ferd; are mus beschlagen wareden; are ist laam; deeser zaum, girtel, reem, ist gebrochen, laast es weeder zu rechte machen; brinkt mine rehcnung.

DUTCH.

Neemt een plaats voor my, twee, drie plaatsen in de post-wagen, voor vanavond, voor morgen, maandag, dingsdag, woensdag, dondergag, vrydag, zaturdag, zondag, *of* bespreekt my een aparte Reytuyg; zaald en brengt myn Paard beyten, het moet beslagen werden; het is laam; deeze Toom, buykreim, strop is gebrooken; laat het gemaaket werden; brengt meyn reckning.

Let these things go to the washerwoman,

GERMAN.

GERMAN.

Nehmet diese sachen zu der wäsherin.   As f.
Namet deese sachen zu dare wesherin.

DUTCH.

Zend dit goed naer de waschvrouw.

I am no judge of your charges, but shall keep
your bill and shew it to those who are, and it I
find it reasonable, I shall recommend your
house.

GERMAN.

Ich kann ihne berechnung nicht beurtheilen,
werde aber die rechnung behalten, und es denen
zeigen, welche es können ; finde ich dann das
es billig ist, will ich ihr haus recommandiren.
As f. Ich kann ihre berechnung nicht beurtilen,
warede aaber die rechnung behaalten unt es
danen zigen, welche es kennen, finde ich dann
das es billig ist, will ich ear house recommandiren.

DUTCH.

Ik kan over u reekening niet oordeelen, maer
sal u reckening houden en laeten sien aan die
het konnen, en als ik dezelve reedlyk vinde,
zal ik u huys recommendeeren.

                 F f   These

Thefe fentences, which I have rather thrown into commands than queftions, comprehend all the ufual points of accommodation at an inn, where a traveller intends to ftop only for a day,—night,—or four and twenty hours. The fecond fhall prepare you for a longer ftop,—although, in places where as a ftranger you can be *induced* to make this,—unlefs like me you love to walk

> " along the cool fequefter'd vale of life."

You will find the popular languages of France, Italy, or that of your own country fpoken in common. I therefore begin with a queftion which will decide this neceffary *firft* point— and indeed it would be well to make it a preliminary interrogation every where; becaufe, when anfwered in the affirmative, your bufinefs is done,—as I muft pre-fuppofe you poffefs'd of a knowledge of the two firft of thefe,—or at leaft one of them, in cafe your company fhould be at fault to find you or any perfon converfant in the third—although the Englifh tongue is getting popularity and extending faft. So ends your firft leffon, and I will bid you *farewell.*

LETTER II.

DO you or any of your people speak French, Italian, or English, or any body near you ?

GERMAN.

Sprechen sie oder einige von thre leute, Fransöfch, Italienifch, oder Englifh, oder jemand hier in der nähe ? As f. Sprechen fee oder eynege fon care lyte Fransäfich, Italianifh, oder Englith, oder yemand here in der nayc ?

DUTCH.

Vetftaat gy of iemand van u volk Franfch, Italianfch, of Engelfch, of iemand in de buurt ?

I wifh to ftay fome time, look out fome private lodgings, and fhew me to them, if poffible, where one of thofe languages are fpoken, I want two, three, four beds, rooms, a fuite of apartments, in the beft part of the town, a little out of town.

GERMAN.

Ich wünsche hier einige zeit zu bleiben, fucht aus ein privat logis, und zeigt mir dahin,

WO

wo möglich allwo man eine von diese sprachen
spricht, ich verlange, zwey, drey, vier, betten,
zimmers, eine reihe von zimmern, in den
besten Theil der stadt,—etwas aus der stadt. As
s. Ich winshe here inege zite zu blyben, sucht
aus ine privat logis, unt zygt meer daahin, wo
mäglich allwo maan ine son deese spraachen
spricht, ich ferlaange zwey, dry, fear betten';
zimmers, iyne ryee son zimmern, in den besten,
Tile der stadt,—etwas aus der stadt.

Dutch.

Ik will wat blyven, nae eene a parte wooning
uytzeen, en wyst my zulke aan, zoo't moo-
glykis, daar een van deeze taalen gesprooken
werd. Ik moet twee, drie, vier bedden kebben;
kamers gevoegelyke vertrekken, int best van
de stad; iets buyten de stad.

I shall find my own plate and linen, and vic-
tuals; you must find me plate, &c. and in short
every thing but wines; how much must you
have per week? month? for one, two, three,
four, five, or six persons, but do not ask unrea-
sonably, I cannot afford extravagance, if you
cannot yourself find me in diet, &c. I must
arrange with a traiteur, shew me one; or with
the master of the hotel where I put up.

GERMAN,

German.

Ich bin mit filberzeng & leinewand verfehen, beforge mein eigenes effen ;—ihr must mir mit zilberzeng verfchen, und kurtz mit alles, auffer wein; wieviel verlangt ihr per woche ? monath? für ein, zwey, drey, vier, fünffe, fechs perfonen, aber fördert nicht unbillig, ich darff nicht verfchwenderifh thun. Wenn ihr felbst mich nicht bekoftigen könt, mufs ich mit einen trateur fprechen, zeigt mir einen, oder mit dem wirth bey dem ich abftieg, As f. Ich bin mit filberzyg unt linewand verfehen, beforge mine eygenes effen; eer muft meer mit zilberzyg ferfaen, unt kurtz mit alles, auffer wine, we feel ferlangt eer per woche ? monaat? fear ine, zwy, drey, fear, finffee, fex perfonen, Aaber fördert nicht unbillig, ich daarf nicht ferfwenderifh toon. Wenn ear felbst mich nicht bekoftigen kent, mufs ich mit inen trateur fprechen, zygt mir inen;—oder mit dem wurt by dem ich aapftyg.

Dutch.

Ik zal myn eygen bord & tafelgoed houden en ecten,—gy moet my met bord en tafelgoed voorzien, en in't kort van alles behalven wynen. Hoe veel moet gy per week hebben ?

per

per maand? voor een, twee, drie, vier, vyf, fes perfoonen, maan vraagt niet onreedelyk. Ik kan niet veel befteeden,—als gy zelfs my niet in de koft neemen kan, moet ik my by en ordeen- aris befteeden,—wyft my een—of by de cafte- leyn van 't logement daar ik aangekomen ben.

Agreed—I fhall come to morrow, prepare them—Next day—Day after.

GERMAN.

Accordirt—Ich werde morgen kommen, macht es fertig—Ubermorgen—Uber zwey tage. As f. Accordirt—Ich werde morgen kommen, macht es fertig—ebermorgen—eber zy tage.

DUTCH.

Gedaan—Ik zal morgen komen, Maakt het gereed—over morgen—over twee dagen.

SUPPLEMENTARY QUESTIONS.

How many hours to—by water, by poft wag- gon—by private carriage—with two—three— four horfes.—I will go there by water at— hour—poft-waggon—private. Call me at— hour—bring my bill—take my baggage.

GERMAN.

GERMAN.

Wieviel ſtunden nach—zu waſſer—im poſtwaagen,—mit extra poſt, mit zwey, drey, vier
pferde. Ich will den zu waſſer gehen um—
ſtunde, im poſtwaagen, mit extra poſt. Ruft
mir um—ſtunde—bringt meine recknung—
nehm't meine baggage. As ſ. Wefeel ſtunden
nach—zu waſſer—Im poſtwaagen,—mit extra
poſt—mit zy, dry, fear ferde. Ich will den zu
waſſer gain um—ſtunde—im poſtwaagen—mit
extra poſt. Rooft mir um—ſtunde. Brinkt
mine rechnung. Namet mine baggage.

DUTCH.

Hoeveel uuren is het naar—met de ſchuyt,
met de poſtwaagen, met particulier rytuyg,—
met twee, drie, vier paarden. Ik ſal den te
waater gaan ten—uuren—met de poſtwagen—
particulier. Wekt my ten—uuren. Brengt
myn reckening. Neemt myn goed, baggage.

F I N I S.

ERRATA, VOL. III.

Page 13, line 2 penult, for, *make*, read—*made.*
Page 14, line 15, dele—*were.*
Page 62, line 4, for, *monofyllables*, read—*words.*
Page 100, line 10, for, *meant to fignify*, read—*fignified.*
Page 123, line 4, for, thirty *or* forty, read—*and* forty.
Page 139, line 10, for, *be fuppofed of*, read—*be fufpected of.*
Page 187, line 10, for, *this*, read—*his* Ifabel.
Page 205, line 5, for, *extends*, read—*expands.*
Page 245, line 10 penult, for, *appears*, read—*appear.*
Page 279, line 6, for, *prefented*, read—*prefenting.*
Page 321, line 5, for, *that* injur'd, read—*an* injur'd.
Ibid, line 8, for, on *their*, read—*on its.*
Page 324, line 6, for, entering *its*, read—*into.*
Page 325, line 3 penult, for, UNITS AND CYPHERS, read—
     CYPHERS.
Page 327, line 11, for, *which*, read—*when.*